ROSE REISMAN
BRINGS HOME
LIGHT
PASTA

ROSE REISMAN
BRINGS HOME
LIGHT
PASTA

Robert
ROSE

ROSE REISMAN BRINGS HOME LIGHT PASTA

Copyright © 1995 Rose Reisman

For complete cataloguing data, see page 228.

DESIGN AND PAGE COMPOSITION:	MATTHEWS COMMUNICATIONS DESIGN
PHOTOGRAPHY:	MARK SHAPIRO/IN CAMERA STUDIO
FOOD STYLIST:	KATE BUSH
MANAGING EDITOR:	PETER MATTHEWS/MATTHEWS COMMUNICATIONS DESIGN
COPY EDITOR:	WENDY THOMAS
INDEXER:	BARBARA SCHON

Cover photo: Orange and Pineapple Chicken Stir-Fry over Linguine (page 91)

Distributed in the U.S. by:

Firefly Books (U.S.) Inc.
P.O. Box 1338
Ellicott Station
Buffalo, NY 14205

ORDER LINES
Tel: (416) 499-8412
Fax: (416) 499-8313

Published by:

Robert Rose Inc.
156 Duncan Mill Road, Suite 12
Toronto, Ontario, Canada M3B 2N2
Tel: (416) 449-3535

Printed in Canada

34567 BP 99 98 97 96 95

CONTENTS

To my family: Sam, Natalie, David, Laura and Adam.
There was never a better source of inspiration
for my life and work.

Also to the Canadian Breast Cancer Foundation and
Y-ME National Breast Cancer Organization,
whose tireless efforts have helped so many.

ACKNOWLEDGMENTS

My very special thanks to the incredible team of people that made this book happen in record-breaking time!

The Canadian Breast Cancer Foundation and Y-ME National Breast Cancer Organization, for giving me an additional opportunity to raise funds for their organizations with this cookbook. A special thanks to Susan Davidson, Carole Grafstein, Andrea Thomas, Sharon Green and Debbie Fishbein.

Helen Chambers and Lorraine Fullum-Bouchard, from A.D. Harvey Nutrition Consultants, for providing a comprehensive nutritional analysis of each recipe, as well as an excellent and informative introduction on pasta and nutrition. Thanks also to our U.S. nutrition consultant, Carolyn Guyton-Ringbloom, for her valuable contribution to the introduction.

Dr. Roy Clark, Chairman of the Medical Advisory Committee (Canadian Breast Cancer Foundation), for his continued support and for his informative foreword on breast cancer.

A special thanks to Robert Dees who initiated this project and was "determined" to have it in time.

Matthews Communications Design for their intense, around-the-clock work on this book: Peter Matthews who directed the editorial, design, and pre-press work; and a special thanks to Sharon for her expert page design and photo art direction. The book looks fabulous.

Mark Shapiro of In-Camera Studio, who may have given me ulcers with his conscientiousness, but made certain each picture was brilliantly shot. And to his assistant Jay Town for his humor in getting my beautiful children to have the fun they exhibited on the back cover.

Kate Bush, the food stylist, whose expertise a cookbook can not be without.

Shelley Vlahantones, the food props coordinator, whose eclectic collection of tableware and props added so much to the photography. Also to the fine suppliers of products that appear in the food shots: B.B. Bargoons (fabrics); Villeroy and Boch, The Compleat Kitchen, and DeVerre (tableware); and Country Floors (tiles).

Dianne Hargrave, my "forever" publicist, who has worked relentlessly to provide me and my books with media exposure, and is now planning another whirlwind national tour.

My testing kitchen, with a special thanks to Lesleigh Landry, Edit Vendel and Irene Patrao.

The "boys" from the office — Charlie, Stephen, Norm, Marty and Dick — for their lunchtime testing.

INTRODUCTION

I love pasta. In fact, three years ago, before I mended my "unlight" ways, I "brought them home" with the publication of my fourth book, *Rose Reisman Brings Home Pasta Dishes*. Bob Dees (my friend, mentor and publisher) loved the recipes from that book, and never a "light" convert himself, challenged me to demonstrate how rich pasta recipes could be made light and delicious. Why not? Pasta is versatile, quick to prepare, economical, healthy, and when properly prepared, absolutely delicious. Well, Bob, here's the proof, and my bet is that I have another convert!

Nothing — absolutely nothing — has energized me like the overwhelming reception my last book, *Rose Reisman Brings Home Light Cooking*, received. I have no other excuse for having found the energy to write this book, scarcely 18 months after my last was published. It was not intended to happen so soon. Shortly after I had the idea for a light pasta book, I went to my publisher to seek their support. That was when circumstances began to develop their own momentum. While I was anticipating a workable time frame so as to allow for an enjoyable summer with my family, my publisher was, apparently, "taste-testing" the market. You might say they "ate up" the idea (pun intended), and while I may have reasoned a more digestible pace, they, (n)ever concerned for my family life, informed me that favorable market conditions dictated the book be ready for Fall . . . Fall '94! When I "finally" relented, my immediate concern was, "How am I going to tell my official (exhausted from my last book) taste-tester husband, Sam?" The romantic bit may have worked last time, but a six-course, all-pasta dinner is not exactly saying "I Love You."

At any rate, the challenge was on. Working quickly has its advantages, I learned. Nothing quite so focuses the mind like an important publishing date, and nothing quite compares to testing 200 recipes three to four times over the course of 60 days. While I worked hard and fast, I believe that I did so without compromise. I had a clear objective: Could I create recipes that would, on a fat- and calorie-reduced basis, taste as rich and delicious as the recipes in my previously-published pasta book? The challenge daunted me, especially given the time frame, but I feel thrilled with the results. In fact, I can unequivocally say this book is not as good as my other pasta book — it's better!

As a result, this book is not only an alternative eating guide ideally suited for weight-watchers, it's also ideal for people like you and me who love to eat. The recipes have been engineered and tested until they passed my personal (and Sam's) standards of excellence. These recipes are simply sublime.

The 175 pasta recipes in this book are light, delicious, easy to prepare, and are all nutritionally analyzed. Sauces to complement pasta dishes can be prepared quickly, served immediately, or later, by gently reheating, or frozen for future use. While lessening the fat content in each recipe, I was able to include interesting ingredient combinations which enhanced taste and texture...see for yourself by trying these wonderful recipes, and change forever the way you think of pasta. Pasta is a popular staple in the North American diet, traditionally accompanied by heavy cheese, oil and cream sauces. However, because pasta is naturally rich in carbohydrates and low in fat, it is highly recommended by food guides in Canada and the United States as an important addition to our diet. When combined with vegetables, meat, chicken, fish or cheese, together with a delicious sauce, a pasta dish becomes a completely nutritious meal, very satisfying. For example, try these recipes: Pasta with Salmon in Teriyaki Sauce; Pesto Lasagna with Roasted Peppers; Orange and Pineapple Chicken Stir-Fry over Linguine; Hoisin Beef, Red Peppers and Snow Peas over Fettucine; Four-Cheese Macaroni; and my newly introduced Pizza Pastas!!

It has been my great privilege to be involved in a career I love, while raising funds for a worthwhile cause. The value of life and health has been incomparably reinforced by my concern for my family's welfare. Breast cancer is a family disease: when one member is stricken, all are stricken. *Rose Reisman Brings Home Light Cooking*, my last book, is continuing to raise funds to fight breast cancer in the United States and Canada. At this writing, the book has raised in excess of $400,000 for this purpose. I plan to continue to support this worthwhile cause and a portion of the proceeds from each *Light Pasta* book sold will go towards breast cancer research and awareness. Whether or not you purchase a copy, please support Y-ME and the Canadian Breast Cancer Foundation in their efforts to eradicate this disease.

I'd love to hear from you. Write to me at:

P.O. Box 55176
Fairview Mall
1800 Sheppard Avenue East
North York, Ontario CANADA
M2J 5B9

Rose Reisman

FOREWORD

We do not know the exact cause of breast cancer. While there has been considerable excitement over the recent localization of a breast cancer predisposing gene called BRCAI, the gene accounts for only a small fraction of patients with breast cancer.

Research continues, however, and is now being focused on methods of reversing or blocking tumor growth and spread. In the future we shall see forms of treatment evolving from genetic engineering, with sophisticated gene control systems, less emphasis on the destruction of cells and more emphasis on reversing the malignant process. Breast cancer research benefits all other types of cancer, giving insight into causation, how tumors grow and spread and how this process can be prevented.

For now, however, breast cancer remains the leading killer of women between the ages of 35 and 55. An estimated 17,000 Canadian and 182,000 American women developed breast cancer in 1994. Deaths in that year numbered 5,400 and 46,000, respectively. Clearly, it is imperative that we find methods of preventing this all-too-common and distressing disease.

We can start by identifying the most important risk factors: increasing age and family history. Age at first pregnancy is also significant, since a first pregnancy after the age of 35 increases the risk threefold compared with pregnancy before the age of nineteen.

Still, 70% of women developing breast cancer have no obvious risk factors. What other factors might we consider?

We do know that there is an increased incidence of breast cancer amongst populations with a high intake of fatty food. Excessive body weight seems to produce the same effect, and results in a poorer outlook for those who have been treated for the disease. Although trials are under way to examine this link, it will take many years to assess the results. So we cannot say definitively that a low-fat diet or losing weight will have any impact on the incidence of breast cancer or improve the outlook for those with the disease.

For now, however, it makes sense to reduce your fat intake. This has a proven impact on weight loss and the risk of coronary artery disease, which becomes a more important factor after menopause. It is also imperative to impress upon girls and young women that exercise and healthy eating habits are a vital necessity during their formative years when critical changes are occurring in the maturation of their sexual organs.

Pasta has become a very popular component of our diet in recent years and lends itself to appetizing dishes that are low in fat. *Rose Reisman Brings Home Light Pasta* provides an excellent opportunity to experience this cuisine.

Do yourself a favor. Treat your family to these low-fat pasta recipes and, at the same time, take satisfaction in the fact that you are providing much-needed funding for breast cancer research.

R.M. Clark MB, BS, FRCR, FRCPC

Princess Margaret Hospital, Toronto
Professor, University of Toronto

Y-ME

Dear Friends,

The Y-ME National Breast Cancer Organization was founded in 1978 by the late Mimi Kaplan and Ann Marcou to offer information and support to breast cancer patients, their families and friends.

It was founded on the belief that a well-informed patient could better cope with her diagnosis. Y-ME believes that it is crucial for women to be full partners with their medical team so the decisions made will reflect the personal needs of the patient. Today, Y-ME helps empower hundreds of women every month through its national hotline and support groups. Our twenty Chapters help bring Y-ME services to cities from coast to coast. In addition to our programs for survivors, Y-ME volunteers educate the general public on the importance of early detection.

Most recently, Y-ME has been representing women with breast cancer in Washington, D.C., lobbying for more research dollars to end this epidemic. In three years, the funding for breast cancer research has increased sixfold. Until there is a cure, Y-ME will continue to voice the concerns of the women and men touched by this disease.

Y-ME is delighted to join our sisters at the Canadian Breast Cancer Foundation in promoting **Rose Reisman Brings Home Light Pasta**. The funds raised through this project will help our organizations meet the ultimate goal — a world without breast cancer.

Sincerely,

Sharon Green

Executive Director
Y-ME National Breast Cancer Organization

**CANADIAN
BREAST CANCER
FOUNDATION**

An Appreciation

Since it began in 1986, the Canadian Breast Cancer Foundation has been honoured by the strong support of many individuals and corporations. They, working side by side with our hundreds of committed volunteers, have made it possible for the Foundation to award grants totalling over $1.6 million to support breast cancer research, treatment, and education projects across Canada.

Rose Reisman, by donating a significant portion from the sale of **Rose Reisman Brings Home Light Cooking** *and* **Rose Reisman Brings Home Light Pasta**, *is one of those who has made a major contribution — not just in dollars raised, but in providing recipes that are simple to make, tasty, fun to eat, and healthy. Her efforts have also helped us to raise public awareness, and for this we are very grateful.*

If we are to succeed in our stated goal of helping to eradicate the terrible scourge of breast cancer, we need the commitment and energy of many more people and companies to join with those who are already involved. You can help by donating, by supporting, and by volunteering.

On behalf of the thousands of women touched by your participation, please accept our deepest thanks.

We look forward to hearing from you.

*Maureen Molaro and Susan Davidson
Canadian Breast Cancer Foundation*

PASTA AND NUTRITION

LIGHT PASTA? It almost sounds too good to be true. After all, pasta dishes are not exactly what most people think of as a "health food" — they're simply too good-tasting, too satisfying.

Nevertheless, as this book demonstrates so convincingly, you can enjoy pasta in a variety of delicious ways, and still maintain a sensible, low-fat diet.

How? The secret, you might say, is in the sauce: On its own, pasta is an exceptionally healthy food, packed with energy-providing carbohydrates; it's only when we load pasta with a high-fat sauce, that it becomes nutritionally less desirable. But pasta doesn't need a heavy sauce to taste great. And that's what this book is all about.

WHY YOU SHOULD EAT PASTA

Our food supply includes many different forms of carbohydrates. Some are refined simple sugars that provide very few minerals and vitamins and need to be consumed in limited quantities. Fortunately, however, pasta is a starch, or complex carbohydrate — as are breads, cereals, legumes, potatoes, rice, barley, oats and corn — which has much greater nutritional value.

Many of these foods were once considered fattening. In fact, even now, many people do not allow themselves to enjoy a plate of pasta. What they fail to recognize is the importance of a healthy balance of carbohydrates, protein and fat — something that these *Light Pasta* recipes have built right in. The carbohydrates are more than adequate, the protein is moderate, and the fat is low. That's the balance we're looking for.

LOW FAT, HIGH FIBER

A healthy diet is characterized by many factors (including plenty of variety), but two of the most important are **low fat** and **high fiber**. This is important for a number of reasons, among which is the need to maintain a healthy body weight — particularly since it appears that a high-fat diet may increase the risk of medical problems, such as breast cancer, heart disease, diabetes and hypertension.

Of course, that's not to say you must avoid fat at all costs. Remember, balance is the goal. We have dismissed the concept of "good" foods and "bad" foods. By planning meals, the occasional high-fat food or meal can be included in a healthy diet when it is balanced with low-fat foods for the rest of the day or week.

As a rule, no more than 30% of total calories should be derived from fats, although some authorities suggest a 20% limit. This refers to total daily caloric intake, not just the percentage of fats per meal or per food item. Here are some examples of recommended fat consumption for various caloric intake levels.

	Recommended fat intake (grams)	
Total Calories	30% of Total	20% of Total
1500	50	35
1800	60	40
2100	70	45
2400	80	55

SOURCES OF FAT

One teaspoon of foods such as oil, butter, margarine or regular mayonnaise contains 4 to 5 grams of fat. These are visible fats and are relatively easy to control. But other sources of fats are less visible. These include: whole or partially skimmed dairy products such as milk, cheese and yogurt; meats, fish and poultry; many cookies, crackers and desserts; and, of course, fried foods. The control of invisible fats requires more knowledge of the fat content of the foods consumed, so a full nutritional analysis is given with the recipes in this book.

You can eliminate all visible fat in cooking by using nonstick cookware, nonstick vegetable sprays, and by sautéeing vegetables in water. Other fat-reduction strategies include replacing 2% milk with skim milk, experimenting with the many low-fat cheeses that are now available, and selecting only lean cuts of meat. Lean cuts of beef can usually be identified by the words "round" or "loin" in their names. You can make good use of herbs (preferrably fresh) and spices to fill the "flavor void" that can result from the diminished fat content.

While the quantity of fat used in cooking is important, so is the *type* of fat used. In testing the recipes for this book, when a vegetable oil was called for, we used canola oil. This is a good all-purpose oil which contains very little saturated fat and has a large percentage of monounsaturated fat. Olive oil was used for certain recipes where its special flavor enhances the overall enjoyment of a particular pasta dish. Olive oil and canola oil have similar chemical properties. Because they are in a liquid state, they do not contain trans-fatty acids. (Trans-fatty acids are formed when liquid oils are processed into solid fats and are believed to behave in a manner similar to saturated fats.)

SOURCES OF FIBER

Another mainstay of healthy eating, fiber is derived largely from plant foods. By eating the recommended 5 to 10 servings of vegetables and fruits and the 5 to 12 servings of grain products each day, you should obtain the average suggested intake of approximately 25 grams of fiber daily. Choose whole-grain products frequently, as well as legumes (beans, peas and lentils) to ensure an adequate intake of fiber. Vegetarian meals that combine pasta and legumes offer an endless variety of interesting meals. Check the soup section in this book for some great ideas.

A WORD ABOUT PHYTOCHEMICALS

The importance of plant foods in our diet is being stressed more and more. This is because research has identified the potential benefits of many naturally occurring substances in plant foods, known as phytochemicals. These appear to offer protection from a number of major medical problems, and may even slow the aging process.

Most people enjoy eating vegetables and fruits, but few consume the recommended 5 to 10 servings daily — often choosing to pop vitamin pills instead of eating well. Until research has produced more specific recommendations, do what your mother always said: Eat your vegetables!

Some highly recommended vegetables and fruits are:

▼ Cruciferous vegetables such as broccoli, brussels sprouts, cauliflower and cabbage.

▼ Umbelliferous vegetables such as carrots, parsley, parsnips and celery.

▼ Allium vegetables such as garlic, onions and chives.

▼ Citrus fruits and others that are good sources of vitamin C.

▼ Dark green and orange-yellow vegetables and fruit.

▼ Legumes.

Many of these vegetables and fruits are ingredients used by the recipes in this book.

GUIDELINES FOR HEALTHY EATING

Finally, consider the following recommendations, taken from government food guides in the United States and Canada:

1. Enjoy a variety of foods.

2. Emphasize cereals, breads, other grain products, vegetables and fruits.

3. Choose lower-fat dairy products, leaner meats and foods prepared with little or no fat.

4. Achieve and maintain a healthy body weight by enjoying regular physical activity and healthy eating.

5. Limit salt, alcohol and caffeine.

Note the #1 recommendation: variety. Pasta comes in so many shapes and sizes, colors and flavors that the variety is almost endless!

These common-sense principles are at the heart of a balanced, healthy diet — and of this book.

Enjoy your Light Pasta!

Helen Chambers RD

Lorraine Fullum-Bouchard RD

Carolyn Guyton-Ringbloom MBA, RD
U.S. Nutrition Consultant

Nutritionist's Note: *All recipes have been analyzed for the ingredients given in the main body of the recipe. Where substitute or optional ingredients are used (for example, as suggested in the Tips portion of the recipe), nutritional values may change.*

PASTA BASICS

COOKING TIPS

1. Cook pasta in a large pot of boiling water. Use 12 to 16 cups (3 to 4L) water for each pound (500 g) of pasta. Add a little oil to prevent pasta from sticking. Stir pasta occasionally while cooking.

2. Cook pasta "al dente," or firm to the bite. Never overcook or it will become soft and loses all its texture. When cooked, drain in colander, then transfer to a serving dish. If pasta is to be eaten right away, add sauce immediately and toss. If not, add a little sauce, water or chicken stock (so pasta does not stick), then cover and set aside. Do not add sauce to pasta until just ready to serve, or pasta will absorb the sauce, leaving the appearance of not enough.

3. Prepare the sauce while the pasta is cooking. Plan ahead so the sauce will be completed at the same time the pasta is cooked.

4. For these recipes, 1/2 lb (250 g) dry pasta serves 4 people, 3/4 lb (375 g) serves 6 people, and 1 lb (500 g) serves 8 people.

5. You can prepare the pasta early in the day if necessary. Drain cooked pasta, rinse with cold water and add 3 tbsp (45 mL) of stock or 3 tbsp (45 mL) of the sauce to be used, or 3 tbsp (45 mL) of the water in which the pasta was cooked. (This will ensure that pasta strands do not stick.) Let sit at room temperature. Before serving, either warm slightly in a microwave for 1 minute at High (be careful not to overcook the pasta), or heat sauce well and pour over pasta immediately.

6. Heavier pasta such as rigatoni or jumbo shells needs a heavier, more robust sauce. Lighter pasta such as fettucine, linguine or

spaghetti need a finer sauce and more finely diced vegetables. Sauces for rotini or penne should be somewhere between fine and robust.

7. Homemade pastas can be delicious (see page 223 for information on making fresh pasta), but most of the time I use dried pasta. There are several reasons for this:

   • It is easier to find, store, and costs much less than fresh.

   • It lacks the fat and cholesterol of the fresh types, which have eggs added.

   • There are more varieties of dry pasta readily available.

   • Dried pastas have consistent flavor and texture. Fresh pasta can stick, even if cooked properly, and is best only if cooked immediately after the pasta is made.

   • It can be stored at room temperature for up to 1 year.

8. If reheating leftover pasta, add more stock or tomato sauce to provide extra moisture.

THE COMPLETE PASTA PANTRY

There are a number of key ingredients that you'll find useful to have on hand for the recipes in this book.

ARTICHOKES

You can use canned, drained artichokes or cook your own. If using fresh artichokes, cook them in boiling, salted water or a dry white wine that has been flavored with herbs and oil. Cook just until tender, approximately 30 minutes, for larger hearts. Test doneness by pulling off an outer leaf. If it pulls off easily, the artichoke is ready. Peel off leaves until you reach the heart.

BUTTER OR MARGARINE

In this book butter or margarine can be used interchangeably, depending on one's preference. Butter is a saturated (animal) fat, and therefore contains cholesterol. Margarine has no cholesterol, and is not a saturated fat. Both contain similar amounts of fat and calories.

Unsalted butter has a fresher and healthier taste. It can be kept frozen so that you can always have it on hand. If cholesterol is a concern, substitute a good-quality vegetable margarine.

CHEESES

There is no "perfect" cheese for a specific pasta dish. The recipes give recommendations, but feel free to substitute. If you feel the taste of a cheese is too strong, substitute a milder cheese and vice versa. Below is a list of common cheeses used with pasta.

In light pasta cooking, the key is lowering the amount of cheese used, not eliminating it. I use whole-fat cheeses for their taste, but use lesser amounts.

The Best Hard Cheeses for Grating

Parmesan is probably the most common cheese used with pasta. It is always better to buy it fresh and grate it yourself. If you need grated cheese on hand, most groceries have a deli department where they sell it freshly grated. The packaged grated cheese is not as fresh and does not always contain the best parmigiana cheeses. Parmesan should have a good golden colour, which indicates a younger cheese. The best Parmesan will be labelled "Parmigiano-Reggiano."

Either grated or whole, Parmesan cheese can be stored for long periods in the refrigerator. If storing in whole pieces, wrap each piece tightly with plastic wrap and then with foil; this will keep for several months. Grate these just before serving.

Asiago. A hard, dry cheese with a strong flavor.

Aged Provolone. A pear-shaped cheese. The aging gives it a strong taste.

Aged Gouda. Hard and tasty.

Romano. Very sharp and salty. If you do not like the taste, substitute Parmesan.

Soft Cheeses

Blue Cheeses. These include **Roquefort, Gorgonzola, Danish Blue,** and **Stilton.** Soft and creamy with a blue mold. Very distinct flavor. They are usually used in combination with a milder cheese.

Cottage Cheese. White, soft curds; can be used interchangeably with Ricotta cheese. I use 2% cottage cheese for the best flavor and texture.

Cream Cheese. Soft and creamy. Ricotta or cottage cheese can be substituted, or light cream cheese (with 25% fewer calories) can be used.

Goat Cheese (chevre). Distinctive flavor, made from goat's milk. When wrapped tightly, will keep for 3 to 4 weeks in the refrigerator.

Mascarpone. A delicious double cream, soft and creamy Italian cheese usually used in Tiramisu, an Italian dessert. Can be substituted for ricotta or cream cheese.

Ricotta. Creamy and bland. Use in place of cottage cheese, cream cheese or mascarpone cheese. Ricotta comes in 5% or 10% fat. Either can be used. Read expiry date on package container. This cheese can usually be kept for 7 to 10 days.

Semi-Soft Cheeses

Brie. Soft, mild and sweet cheese.

Emmentaler. Type of Swiss cheese. Firm texture with a pleasant, nutty flavor.

Fontina. Creamy and buttery whole-fat cheese. Any mild cheese can be substituted.

Havarti. Mild and sweet. Any mild cheese can be substituted.

Gruyère. A type of Swiss cheese with a tasty, delicate flavor. Sweeter than Emmentaler.

Jarlsberg. Nutty, Swiss-like flavor. An excellent cheese for cooking or eating.

Mozzarella. Creamy, mild, and sweet. Can be kept for 2 to 3 weeks if wrapped tightly. This cheese can be replaced with low-fat versions because of its mild taste.

Monterey Jack. Soft and mild. Any mild cheese can be substituted.

Muenster. Creamy and bland. Any creamy, mild cheese can be substituted.

CHICKEN AND MEAT

Meat recipes generally call for quantities of 1/2 to 3/4 lb (250 to 375 g). These include: ground beef, chicken or veal; boneless, skinless chicken breast; lean steak; boneless pork; stewing beef or veal; spicy and sweet sausages.

FISH AND SEAFOOD

Except where noted, fish and seafood ingredients are interchangeable in most recipes. Buy fresh where possible, although frozen ingredients work well, too. Keep in mind that shellfish freezes better than fish fillets. Shrimps, scallops or squid, when well wrapped, can be kept in the freezer for up to 2 months.

Canned clams are extremely useful to have on hand, since they make a good seafood sauce if fresh fish is unavailable. The liquid can be used as a seafood stock.

GARLIC

Fresh, whole, firm heads of garlic are always the best to use. Stored in a cool, dry, airy spot, they will stay fresh for 2 to 3 weeks. Garlic powder or salt should not be used if a true garlic taste is required. Chopped garlic, packed in a jar of oil, can be quite good (refrigerate after opening). Still, the fullest garlic flavor comes only from fresh cloves.

HERBS

Fresh herbs such as basil, coriander (also called Chinese parsley), dill, parsley and oregano are most commonly used for pasta dishes. Fresh herbs are almost always preferable to dried. (The exception is for sauces that require longer cooking times, in which case dried herbs provide a more intense flavor.)

When fresh herbs are not in season, use dried herbs. Be sure to keep them in airtight jars, stored in a cool, dry place.

Good dried herbs to keep on hand include basil, oregano, dill, chili powder, chili flakes and cayenne pepper.

The recipes in this book include measurements for both fresh and dried herbs. A good rule to follow is 1/2 tsp (2 mL) of dried for 1 tbsp (15 mL) of fresh herbs.

MISCELLANEOUS ESSENTIALS

Beans. Keep a good variety of canned beans on hand, including red and white kidney beans, chick peas and black beans. These are great in pasta salads and soups.

Black olives. Canned, pitted black olives are easy to measure and can be used in a number of pasta dishes.

Oriental ingredients. These are handy to have for Asian pasta dishes: rice wine vinegar, hoisin sauce, soya sauce, sesame oil, oyster sauce and ginger root (fresh or marinated in oil).

Pine nuts. Store in freezer and toast before use. Toast either in 400°F (200°C) oven for 10 to 15 minutes until golden or on top of oven in skillet for 2 to 3 minutes.

MUSHROOMS

Regular white mushrooms are called for in most recipes, but you can substitute wild mushrooms such as oyster, cremini, portobello or shiitake. They give an exotic flavor and texture to the pasta dish and are well worth the extra expense. Many groceries now carry a variety of different mushrooms.

Dried mushrooms can also be used. They should be soaked in approximately 1 cup (250 mL) of warm water or stock for 30 minutes. Drain well before using. Usually, 1 oz (30 g) of dry mushrooms equals 1/2 lb (250 g) of fresh.

OIL

Vegetable or olive oil is specified in each recipe. Canola oil is the best vegetable oil to use.

For olive oil, the "first pressed" or "extra virgin" varieties are best because of their rich, fruity consistency. The first pressing is important because the oil has not been heated and is free from chemical additives. The darker the oil, the richer the olive taste. If the flavor is too strong for you, high-quality lighter oils are available and provide a more subtle taste. Oils labelled "cold-pressed" are good when you want the olive taste to be dominant, or if dipping bread.

The least expensive olive oil is labelled "pure olive oil," and is made from the second or third pressings. This can be used as a substitute for other vegetable oils, when the taste of olive oil is not important.

Both vegetable and olive oils should be stored in dark cool places for 1 1/2 to 2 years. After opening, use within 8 to 12 weeks.

STOCK

For chicken, beef, vegetable and seafood stock, try to find the time to make your own. It's simple and yields the best results.

In 12 cups (3 L) of water, boil a variety of vegetables such as carrots, onions and celery with your favorite dried herbs and spices. For chicken, meat or fish stocks, add 2 lbs (1 kg) of chicken, beef or fish bones, and simmer for 2 hours. Strain the liquid and use immediately, or freeze for up to 2 months.

If homemade stock is unavailable, use canned broth. Otherwise, use bouillon powders or cubes for chicken or beef stock (1 tsp [5 mL] added to 1 cup (250 mL) of hot water). Keep in mind, however, that these substitutes can be high in sodium.

Bottled clam juice or liquid from canned clams makes a good substitute for fish broth.

TOMATOES

Many of the recipes call for chopped or crushed tomatoes. When in season, fresh, ripe plum tomatoes are best. Do not ripen tomatoes in direct sunlight. Place them in a paper bag and leave in indirect sunlight. Chop them and try to save the juice for the sauce.

Canned tomatoes. When tomatoes are not in season, it is better to use canned tomatoes, preferably Italian plum. Use whole and break up with back of spoon while cooking. For crushed tomatoes place contents of can in food processor; switch on and off quickly until desired consistency is achieved.

Try not to use canned tomato sauce or seasoned tomatoes because the seasoning is not fresh, and the salt content is very high.

Tomato paste, a concentrated form of tomatoes, adds great flavor to sauces. It also helps to thicken the sauce. Buy small cans of paste. Refrigerate after opening, or freeze in small containers.

Tomato concentrate comes in a tube and is twice as intense as tomato paste. It has a better flavor than paste and leaves no bitter taste afterward.

Sun-dried tomatoes are available packaged dry or in bulk, or packed in oil. Pour boiling water over dry tomatoes and let soften for 15 minutes. Drain, then use. Use dry for less fat and calories.

VEGETABLES

A wide range of vegetables are used in my recipes. Most will keep for at least a week in the proper section of the refrigerator. In addition to tomatoes and mushrooms (discussed separately in this section), some that you may want to keep on hand include: green, red and/or yellow sweet bell peppers; red, white and yellow onions; carrots; zucchini; eggplant; broccoli; snow peas; green onions; potatoes and yams; and, in the freezer, sweet green peas and chopped spinach.

VINEGARS

Balsamic vinegar provides the mildest, sweetest taste. Other vinegars to have include those made from rice wine and red wine.

SOUPS

 SOUP TIPS

1. For soup stock, use 1 tsp (5 mL) powdered stock to 1 cup (250 mL) of boiling water for 1 cup (250 mL) of stock. Or use stock cubes, following package instructions. Homemade stock is excellent. Stocks can be frozen. Low-sodium stock is now available.

2. Using a large nonstick saucepan sprayed with vegetable spray allows you to sauté vegetables with minimal fat, and ensures that the food will not stick to the pan.

3. Always simmer soup covered, on a medium-low heat, stirring occasionally.

4. When puréeing soup, process in batches to achieve an even, smooth texture.

5. If soup appears too thick after cooking , add more stock.

6. For more fiber, use unpeeled vegetables.

7. Leftover vegetables are ideal for soups.

8. To ensure that vegetables such as broccoli, asparagus or zucchini retain maximum color, add during the last 5 minutes of cooking.

9. To avoid overcooking pasta, do not add to soup until the last 10 minutes of cooking. Stir occasionally so pasta does not clump together or stick to the bottom of the saucepan.

10. Since carrots take longer to become tender, chop them more finely than other vegetables.

11. When a recipe calls for canned crushed tomatoes, you can use whole canned tomatoes, puréed in a food processor with the juice, or use fresh puréed tomatoes.

PASTA AND BEAN SOUP (FAGIOLI)

Serves 6.

TIP

A combination of red and white kidney beans can be used. Mashing 1 cup (250 mL) of beans adds thickness to the soup.

MAKE AHEAD

Prepare early in day, but do not add pasta until 10 minutes before serving.

2 tsp	vegetable oil	2 F	10 mL
2 tsp	crushed garlic	—	10 mL
1/2 cup	chopped onions	1 ✓	125 mL
1/3 cup	chopped carrots	1 ✓	75 mL
1/3 cup	chopped celery	1 ✓	75 mL
2 cups	canned crushed tomatoes	4 ✓	500 mL
3 1/2 cups	beef or chicken stock	10 oc	875 mL
1 tsp	dried basil	—	5 mL
1/2 tsp	dried oregano	—	2 mL
3 cups	canned red kidney beans, drained	22 oz	750 mL
1/2 cup	macaroni or small shell pasta	2B	125 mL
3 tbsp	grated Parmesan cheese		45 mL

1. In large nonstick saucepan sprayed with vegetable spray, heat oil; sauté garlic, onions, carrots and celery for 5 minutes. Add tomatoes, stock, basil, oregano and 2 cups (500 mL) of beans. Mash remaining 1 cup (250 mL) of beans and add to soup.

2. Simmer for 15 minutes, stirring occasionally. Add pasta and simmer for 5 to 8 minutes or just until pasta is done. Add cheese.

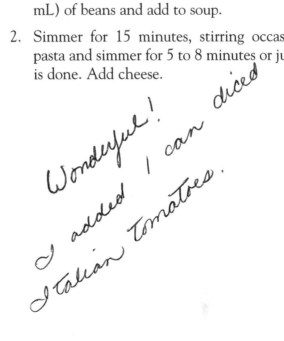

Wonderful! I added 1 can diced Italian tomatoes.

PER SERVING

Calories	250
Protein	12 g
Fat, total	5 g
Fat, saturated	2 g
Carbohydrates	40 g
Sodium	1210 mg
Cholesterol	6 mg
Fiber	9 g

 # WHITE BEAN SPINACH PASTA SOUP

Serves 6.

TIP

Chick peas or navy beans can replace white kidney beans.

Half a 10-oz (300 g) package of fresh chopped spinach can be used instead of frozen.

MAKE AHEAD

Prepare soup early in day, but do not add pasta until 10 minutes before serving.

2 tsp	vegetable oil	10 mL
1 1/2 tsp	chopped garlic	7 mL
1 cup	chopped onions	250 mL
2/3 cup	finely chopped carrots	150 mL
1/2	package (10 oz [300 g]) frozen spinach (chopped, thawed and squeezed dry)	1/2
4 cups	chicken broth	1 L
1	can (19 oz [540 mL]) crushed tomatoes	1
1 1/2 cups	canned white kidney beans, drained	375 mL
1 1/2 tsp	dried basil	7 mL
1	bay leaf	1
1/3 cup	macaroni	75 mL
1 tbsp	grated Parmesan cheese	15 mL

1. In nonstick saucepan sprayed with vegetable spray, heat oil; sauté garlic, onions and carrots until softened, approximately 5 minutes.

2. Add spinach, broth, tomatoes, beans, basil and bay leaf; cover and simmer for 15 minutes. Add pasta and cook for 10 minutes or until pasta is just tender. Sprinkle with Parmesan cheese.

PER SERVING

Calories	188
Protein	9 g
Fat, total	3 g
Fat, saturated	0.7 g
Carbohydrates	33 g
Sodium	1040 mg
Cholesterol	2 mg
Fiber	8 g

VEGETABLE, BEAN AND PLUM TOMATO SOUP

Serves 6.

TIP

Any combination of beans can be added, not exceeding 1 1/2 cups (375 mL). Chick peas, red kidney beans and/or black beans can be used.

MAKE AHEAD

Prepare early in day, but do not add macaroni until 10 minutes before serving.

2 tsp	vegetable oil	10 mL
2 tsp	crushed garlic	10 mL
1 cup	diced sweet red peppers	250 mL
1 cup	thinly sliced carrots	250 mL
1 cup	diced zucchini	250 mL
3/4 cup	chopped onions	175 mL
5	medium plum tomatoes, diced	5
5 cups	chicken or vegetable stock	1.25 L
1 1/2 tsp	dried basil	7 mL
1 tsp	dried oregano	5 mL
1 1/2 cups	canned white kidney beans, drained	375 mL
1/3 cup	macaroni	75 mL
	Pepper	
1/4 cup	grated Parmesan cheese	50 mL

1. In large nonstick saucepan sprayed with vegetable spray, heat oil; sauté garlic, red peppers, carrots, zucchini and onions until softened, approximately 5 minutes. Add tomatoes and sauté for 2 minutes. Add stock, basil and oregano. Simmer covered, on medium heat, for 20 minutes.

2. Add beans and pasta; cook for 10 more minutes. Add pepper and cheese.

PER SERVING

Calories	221
Protein	8 g
Fat, total	4 g
Fat, saturated	1 g
Carbohydrates	30 g
Sodium	1060 mg
Cholesterol	3 mg
Fiber	9 g

VEGETABLE, SWEET POTATO AND BEAN MINESTRONE

Serves 6.

TIP

Orzo resembles large rice but is really a small pasta.

Any cooked beans can replace white kidney beans.

MAKE AHEAD

Prepare soup up to a day ahead, but add pasta 10 minutes before serving.

2 tsp	vegetable oil	10 mL
2 tsp	crushed garlic	10 mL
1 1/2 cups	finely chopped onions	375 mL
1/2 cup	finely chopped carrots	125 mL
1/2 cup	finely chopped celery	125 mL
4 1/2 cups	chicken or vegetable stock	1.125 L
1 1/2 cups	sweet potatoes, peeled and finely chopped	375 mL
1 1/2 cups	sliced zucchini	375 mL
1	can (19 oz [540 mL]) tomatoes, crushed	1
3/4 cup	canned white or red kidney beans, drained	175 mL
1	bay leaf	1
2 tsp	dried basil	10 mL
1 tsp	dried oregano	5 mL
	Pepper	
1/3 cup	orzo or small shell pasta	75 mL
3 tbsp	grated Parmesan cheese	45 mL

1. In large nonstick saucepan, heat oil; sauté garlic, onions, carrots and celery until softened, approximately 5 minutes.

2. Add stock, potatoes, zucchini, tomatoes, kidney beans, bay leaf, basil and oregano; cover and simmer for approximately 40 minutes or until vegetables are tender, stirring occasionally. Remove bay leaf. Season with pepper to taste.

3. Add pasta; cook for 10 to 15 minutes, stirring often, or until orzo is firm to the bite. Sprinkle with cheese and pepper.

PER SERVING

Calories	247
Protein	10 g
Fat, total	5 g
Fat, saturated	2 g
Carbohydrates	43 g
Sodium	1100 mg
Cholesterol	6 mg
Fiber	9 g

CHICKEN PASTA VEGETABLE BEAN MINESTRONE (PAGE 24) ➤

Sweet Potato, White Bean and Orzo Soup

Serves 6.

TIP

Orzo looks like large rice but is really a pasta. The texture is excellent for this soup.

Be certain to stir after adding orzo, so they do not sink to bottom of pan.

MAKE AHEAD

Prepare early in day, up to the point of adding orzo. Add orzo 10 minutes before serving.

2 tsp	vegetable oil	10 mL
1 tsp	crushed garlic	5 mL
1 cup	chopped onions	250 mL
1/2 cup	chopped celery	125 mL
3 cups	diced sweet potatoes	750 mL
1/2 cup	diced carrots	125 mL
4 cups	chicken stock	1 L
1 cup	canned white kidney beans, drained	250 mL
1/3 cup	orzo or small shell pasta	75 mL
1 cup	2% milk	250 mL
	Chopped parsley	

1. In large nonstick saucepan, heat oil; sauté garlic, onions and celery until tender, approximately 4 minutes.

2. Add potatoes, carrots and stock. Cover and simmer on medium heat for 20 to 30 minutes or until potatoes are tender. Purée in food processor until smooth. Pour back into saucepan; add kidney beans and pasta. Cover and simmer for 10 minutes or until pasta is tender.

3. Add milk. Heat, then sprinkle with chopped parsley.

PER SERVING

Calories	242
Protein	8 g
Fat, total	3 g
Fat, saturated	0.7 g
Carbohydrates	47 g
Sodium	799 mg
Cholesterol	3 mg
Fiber	8 g

◄ Mango Salsa over Vermicelli (page 43)

TOMATO, ZUCCHINI AND TORTELLINI SOUP

Serves 6.

TIP

Small ravioli or gnocchi can replace tortellini.

MAKE AHEAD

Prepare early in day, but do not add pasta until 10 minutes before serving.

2 tsp	vegetable oil	10 mL
1 1/2 tsp	crushed garlic	7 mL
1 cup	chopped onions	250 mL
1/3 cup	chopped carrots	75 mL
2 cups	chicken stock	500 mL
1	can (28 oz [796 mL]) crushed tomatoes	1
2 tsp	dried basil	10 mL
1 tsp	dried oregano	5 mL
6 oz	cheese tortellini	150 g
1 cup	diced zucchini	250 mL

1. In large nonstick saucepan, heat oil; sauté garlic, onions and carrots until tender, approximately 5 minutes.

2. Add stock, tomatoes, basil and oregano. Simmer on medium heat for 15 minutes, stirring occasionally.

3. Add tortellini and zucchini and cook for 10 minutes or just until pasta is cooked.

PER SERVING

Calories	151
Protein	6 g
Fat, total	4 g
Fat, saturated	0.5 g
Carbohydrates	25 g
Sodium	577 mg
Cholesterol	0.2 mg
Fiber	5 g

TOMATO VEGETABLE PASTA SOUP

Serves 6.

TIP

A medium onion can replace leek.

Sweet potatoes can replace regular potatoes to give a unique sweetness to soup.

Any small shell pasta can be used.

MAKE AHEAD

Prepare soup early in day. Do not add pasta until 10 minutes before serving.

2 tsp	vegetable oil	10 mL
1 1/2 tsp	crushed garlic	7 mL
1	medium leek, sliced	1
1 cup	thinly sliced carrots	250 mL
1 cup	sliced celery	250 mL
1 cup	diced potatoes	250 mL
4 cups	chicken broth	1 L
1	can (19 oz [540 mL]) crushed tomatoes	1
1 1/2 cups	canned white kidney beans, drained	375 mL
1	bay leaf	1
1 1/2 tsp	dried basil	7 mL
1 tsp	dried oregano	5 mL
1/3 cup	broken linguine	75 mL

1. In large nonstick saucepan sprayed with vegetable spray, heat oil; sauté garlic, leek, carrots and celery until tender.

2. Add potatoes, broth, tomatoes, beans, bay leaf, basil and oregano. Cover and simmer on medium heat for 20 minutes or until potatoes are tender.

3. Add pasta and cook for 10 minutes or until pasta is cooked.

PER SERVING

Calories	202
Protein	8 g
Fat, total	3 g
Fat, saturated	0.3 g
Carbohydrates	39 g
Sodium	1140 mg
Cholesterol	0 mg
Fiber	8 g

MEXICAN CORN, BEAN AND PASTA SOUP

Serves 6 to 8.

TIP

Chick peas or other beans can replace kidney beans.

Any small shell pasta can be used.

MAKE AHEAD

Prepare soup up to a day ahead, but do not add pasta until 10 minutes before serving.

2 tsp	vegetable oil	10 mL
2 tsp	crushed garlic	10 mL
1 cup	chopped onions	250 mL
1 1/2 cups	chopped sweet green peppers	375 mL
1	can (28 oz [796 mL]) crushed tomatoes	1
2 1/2 cups	chicken stock	625 mL
2 cups	canned red kidney beans, drained	500 mL
1 cup	corn niblets	250 mL
1 tbsp	chili powder	15 mL
1/4 tsp	cayenne pepper	1 mL
1/2 cup	macaroni	125 mL
Dollop	yogurt	Dollop
	Coriander	

1. In large nonstick saucepan, heat oil; sauté garlic, onions and green peppers until soft, approximately 5 minutes.

2. Add tomatoes, stock, beans, corn niblets, chili powder and cayenne. Cover and simmer on low heat for 20 minutes.

3. Add pasta, simmer for 10 to 12 minutes or until pasta is "al dente" (firm to the bite). Garnish with yogurt and fresh coriander.

PER SERVING (8)

Calories	187
Protein	7 g
Fat, total	3 g
Fat, saturated	0.2 g
Carbohydrates	37 g
Sodium	682 mg
Cholesterol	0 mg
Fiber	7 g

Chili, Chicken, Bean and Pasta Stew

Serves 4 to 6.

TIP

Ground pork or veal can replace chicken.

▼

Sweet potatoes are a nice change from white potatoes.

▼

Adjust spiciness by adding more cayenne.

MAKE AHEAD

Prepare soup up to a day ahead, but do not add pasta until 10 minutes before serving.

PER SERVING (6)

Calories	245
Protein	16 g
Fat, total	4 g
Fat, saturated	0.4 g
Carbohydrates	39 g
Sodium	737 mg
Cholesterol	24 mg
Fiber	6 g

2 tsp	vegetable oil	10 mL
2 tsp	crushed garlic	10 mL
1 cup	chopped onions	250 mL
8 oz	ground chicken	250 g
1	can (19 oz [540 mL]) crushed tomatoes	1
2 1/2 cups	chicken stock	625 mL
1 1/2 cups	diced peeled potatoes	375 mL
1/2 cup	canned red kidney beans, drained	125 mL
1/2 cup	canned chick peas, drained	125 mL
2 tbsp	tomato paste	25 mL
1 tbsp	chili powder	15 mL
2 tsp	dried basil	10 mL
1 tsp	dried oregano	5 mL
Pinch	cayenne	Pinch
1/3 cup	macaroni	75 mL

1. In large nonstick saucepan, heat oil; sauté garlic and onions until softened, approximately 5 minutes.

2. Add chicken and cook, stirring to break up chunks, until no longer pink; pour off any fat.

3. Add tomatoes, stock, potatoes, kidney beans, chick peas, tomato paste, chili powder, basil, oregano and cayenne. Cover and reduce heat; simmer for 40 minutes, stirring occasionally.

4. Add pasta; cook until firm to the bite, approximately 10 minutes.

 # CHICKEN PASTA VEGETABLE ✕ BEAN MINESTRONE

Serves 6.

TIP

The unusual sweet chicken flavor is due to the sweet potatoes. White potatoes can be used or a combination of both.

By adding the chicken at the end, the meat does not become overcooked.

MAKE AHEAD

Prepare early in day, but set aside the broccoli, linguine and chicken. Reheat gently and add the three ingredients 10 minutes before serving.

PER SERVING

Calories	213
Protein	12 g
Fat, total	4 g
Fat, saturated	0.5 g
Carbohydrates	35 g
Sodium	877 mg
Cholesterol	18 mg
Fiber	6 g

2 tsp	vegetable oil	10 mL
1 tsp	crushed garlic	5 mL
3/4 cup	chopped onions	175 mL
3/4 cup	finely chopped carrots	175 mL
1 cup	sliced mushrooms	250 mL
1 cup	diced sweet potatoes	250 mL
5 cups	chicken stock	1.25 L
1 cup	canned red kidney beans or chick peas, drained	250 mL
6 oz	skinless, boneless, chicken breast, diced	150 g
1 cup	chopped broccoli	250 mL
1/3 cup	small shell pasta or broken linguine	75 mL
1/4 cup	chopped parsley	50 mL

1. In large nonstick saucepan, heat oil; sauté garlic, onions and carrots until tender, approximately 7 minutes. Add mushrooms and sauté for 4 minutes.

2. Add sweet potatoes, stock and beans. Cover and simmer on low heat for 12 minutes or until sweet potatoes are just tender.

3. Add chicken, broccoli and pasta; simmer for 7 minutes or until pasta and chicken are cooked. Sprinkle with parsley.

 # BOK CHOY NOODLE AND TOFU CHICKEN SOUP

Serves 6.

TIP

Nappa cabbage, found in the lettuce section of grocery stores, can replace bok choy.

Spaghettini or capellini can also be used.

Try adding 3 oz (75 g) of shrimp or cubed boneless chicken with pasta.

MAKE AHEAD

This soup is best prepared just before serving so the pasta and vegetables do not get overcooked and lose their color.

2 tsp	sesame oil	10 mL
1 1/2 tsp	minced ginger root	7 mL
1 tsp	crushed garlic	5 mL
2 1/2 cups	chopped bok choy	625 mL
2/3 cup	chopped green onions	150 mL
1/3 cup	chicken stock	75 mL
6 cups	chicken stock	1.5 L
2 tbsp	soya sauce	25 mL
3/4 cup	broken rice vermicelli	175 mL
1/2 cup	chopped snow peas	125 mL
1/2 cup	diced sweet red peppers	125 mL
1 cup	firm tofu, cut into small cubes	250 mL

1. In large nonstick saucepan, heat oil; sauté ginger, garlic, bok choy and green onions with 1/3 cup (75 mL) stock, covered, for approximately 5 minutes.

2. Add stock; bring to boil and add soya sauce, vermicelli, snow peas, red peppers and tofu. Cook for 3 minutes on medium heat until pasta is cooked.

PER SERVING

Calories	162
Protein	8 g
Fat, total	6 g
Fat, saturated	0.6 g
Carbohydrates	20 g
Sodium	1020 mg
Cholesterol	0 mg
Fiber	3 g

Chunky Veal, Corn and Pasta Soup

Serves 6.

TIP

Stewing beef can replace veal.

▼

Sweet potatoes make an unusual replacement for white potatoes.

▼

Macaroni, tubetti or orzo pasta can be used.

MAKE AHEAD

Prepare early in day, not adding pasta until 10 minutes before serving.

1 tbsp	vegetable oil	15 mL
2 tsp	crushed garlic	10 mL
12 oz	stewing veal, cut into 1-inch (2.5-cm) pieces	375 g
1 cup	chopped onions	250 mL
3/4 cup	chopped celery	175 mL
1 cup	finely chopped carrots	250 mL
1 cup	sliced mushrooms	250 mL
1 cup	green beans, cut in half	250 mL
1 cup	diced potatoes	250 mL
4 cups	beef or chicken stock	1 L
1/2 cup	corn niblets	125 mL
1	can (19 oz [540 mL]) crushed tomatoes	1
1	bay leaf	1
2 tsp	basil	10 mL
1 1/2 tsp	oregano	7 mL
1/3 cup	small shaped pasta	75 mL

1. In large nonstick saucepan, heat oil; sauté garlic and veal just until veal is browned on all sides, approximately 3 minutes.

2. Add onions, celery and carrots; cook on medium heat for 10 minutes or until soft.

3. Add mushrooms and green beans; cook for 2 minutes. Add potatoes, stock, niblets, tomatoes, bay leaf, basil and oregano; cover and simmer on low heat for 30 minutes, stirring occasionally.

4. Add pasta; cook just until firm to the bite, approximately 10 minutes.

PER SERVING

Calories	245
Protein	22 g
Fat, total	8 g
Fat, saturated	3 g
Carbohydrates	22 g
Sodium	472 mg
Cholesterol	58 mg
Fiber	7 g

CHUNKY VEAL STEW over RIGATONI

Serves 6.

TIP

Stewing beef or pork can replace veal.

Substitute other vegetables of your choice.

MAKE AHEAD

Prepare stew up to the day before. Reheat gently, adding more stock if too thick.

12 oz	rigatoni	375 g
2 tsp	vegetable oil	10 mL
12 oz	boneless stewing veal, cut into 1-inch (2.5-cm) cubes	375 g
2 tsp	crushed garlic	10 mL
1 cup	chopped onions	250 mL
3/4 cup	diced carrots	175 mL
1 cup	sliced zucchini	250 mL
1/3 cup	dry red wine	75 mL
1 cup	sliced mushrooms	250 mL
1 cup	beef or chicken stock	250 mL
1	can (19 oz [540 mL]) crushed tomatoes	1
2 tbsp	tomato paste	25 mL
1	bay leaf	1
2 tsp	chili powder	10 mL
2 tsp	dried basil	10 mL
1 1/2 tsp	dried oregano	7 mL
1/3 cup	grated Parmesan cheese	75 mL
	Pepper	

PER SERVING

Calories	285
Protein	20 g
Fat, total	5 g
Fat, saturated	0.8 g
Carbohydrates	43 g
Sodium	986 mg
Cholesterol	53 mg
Fiber	6 g

1. Cook pasta in boiling water according to package instructions or until firm to the bite. Drain and place in serving bowl.

2. In medium nonstick saucepan sprayed with vegetable spray, add 1 tsp (5 mL) oil. Sauté veal until browned on all sides, approximately 4 minutes. Remove meat and set aside.

3. Add the remaining 1 tsp (5 mL) oil to saucepan and sauté garlic, onions, carrots and zucchini until tender, approximately 5 minutes. Add wine and cook for 2 minutes. Add mushrooms and sauté for 4 minutes. Add stock, tomatoes and tomato paste, bay leaf, chili powder, basil, oregano and veal. Cover and simmer for 50 to 60 minutes or until veal is tender. Pour over pasta. Sprinkle with cheese and pepper, and toss.

CLAM AND PASTA CHOWDER

Serves 6.

TIP

Sweet potatoes are a nice substitute for white potatoes. The soup acquires a sweeter taste.

MAKE AHEAD

Prepare early in day, not adding pasta until 10 minutes before serving.

2 tsp	vegetable oil	10 mL
1 1/2 tsp	crushed garlic	7 mL
1 cup	chopped onions	250 mL
1/2 cup	finely chopped carrots	125 mL
2/3 cup	chopped sweet green peppers	150 mL
1 1/2	cans (5 oz [140 mL]) clams, reserving juice from 1 can	1 1/2
1 cup	diced potatoes	250 mL
2 1/2 cups	canned or fresh tomatoes, crushed	625 mL
2 1/2 cups	seafood or chicken stock	625 mL
1/3 cup	tubetti or macaroni	75 mL

1. In large nonstick saucepan, heat oil; sauté garlic, onions, carrots and green peppers until tender, approximately 5 minutes.

2. Add juice of 1 can of clams, potatoes, tomatoes and stock. Cover and simmer for 20 minutes.

3. Add reserved clams and tubetti. Simmer for 10 minutes or until pasta is cooked.

PER SERVING

Calories	225
Protein	17 g
Fat, total	3 g
Fat, saturated	0.3 g
Carbohydrates	33 g
Sodium	636 mg
Cholesterol	32 mg
Fiber	4 g

SALADS

SALAD TIPS

1. Use fresh crisp vegetables for salads.

2. Fresh herbs are preferable to dried, since the intensity of flavors is more pronounced.

3. Wash and dry vegetables carefully before adding to salad to avoid excess liquid. If skins are not bruised, leave skins on for extra fiber.

4. Prepare pasta salad early in day before serving, without dressing. Cover and refrigerate. If prepared earlier, the vegetables will give off excess liquid and lose their crispness.

5. Prepare the dressing early in the day or up to 2 days before. Keep covered and refrigerated. Do not pour over salad until just ready to use. These pasta salads are best served at room temperature.

6. If serving the leftover pasta salad the next day, add a little more of a liquid called for in the recipe — such as lemon juice, stock or vinegar, but **not** oil — to provide extra moisture. Then toss well. If the recipe calls for chopped tomatoes, add more to add extra liquid.

7. To reduce the fat, cholesterol and calories of high-fat dressings, use 2% yogurt or light sour cream instead of mayonnaise. For dressings that serve 4 people, reduce the oil to 3 tbsp (45 mL) and increase the juices, stocks, vinegar or water.

ROTINI SALAD WITH ORIENTAL VEGETABLE SAUCE

Serves 6 to 8 as an appetizer.

TIP

Zucchini can replace the cucumber.

Use ginger marinated in oil, available in the vegetable section of the grocery store. It's easy to use and keeps indefinitely in the refrigerator.

MAKE AHEAD

Prepare pasta and sauce early in day. Toss up to 2 hours earlier. Toss again just before serving.

12 oz	rotini	375 g
Sauce		
1 cup	diced cucumbers	250 mL
1 cup	diced carrots	250 mL
1 cup	diced sweet red peppers	250 mL
1/3 cup	chopped green onions	75 mL
1/4 cup	chopped coriander or parsley	50 mL
3 tbsp	vegetable oil	45 mL
2 tsp	sesame oil	10 mL
3 tbsp	rice wine vinegar	45 mL
1/4 cup	chicken stock	50 mL
1 tbsp	soya sauce	15 mL
2 tsp	minced ginger root	10 mL
2 tsp	crushed garlic	10 mL

1. Cook pasta in boiling water according to package instructions or until firm to the bite. Rinse with cold water. Drain and place in serving bowl.

2. Make the sauce: In food processor, combine cucumbers, carrots, red peppers, onions, coriander, both oils, vinegar, stock, soya sauce, ginger and garlic. Process on and off for 30 seconds until finely diced. Pour over pasta, and toss.

PER SERVING (8)

Calories	256
Protein	7 g
Fat, total	7 g
Fat, saturated	0.6 g
Carbohydrates	41 g
Sodium	167 mg
Cholesterol	0 mg
Fiber	2 g

ITALIAN BEAN PASTA SALAD

Serves 6 to 8 as an
appetizer.

TIP

Use any combination of
cooked beans. Try black
beans or lima beans.

MAKE AHEAD

Prepare salad and dressing
early in the day. Toss up to
2 hours ahead.

12 oz	medium shell pasta	375 g
2 1/2 cups	chopped tomatoes	625 mL
3/4 cup	diced sweet green peppers	175 mL
3/4 cup	diced red onions	175 mL
2/3 cup	canned red kidney beans, drained	150 mL
2/3 cup	canned white kidney beans, drained	150 mL
2/3 cup	canned chick peas, drained	150 mL
3 oz	feta cheese, crumbled	75 g

Dressing

1/4 cup	lemon juice	50 mL
3 tbsp	olive oil	45 mL
1 tbsp	red wine vinegar	15 mL
2 tsp	crushed garlic	10 mL
2 1/2 tsp	dried basil	12 mL
1 1/2 tsp	dried oregano	7 mL

1. Cook pasta in boiling water according to package instructions or until firm to the bite. Rinse with cold water. Drain and place in serving bowl.

2. Add tomatoes, green peppers, onions, three beans and feta cheese.

3. Make the dressing: In small bowl add lemon juice, oil, vinegar, garlic, basil and oregano. Mix well. Pour over pasta, and toss.

PER SERVING (8)

Calories	333
Protein	11 g
Fat, total	9 g
Fat, saturated	2 g
Carbohydrates	53 g
Sodium	266 mg
Cholesterol	8 mg
Fiber	7 g

 # BOW-TIE PASTA SALAD WITH SHRIMP, SNOW PEAS AND RED PEPPERS IN ORANGE DRESSING

Serves 6 to 8 as an appetizer.

TIP

Substitute any other seafood or firm white fish fillet such as swordfish or orange roughy.

Fresh tarragon can replace cilantro for an unusual sweet flavor.

MAKE AHEAD

Prepare salad and dressing early in day. Do not toss until ready to eat.

12 oz	bow-tie pasta or rotini	375 g
12 oz	shrimp, peeled, deveined, and cut in half	375 g
1 cup	thinly sliced sweet red peppers	250 mL
1 cup	snow peas, cut in half	250 mL
1 cup	canned mandarin orange segments, drained	250 mL
1 cup	sliced water chestnuts	250 mL

Dressing

4 tbsp	olive oil	60 mL
4 tbsp	frozen orange juice concentrate, thawed	60 mL
4 tbsp	lemon juice	60 mL
2 tbsp	balsamic vinegar	25 mL
1 1/2 tsp	crushed garlic	7 mL
1/2 cup	chopped cilantro or parsley	125 mL

1. Cook pasta in boiling water according to package instructions or until firm to the bite. Rinse with cold water. Drain and place in serving bowl.

2. In medium nonstick skillet sprayed with vegetable spray, sauté shrimp just until pink, approximately 4 minutes. Do not overcook. Add to pasta.

3. Add red peppers, snow peas, orange segments and water chestnuts.

4. Make the dressing: In small bowl combine oil, orange juice concentrate, lemon juice, vinegar, garlic and cilantro. Pour over salad, and toss.

PER SERVING (8)

Calories	385
Protein	18 g
Fat, total	9 g
Fat, saturated	1 g
Carbohydrates	57 g
Sodium	52 mg
Cholesterol	71 mg
Fiber	3 g

CREAMY SEAFOOD PASTA SALAD

Serves 6 to 8 as an appetizer.

TIP

Firm fish fillets can be used with or instead of mixed seafood. Be careful not to overcook.

Grilled fish instead of sautéed makes an excellent variation.

MAKE AHEAD

Pasta salad and dressing can be prepared early in day. Do not toss until ready to serve.

12 oz	medium shell pasta	375 g
1 lb	mixed seafood (combination of scallops, shrimp, squid and/or firm white fish fillets) cut into 2-inch (5-cm) pieces	500 g
1 1/2 cups	diced sweet red peppers	375 mL
1 cup	diced sweet green peppers	250 mL
3/4 cup	diced red onions	175 mL
3/4 cup	thinly sliced carrots	175 mL
1/2 cup	chopped green onions	125 mL

Dressing

1 cup	2% yogurt	250 mL
1/3 cup	light mayonnaise	75 mL
1/2 cup	chopped fresh dill (or 1 1/2 tbsp [20 mL] dried)	125 mL
2 tbsp	lemon juice	25 mL
2 tsp	crushed garlic	10 mL
1 tsp	Dijon mustard	5 mL

1. Cook pasta in boiling water according to package instructions or until firm to the bite. Rinse with cold water. Drain and place in serving bowl.

2. In medium nonstick skillet sprayed with vegetable spray, sauté seafood just until cooked, approximately 3 minutes. Set aside.

3. Add red and green peppers, onions, carrots and green onions to pasta. Add seafood.

4. Make the dressing: In small bowl combine yogurt, mayonnaise, dill, lemon juice, garlic and mustard. Pour over pasta. Toss and chill.

PER SERVING (8)

Calories	374
Protein	23 g
Fat, total	6 g
Fat, saturated	0.9 g
Carbohydrates	59 g
Sodium	191 mg
Cholesterol	89 mg
Fiber	7 g

 # PENNE SALAD WITH TOMATOES, GOAT CHEESE AND BASIL

Serves 6.

TIP

Apple cider vinegar can replace balsamic vinegar.

Try feta cheese instead of goat cheese.

Use juicy ripe tomatoes to give the salad enough liquid.

MAKE AHEAD

Prepare tomato dressing early in day to marinate. Do not toss until ready to serve.

12 oz	penne	375 g
3 cups	chopped tomatoes	750 mL
2 tsp	crushed garlic	10 mL
2 tbsp	olive oil	25 mL
2 tbsp	balsamic vinegar	25 mL
3 oz	goat cheese, crumbled	75 g
3/4 cup	chopped fresh basil (or 2 tsp [10 mL] dried)	175 mL
1/3 cup	sliced black olives	75 mL
	Pepper	

1. Cook pasta in boiling water according to package instructions or until firm to the bite. Rinse with cold water. Drain and place in serving bowl.

2. Add tomatoes, garlic, oil, vinegar, cheese, basil, olives and pepper. Toss until cheese begins to melt.

PER SERVING

Calories	333
Protein	11 g
Fat, total	8 g
Fat, saturated	2 g
Carbohydrates	54 g
Sodium	167 mg
Cholesterol	4 mg
Fiber	4 g

PASTA WITH LIME, CORIANDER AND SCALLOP SEVICHE

Serves 6 to 8 as an appetizer.

TIP

Thinly sliced tuna or salmon can replace scallops.

Fresh herbs, not dried, are a must here.

MAKE AHEAD

Prepare scallop marinade 3 to 4 hours ahead. Do not add pasta until ready to serve.

12 oz	penne	375 g
12 oz	scallops, sliced in 1/2-inch (1-cm) pieces	375 g
1 1/2 cups	diced sweet red peppers	375 mL
1 3/4 cups	diced tomatoes	425 mL
3/4 cup	diced red onions	175 mL
3/4 cup	diced sweet green peppers	175 mL
1/2 cup	chopped coriander or parsley	125 mL
1/4 cup	olive oil	50 mL
1/4 cup	lime or lemon juice	50 mL
2 1/2 tsp	crushed garlic	12 mL

1. Cook pasta in boiling water according to package instructions or until firm to the bite. Rinse with cold water. Drain and place in serving bowl. Cover and set aside.

2. In small bowl add scallops, red peppers, tomatoes, onions, green peppers, coriander, oil, lime juice and garlic. Toss and chill for at least 1 to 2 hours. Pour over pasta and toss.

PER SERVING (8)

Calories	309
Protein	16 g
Fat, total	10 g
Fat, saturated	1 g
Carbohydrates	46 g
Sodium	309 mg
Cholesterol	16 mg
Fiber	4 g

 CREAMY CRABMEAT SALAD ✕
OVER MACARONI

**Serves 6 to 8
as an appetizer.**

TIP

Cooked shrimp, scallops
or squid or a combination
are delicious as a
replacement for crabmeat.

Sweet red or yellow
peppers can replace
green peppers.

MAKE AHEAD

Prepare sauce up to a
day ahead. Do not toss
until ready to serve.

8 oz	macaroni or small shell pasta	250 g
12 oz	crabmeat, chopped	375 g

<u>Sauce</u>

1 cup	tomato juice	250 mL
1/4 cup	chili sauce	50 mL
1 tsp	crushed garlic	5 mL
3/4 cup	chopped cucumbers	175 mL
1/2 cup	chopped celery	125 mL
1/2 cup	chopped sweet green peppers	125 mL
1/3 cup	chopped red onions	75 mL
1/2 cup	chopped parsley	125 mL
1/4 cup	light mayonnaise	50 mL

1. Cook pasta in boiling water according to package instructions or until firm to the bite. Rinse with cold water. Drain and place in serving bowl. Add chopped crabmeat.

2. Make the sauce: In food processor combine tomato juice, chili sauce, garlic, cucumbers, celery, green peppers, onions, parsley and mayonnaise. Process on and off just until vegetables are finely chopped. Pour over pasta; toss and chill for at least 1 hour.

PER SERVING (8)

Calories	205
Protein	14 g
Fat, total	3 g
Fat, saturated	0.3 g
Carbohydrates	30 g
Sodium	510 mg
Cholesterol	26 mg
Fiber	2 g

 ROTINI NIÇOISE ⋙⋘

**Serves 6 to 8
as an appetizer.**

TIP

Serves 4 as a main meal.

For cucumber garnish, use
a vegetable peeler down
the length of the cucumber
to create thin shavings.

MAKE AHEAD

Prepare salad and dressing
early in day, but do not
toss until ready to serve.

12 oz	rotini	375 g
6 oz	green beans, cut in pieces	150 g
1 3/4 cups	chopped tomatoes	425 mL
3/4 cup	diced cucumbers	175 mL
3/4 cup	diced sweet red or green peppers	175 mL
1/2 cup	sliced red onions	125 mL
1	can (6.5 oz [185g]) flaked tuna packed in water, drained	1
1/3 cup	sliced olives	75 mL
1/2 cup	chopped fresh dill (or 1 tbsp [15 mL] dried)	125 mL
5	anchovies, minced	5

<u>Dressing</u>

1/3 cup	olive oil	75 mL
1/4 cup	lemon juice	50 mL
1/4 cup	balsamic vinegar	50 mL
2 tbsp	water	25 mL
2 tsp	crushed garlic	10 mL
	Cucumber shavings	

PER SERVING (8)
⋙⋘⋙⋘⋙⋘

Calories	333
Protein	14 g
Fat, total	12 g
Fat, saturated	2 g
Carbohydrates	45 g
Sodium	307 mg
Cholesterol	4 mg
Fiber	4 g

⋙⋘⋙⋘⋙⋘

1. Cook pasta in boiling water according to package instructions or until firm to the bite. Rinse with cold water. Drain and place in serving bowl.

2. Blanch green beans in boiling water just until still crisp, approximately 2 minutes. Drain, rinse with cold water and add to pasta. Add tomatoes, cucumbers, sweet peppers, onions, tuna, olives, dill and anchovies.

3. Make the dressing: In small bowl combine oil, lemon juice, vinegar, water and garlic. Pour over pasta, and toss. Garnish with cucumber shavings.

 # GREEK PASTA SALAD

Serves 6 to 8
as an appetizer.

TIP

Penne, rotini or medium
shell pasta can be used.

Sweet Vidalia onions are
excellent when in season.

Fresh oregano makes this
salad exceptional.

MAKE AHEAD

Prepare salad and dressing
early in day, except for
oregano. Toss just before
serving, then add oregano.

12 oz	bow-tie pasta	375 g
2 3/4 cups	diced tomatoes	675 mL
1 cup	diced cucumbers	250 mL
1 cup	diced sweet green peppers	250 mL
3/4 cup	sliced red onions	175 mL
3 1/2 oz	crumbled feta cheese	90 g
1/3 cup	sliced black olives	75 mL
1/2 cup	chopped fresh oregano (or 1 tbsp [15 mL] dried)	125 mL

Dressing

1/4 cup	olive oil	50 mL
3 tbsp	lemon juice	45 mL
2 tbsp	water	25 mL
2 tbsp	balsamic vinegar	25 mL
2 tsp	crushed garlic	10 mL

1. Cook pasta according to package instructions or until firm to the bite. Rinse in cold water. Drain and place in serving bowl.

2. Add tomatoes, cucumbers, green peppers, onions, feta cheese, olives and oregano.

3. Make the dressing: In small bowl combine oil, lemon juice, water, vinegar and garlic until mixed. Pour over pasta, and toss.

PER SERVING (8)

Calories	318
Protein	9 g
Fat, total	11 g
Fat, saturated	3 g
Carbohydrates	47 g
Sodium	224 mg
Cholesterol	10 mg
Fiber	5 g

PENNE WITH BRIE CHEESE, TOMATOES AND BASIL

Serves 6 to 8
as an appetizer.

TIPS

This recipe needs little oil because the tomatoes give it the necessary liquid. Use ripe juicy tomatoes.

Sweet Vidalia onions are great to use in season.

MAKE AHEAD

Prepare tomato dressing early in day and let marinate. Do not toss until ready to serve.

12 oz	penne	375 g
1 1/2 lb	chopped tomatoes	750 g
2 tsp	crushed garlic	10 mL
1 cup	chopped red onions	250 mL
3 oz	diced Brie cheese	75 g
1/3 cup	sliced black olives	75 mL
2/3 cup	chopped fresh basil (or 2 tsp [10 mL] dried)	150 mL
3 tbsp	olive oil	45 mL
2 tbsp	lemon juice	25 mL
1 tbsp	red wine vinegar	15 mL
	Pepper	

1. Cook pasta in boiling water according to package instructions or until firm to the bite. Rinse with cold water. Drain and place in serving bowl.

2. Add tomatoes, garlic, onions, cheese, olives, basil, oil, lemon juice, vinegar and pepper. Mix well.

PER SERVING (8)

Calories	299
Protein	9 g
Fat, total	10 g
Fat, saturated	3 g
Carbohydrates	43 g
Sodium	155 mg
Cholesterol	9 mg
Fiber	4 g

 COLD PENNE WITH FRESH  TOMATO, SWEET PEPPERS AND CORIANDER

Serves 6.

12 oz	penne	375 g

Vegetable Dressing

2 cups	thinly sliced sweet red and/or yellow peppers	500 mL
2 cups	chopped tomatoes	500 mL
3/4 cup	diced cucumbers	175 mL
3/4 cup	sliced red onions	175 mL
1/4 cup	chopped green onions	50 mL
1/2 cup	chopped coriander or dill	125 mL
3 tbsp	olive oil	45 mL
3 tbsp	lime or lemon juice	45 mL
2 tsp	crushed garlic	10 mL

1. Cook pasta in boiling water according to package instructions or until firm to the bite. Rinse with cold water. Drain and place in serving bowl.

2. Make the dressing: Add sweet peppers, tomatoes, cucumbers, red and green onions, coriander, oil, lime juice and garlic. Toss and serve cold.

TIP

Use juicy ripe tomatoes for extra liquid in salad.

Fresh chopped basil can replace coriander or dill.

MAKE AHEAD

Prepare vegetable dressing early in day and allow to marinate. Toss just before serving.

PER SERVING

Calories	350
Protein	10 g
Fat, total	8 g
Fat, saturated	1 g
Carbohydrates	60 g
Sodium	15 mg
Cholesterol	0 mg
Fiber	4 g

PASTA SALAD WITH APRICOTS, DATES AND ORANGE DRESSING

Serves 6 to 8.

TIP

A delicious sweet pasta salad that goes well with a grilled fish or chicken entrée.

Prunes can replace apricots or dates or use in combination.

MAKE AHEAD

Prepare salad and dressing early in day. Toss just before serving.

12 oz	medium shell pasta	375 g
1 1/2 cups	diced sweet red or green peppers	375 mL
3/4 cup	diced dried apricots	175 mL
3/4 cup	diced dried dates	175 mL
1/2 cup	chopped green onions	125 mL

Dressing

3 tbsp	balsamic vinegar	45 mL
3 tbsp	frozen orange juice concentrate, thawed	45 mL
3 tbsp	olive oil	45 mL
2 tbsp	lemon juice	25 mL
2 tbsp	water	25 mL
1 1/2 tsp	crushed garlic	7 mL
1/2 cup	chopped parsley	125 mL

1. Cook pasta in boiling water according to package instructions or until firm to the bite. Rinse with cold water. Drain and place in serving bowl.

2. Add sweet peppers, apricots, dates and green onions.

3. Make the dressing: In small bowl combine vinegar, orange juice concentrate, oil, lemon juice, water, garlic and parsley. Pour over salad, and toss.

PER SERVING (8)

Calories	307
Protein	7 g
Fat, total	6 g
Fat, saturated	0.8 g
Carbohydrates	58 g
Sodium	8 mg
Cholesterol	0 mg
Fiber	4 g

Mango Salsa over Vermicelli

8 oz	vermicelli or other fine-strand pasta	250 g
1 3/4 cups	diced mangoes	425 mL
3/4 cup	diced sweet red peppers	175 mL
1/2 cup	diced red onions	125 mL
1/2 cup	diced sweet green peppers	125 mL
3 tbsp	olive oil	45 mL
3 tbsp	lemon juice	45 mL
2 tsp	crushed garlic	10 mL
1/2 cup	chopped coriander or parsley	125 mL

1. Cook pasta in boiling water according to package instructions or until firm to the bite. Rinse with cold water. Drain and set aside.

2. In bowl of food processor, combine mangoes, red peppers, onions, green peppers, oil, lemon juice, garlic and coriander. Process on and off just until finely diced. Pour over pasta; serve at room temperature.

Serves 6 as an appetizer.

TIP

Use a ripe sweet mango for a more intense flavor. If unripe, mangoes are unpleasantly sour.

MAKE AHEAD

Prepare salsa early in day and refrigerate. (This will also allow it to develop more flavor.) Pour over pasta just before serving.

PER SERVING

Calories	265
Protein	6 g
Fat, total	3 g
Fat, saturated	1 g
Carbohydrates	44 g
Sodium	6 mg
Cholesterol	0 mg
Fiber	3 g

 # CHICKEN TARRAGON ⟩⟨⟩⟨ PASTA SALAD

Serves 6 to 8 as an appetizer.

TIP

Other vegetables can be used as long as the total amount is not exceeded.

Try coriander or parsley as an herb.

MAKE AHEAD

Salad and dressing can be made up to a day ahead. Do not toss until ready to serve.

12 oz	rotini or fusilli	375 g
12 oz	skinless, boneless chicken breast, cut into 1-inch (2.5-cm) cubes	375 g
1 1/2 cups	chopped broccoli	375 mL
1/2 cup	diced carrots	125 mL
1 1/2 cups	diced red peppers	375 mL
3/4 cup	diced green peppers	175 mL
1/2 cup	diced red onions	125 mL

Dressing

1/2 cup	2% yogurt	125 mL
1/3 cup	light mayonnaise	75 mL
3 tbsp	lemon juice	45 mL
1/3 cup	chopped fresh tarragon or dill (or 3 tsp [15 mL] dried)	75 mL
2 1/2 tbsp	honey	35 mL
2 tsp	crushed garlic	10 mL
1 1/2 tsp	Dijon mustard	7 mL

1. Cook pasta in boiling water according to package instructions or until firm to the bite. Rinse with cold water. Drain and place in serving bowl.

2. In nonstick skillet sprayed with vegetable spray, sauté chicken until no longer pink, approximately 3 minutes. Cool. Add to pasta.

3. Blanch broccoli and carrots in boiling water just until tender, approximately 3 minutes. Drain and refresh with cold water; add to pasta. Add red and green peppers and onions.

4. Make the dressing: In small bowl combine yogurt, mayonnaise, lemon juice, tarragon, honey, garlic and mustard until mixed. Pour over pasta, and toss.

PER SERVING (8)

Calories	331
Protein	19 g
Fat, total	6 g
Fat, saturated	0.9 g
Carbohydrates	51 g
Sodium	131 mg
Cholesterol	34 mg
Fiber	4 g

CORN AND THREE-BEAN SALAD

Serves 6 to 8.

TIP

Use any combination of cooked beans.

For a sweeter salad, try balsamic vinegar.

MAKE AHEAD

Prepare salad and dressing separately up to a day ahead. Pour dressing over top just before serving.

8 oz	pasta wheels or small shell pasta	250 g
1 cup	canned black beans or chick peas, drained	250 mL
3/4 cup	canned red kidney beans, drained	175 mL
3/4 cup	canned white kidney beans, drained	175 mL
3/4 cup	canned corn niblets, drained	175 mL
1 1/4 cups	diced sweet red peppers	300 mL
3/4 cup	diced carrots	175 mL
1/2 cup	diced red onions	125 mL

Dressing

1/4 cup	lemon juice	50 mL
3 tbsp	vegetable oil	45 mL
3 tbsp	red wine or cider vinegar	45 mL
2 tsp	crushed garlic	10 mL
1/2 cup	chopped coriander or parsley	125 mL

1. Cook pasta in boiling water according to package instructions or until firm to the bite. Rinse with cold water. Drain and place in serving bowl.

2. Add all three beans, corn niblets, red peppers, carrots and onions.

3. Make the dressing: In small bowl combine lemon juice, oil, vinegar, garlic and coriander. Pour over dressing, and toss.

PER SERVING (8)

Calories	277
Protein	10 g
Fat, total	7 g
Fat, saturated	0.6 g
Carbohydrates	46 g
Sodium	293 mg
Cholesterol	0 mg
Fiber	7 g

FISH

FISH TIPS

1. Fish must be fresh. It should have a bright color, a firm texture and a sweet smell. Whole fish should look plump and have shiny, clear, protruding eyes.

2. Fish generally fall into two categories: darker, oilier firm fish and the whiter, more delicate and leaner fish. In either case, a firm-fleshed fish suits pasta best because it will not flake. Of these, recommended darker fish include swordfish, tuna, shark and salmon; the best lighter fish are halibut, haddock, orange roughy, Chilean seabass, snapper, grouper and bluefish.

3. Store fish in the coldest part of the refrigerator. Ideally, place whole fish in a dish surrounded with ice. Replace ice when necessary. Do not allow fish to sit in water. Wash fillets, pat dry, then wrap in plastic wrap and keep very cold. Fish will last up to 3 days like this.

4. Wrap frozen fish very tightly so no air can penetrate. Avoid fish with ice crystals or discoloration. These are signs of freezer burn and result in dry fish. Darker, oily fish can be frozen up to 10 weeks, and lean whiter fish up to 4 months.

5. Defrost fish in refrigerator on a plate, pouring off excess liquid as necessary, or in microwave following manufacturer's instructions.

6. Sauté fish in a nonstick skillet sprayed with vegetable spray, without any oil or butter. This reduces calories and fat. Sauté just until fish is opaque and just cooked. Do not overcook, or fish will be dry. The liquid from the fish prevents sticking.

7. If baking, measure fish at the thickest point and bake for 10 minutes per inch (2.5 cm) at 425°F to 450°F (220°C to 230°C). If the fish is frozen, double the time. This guideline can be applied to any cooking method. If not sautéeing, fish can be broiled, baked, steamed, microwaved, grilled or poached.

8. Fish and seafood can replace each other in any of the following recipes.

 # PASTA WITH SALMON IN TERIYAKI SAUCE

Serves 6.

TIP

Another fish, such as tuna or Chilean seabass, can be substituted for the salmon.

If fresh ginger is unavailable, use bottled minced ginger.

MAKE AHEAD

Sauce can be prepared a day ahead and gently reheated.

12 oz	long fusilli or rotini	375 g
12 oz	salmon, cut into 1-inch (2.5-cm) cubes	375 g
1 1/2 cups	thinly sliced sweet yellow or red peppers	375 mL
1 1/2 cups	chopped snow peas	375 mL

<u>Teriyaki Sauce</u>

1/3 cup	sherry or rice wine vinegar	75 mL
1/4 cup	brown sugar	60 mL
1/3 cup	water	75 mL
1/4 cup	soya sauce	60 mL
1/4 cup	vegetable oil	60 mL
2 1/2 tsp	minced ginger root	12 mL
2 1/2 tsp	crushed garlic	12 mL
1 tbsp	all-purpose flour	15 mL
2 tsp	sesame seeds	10 mL
	Parsley	

1. Cook pasta in boiling water according to package instructions or until firm to the bite. Drain and place in serving bowl.

2. In medium nonstick skillet sprayed with vegetable spray, sauté salmon until no longer pink, approximately 4 minutes. Do not overcook. Add to pasta.

3. Blanch yellow peppers and snow peas in boiling water until tender-crisp, approximately 2 minutes. Drain, rinse with cold water and add to pasta.

4. Make the sauce: In small saucepan, combine sherry, sugar, water, soya sauce, oil, ginger, garlic, flour and sesame seeds until smooth. Simmer on medium heat until slightly thickened, approximately 4 minutes. Pour over pasta, and toss gently. Garnish with parsley.

PER SERVING

Calories	444
Protein	22 g
Fat, total	13 g
Fat, saturated	1 g
Carbohydrates	56 g
Sodium	614 mg
Cholesterol	34 mg
Fiber	2 g

 SALMON FETTUCCINE

Serves 4 to 6.

TIP

Use swordfish or tuna
for a change.

Use rotini or penne
instead of fettuccine.

12 oz	fettuccine	375 g
1 tbsp	olive oil	15 mL
2 tsp	crushed garlic	10 mL
1/2 cup	finely diced carrots	125 mL
2/3 cup	finely diced celery	150 mL
1/3 cup	chopped green onions	75 mL
12 oz	salmon fillets, skinned, boned and cut into 1-inch (2.5-cm) cubes	375 g
1/2 cup	dry white wine	125 mL
1 1/4 cups	prepared tomato sauce or Quick Basic Tomato Sauce (see page 205 for recipe)	300 mL
2/3 cup	2% milk	150 mL
1/2 cup	chopped fresh dill (or 1 tbsp [15 mL] dried)	125 mL

1. Cook pasta in boiling water according to package instructions or until firm to the bite. Drain and place in serving bowl.

2. Meanwhile, in large nonstick skillet, heat oil; sauté garlic, carrots and celery until tender, approximately 5 minutes. Add onions and sauté for 1 minute. Add salmon and wine; simmer for 2 minutes, turning fish occasionally. Do not let salmon overcook.

3. Add tomato sauce and milk; simmer just until salmon is cooked, approximately 2 minutes, stirring often. Add dill. Pour over pasta, and gently toss.

PER SERVING (6)

Calories	456
Protein	26 g
Fat, total	10 g
Fat, saturated	2 g
Carbohydrates	64 g
Sodium	161 mg
Cholesterol	36 mg
Fiber	3 g

ROTINI NIÇOISE (PAGE 38) ➤

 # Linguine with Smoked ✕✕ Salmon and Green Peas

Serves 4.

TIP

Fettuccine or penne can be substituted for linguine.

MAKE AHEAD

Sauce can be made a day ahead and gently reheated. Add more milk if too thick.

8 oz	linguine	250 g
1 tbsp	margarine or butter	15 mL
3 1/2 tsp	all-purpose flour	17 mL
3/4 cup	2% milk	175 mL
3/4 cup	fish or chicken stock	175 mL
1 cup	frozen green peas	250 mL
4 oz	smoked salmon, chopped	125 g
1/4 cup	chopped fresh dill (or 2 tsp [10 mL] dried)	50 mL

1. Cook pasta in boiling water according to package instructions or until firm to the bite. Drain and place in serving bowl.

2. In small nonstick skillet, melt margarine; add flour and cook for 1 minute, stirring constantly. Add milk and stock; simmer just until slightly thickened, approximately 3 minutes, stirring constantly. Add peas and cook for 1 minute. Pour over pasta. Add salmon and dill, and toss.

PER SERVING

Calories	386
Protein	20 g
Fat, total	7 g
Fat, saturated	2 g
Carbohydrates	62 g
Sodium	519 mg
Cholesterol	11 mg
Fiber	3 g

◄ Corn and Three-Bean Salad (page 45)

 # SWORDFISH WITH TOMATO  AND SWEET PEPPER CORIANDER SAUCE

Serves 6.

TIP

Tuna can be substituted for swordfish.

Use ripe tomatoes.

If using dried herbs instead of fresh, use dill, not coriander.

MAKE AHEAD

The red pepper and tomato sauce can be prepared a day ahead, and gently reheated. Add more stock if too thick.

12 oz	fettuccine	375 g
12 oz	swordfish, cut into 1-inch (2.5-cm) cubes	375 g
2 tsp	vegetable oil	10 mL
1 1/2 tsp	crushed garlic	7 mL
2 cups	diced sweet red peppers	500 mL
1 cup	diced onions	250 mL
2 cups	diced tomatoes	500 mL
1 1/4 cups	chicken stock	300 mL
1/2 cup	chopped fresh coriander or dill (or 2 tsp [10 mL] dried dill)	125 mL

1. Cook pasta in boiling water according to package instructions or until firm to the bite. Drain and place in serving bowl.

2. In large nonstick skillet sprayed with vegetable spray, sauté fish just until done, approximately 4 minutes. Do not overcook. Drain and add to pasta.

3. In same skillet, heat oil; sauté garlic, red peppers and onions until tender, about 5 minutes. Add tomatoes and sauté for 4 minutes. Add stock and simmer for 2 minutes. Add coriander.

4. Pour over pasta, and toss.

PER SERVING

Calories	387
Protein	23 g
Fat, total	6 g
Fat, saturated	1 g
Carbohydrates	61 g
Sodium	255 mg
Cholesterol	27 mg
Fiber	4 g

 # Linguine with Swordfish in Tomato Basil Sauce

Serves 6.

TIP

Tuna or Chilean seabass are good substitutes for swordfish.

Try plum tomatoes instead of field tomatoes.

MAKE AHEAD

Prepare sauce early in day. Reheat gently while preparing pasta, adding more stock if sauce is too thick.

12 oz	linguine	375 g
1 1/2 tsp	crushed garlic	7 mL
12 oz	swordfish, cut into 1-inch (2.5-cm) cubes	375 g
14 oz	chopped tomatoes	425 g
3/4 cup	fish or chicken stock	175 mL
4 tsp	flour	20 mL
1/2 cup	chopped fresh basil (or 2 tsp [10 mL] dried)	125 mL
3 tbsp	grated Parmesan cheese	45 mL

1. Cook pasta in boiling water according to package instructions or until firm to the bite. Drain and place in serving bowl.

2. In large nonstick skillet sprayed with vegetable spray, sauté garlic and swordfish until fish is just done, approximately 3 minutes. Drain and add to pasta.

3. Add tomatoes to skillet and simmer for 2 minutes.

4. Meanwhile, in small bowl combine stock and flour until smooth. Add to tomatoes and simmer on medium heat just until slightly thickened, approximately 3 minutes. Add basil; pour over pasta. Sprinkle with cheese, and toss.

PER SERVING

Calories	374
Protein	25 g
Fat, total	6 g
Fat, saturated	2 g
Carbohydrates	54 g
Sodium	311 mg
Cholesterol	30 mg
Fiber	3 g

FETTUCCINE WITH SEABASS ✕ TOMATO SAUCE

Serves 6.

TIP

Chop carrots finely so they become tender during cooking.

▼

Repace seabass with swordfish, salmon or orange roughy.

MAKE AHEAD

Sauce can be made a day ahead, but do not add fish to cook until ready to serve.

12 oz	fettuccine	375 g
2 tsp	olive oil	10 mL
2 tsp	crushed garlic	10 mL
3/4 cup	chopped onions	175 mL
3/4 cup	chopped celery	175 mL
1/2 cup	chopped carrots	125 mL
1 cup	chopped sweet green or yellow peppers	250 mL
2 3/4 cups	crushed tomatoes (canned or fresh)	675 mL
1 tbsp	tomato paste	15 mL
1	bay leaf	1
2 tsp	dried basil	10 mL
1 1/2 tsp	dried oregano	7 mL
Pinch	red pepper flakes or cayenne pepper	Pinch
12 oz	Chilean seabass cut into 1-inch (2.5-cm) cubes	375 g
1/3 cup	grated Parmesan cheese	75 mL
	Parsley	

PER SERVING

Calories	436
Protein	28 g
Fat, total	8 g
Fat, saturated	3 g
Carbohydrates	63 g
Sodium	499 mg
Cholesterol	36 mg
Fiber	6 g

1. Cook pasta in boiling water according to package instructions or until firm to the bite. Drain and place in serving bowl.

2. In large nonstick skillet, heat oil; sauté garlic, onions, celery and carrots until tender, approximately 8 minutes. Add sweet peppers and sauté for 3 minutes. Add tomatoes and paste, bay leaf, basil, oregano and pepper flakes. Simmer on low heat for 10 minutes, stirring occasionally, until slightly thickened; add seabass and cook just until done, approximately 3 minutes. Pour over pasta. Sprinkle with cheese and parsley.

 # LINGUINE WITH TUNA, WHITE BEANS AND DILL

Serves 6.

TIP

For color variation, try red kidney beans or black beans instead of white beans.

For a more sophisticated meal, replace canned tuna with cooked tuna or swordfish.

MAKE AHEAD

Prepare sauce up to a day ahead. Reheat gently, adding more stock if too thick.

12 oz	linguine	375 g
1 tbsp	olive oil	15 mL
2 tsp	crushed garlic	10 mL
1	can (19 oz [540 mL]) white kidney beans, drained	1
4 tbsp	lemon juice	60 mL
1 3/4 cups	cold chicken stock	425 mL
4 tsp	all-purpose flour	20 mL
1	can (6.5 oz [185 g]) flaked tuna packed in water, drained	1
1/2 cup	chopped fresh dill (or 1 tbsp [15 mL] dried)	125 mL
1/3 cup	sliced black olives	75 mL
1/4 cup	chopped green onions	50 mL

1. Cook pasta in boiling water according to package instructions or until firm to the bite. Drain and place in serving bowl.

2. In large nonstick skillet, heat oil; add garlic, beans and lemon juice; cook approximately 2 minutes or until hot.

3. Meanwhile, in small bowl combine stock and flour until smooth. Add to bean mixture; simmer until sauce slightly thickens, approximately 3 minutes.

4. Pour over pasta. Add tuna, dill, olives and green onions. Toss.

PER SERVING

Calories	409
Protein	21 g
Fat, total	6 g
Fat, saturated	0.8 g
Carbohydrates	69 g
Sodium	632 mg
Cholesterol	9 mg
Fiber	5 g

Macaroni, Tuna and Cheese Casserole

Serves 6 to 8.

TIP

Great inexpensive
family meal.

Substitute any small
shell pasta for macaroni,
or use tri-colored
dry pasta.

Substitute cooked chicken
or shrimp for the tuna.

MAKE AHEAD

Prepare pasta and sauce
early in day. Reheat sauce
before adding to pasta.
Add more milk if sauce is
too thick. Continue on
with recipe.

PER SERVING (8)

Calories	354
Protein	20 g
Fat, total	9 g
Fat, saturated	4 g
Carbohydrates	50 g
Sodium	298 mg
Cholesterol	24 mg
Fiber	2 g

Preheat oven to broil
13- x 9-inch (3L) baking dish

12 oz	macaroni	375 g
1 tbsp	margarine or butter	15 mL
1 1/2 tsp	crushed garlic	7 mL
1 cup	diced sweet red peppers	250 mL
3 tbsp	all-purpose flour	45 mL
3 1/4 cups	2% milk	800 mL
2/3 cup	shredded Cheddar cheese	150 mL
1/3 cup	shredded mozzarella cheese	75 mL
2 tbsp	grated Parmesan cheese	25 mL
1	can (6.5 oz [185 g]) flaked tuna packed in water, drained	1
1/3 cup	chopped fresh dill (or 2 tsp [10 mL] dried)	75 mL

Topping

1/3 cup	crushed bran flakes or all-bran cereal	75 mL
1 tsp	margarine or butter	5 mL
1/2 tsp	crushed garlic	2 mL

1. Cook pasta in boiling water according to package
   instructions or until firm to the bite. Drain and place in
   baking dish.

2. In medium nonstick saucepan, melt margarine; sauté
   garlic and red peppers for 3 minutes; add flour and cook
   for 1 minute, stirring constantly. Slowly add milk and
   simmer just until slightly thickened, approximately
   4 minutes. Add all three cheeses and cook until they
   are melted, approximately 1 minute. Add tuna and dill.
   Combine well; pour over pasta.

3. Make the topping: In food processor, combine cereal,
   margarine and garlic. Sprinkle over pasta. Broil until
   browned, approximately 2 minutes.

 # Linguine with Curried Fish Pieces

Serves 6.

12 oz	linguine	375 g
12 oz	any firm white fish, chopped into 1-inch (2.5-cm) pieces	375 g
1 tbsp	margarine or butter	15 mL
1 1/2 tsp	chopped garlic	7 mL
1/2 cup	diced onions	125 mL
1/2 cup	diced carrots	125 mL
1/4 cup	diced celery	50 mL
1 1/2 cups	seafood or chicken stock	375 mL
1 tbsp	curry	15 mL
3/4 cup	2% milk	175 mL
2 tbsp	all-purpose flour	25 mL
	Parsley	

1. Cook pasta in boiling water according to package instructions or until firm to the bite. Drain and place in serving bowl.

2. Meanwhile, in large nonstick skillet sprayed with vegetable spray, sauté fish just until done, approximately 4 minutes. Add to pasta.

3. In large nonstick saucepan, heat margarine; sauté garlic, onions, carrots and celery just until tender, approximately 5 minutes. Add stock and curry; simmer on medium-low heat for 5 minutes.

4. Meanwhile, combine milk and flour in small bowl; add to stock and simmer for 3 minutes, stirring constantly, just until slightly thickened. Toss with pasta. Garnish with parsley.

PER SERVING

Calories	359
Protein	20 g
Fat, total	5 g
Fat, saturated	1 g
Carbohydrates	58 g
Sodium	299 mg
Cholesterol	18 mg
Fiber	3 g

LEMON SEABASS WITH MUSHROOMS AND GREEN ONIONS OVER PENNE

Serves 6.

TIP

Substitute another firm white fish fillet such as grouper, snapper or haddock for the seabass.

MAKE AHEAD

Sauce can be made ahead and gently reheated, adding more stock if too thick.

12 oz	penne	375 g
12 oz	Chilean seabass, cut into 1-inch (2.5-cm) cubes	375 g
1 tbsp	margarine or butter	15 mL
1 1/2 tsp	crushed garlic	7 mL
1 1/2 cups	sliced mushrooms	375 mL
2 1/2 tbsp	all-purpose flour	35 mL
1/2 cup	dry white wine	125 mL
1 2/3 cups	chicken stock	400 mL
1/4 cup	lemon juice	50 mL
2 tsp	grated lemon rind	10 mL
2 tbsp	sugar	25 mL
1/3 cup	sliced green onions	75 mL

1. Cook pasta in boiling water according to package instructions or until firm to the bite. Drain and place in serving bowl.

2. In medium nonstick skillet sprayed with vegetable spray, sauté fish just until cooked, approximately 4 minutes. Add fish to pasta.

3. In same skillet melt margarine; sauté garlic and mushrooms until tender, approximately 4 minutes. Add flour and cook for 1 minute, stirring constantly. Add wine, stock, lemon juice and rind. Simmer on medium heat until slightly thickened, for 4 to 5 minutes. Add sugar and green onions. Pour over pasta, and toss.

PER SERVING

Calories	388
Protein	22 g
Fat, total	5 g
Fat, saturated	0.9 g
Carbohydrates	61 g
Sodium	320 mg
Cholesterol	26 mg
Fiber	4 g

 # FETTUCCINE WITH MONKFISH IN A WHITE WINE, RED PEPPER BASIL SAUCE

Serves 6.

TIP

Monkfish is sometimes called imitation lobster. Substitute any firm white fish fillet or seafood.

▼

Try feta cheese instead of goat cheese.

MAKE AHEAD

Prepare sauce early in day but do not add fish or cheese. Reheat gently, adding more stock if too thick. Then add fish and cheese and continue with recipe.

PER SERVING

Calories	371
Protein	20 g
Fat, total	6 g
Fat, saturated	3 g
Carbohydrates	56 g
Sodium	194 mg
Cholesterol	30 mg
Fiber	2 g

12 oz	fettuccine	375 g
1 tbsp	margarine or butter	15 mL
2 tsp	crushed garlic	10 mL
1 1/2 cups	thinly sliced sweet red peppers	375 mL
3 tbsp	white wine	45 mL
2 tsp	dried basil	10 mL
3/4 cup	cold seafood or chicken stock	175 mL
1/2 cup	2% milk	125 mL
1 tbsp	all-purpose flour	15 mL
12 oz	monkfish, cut into 1-inch (2.5-cm) pieces	375 g
3 oz	goat cheese	75 g

1. Cook pasta in boiling water according to package instructions or until firm to the bite. Drain and place in serving bowl.

2. In large nonstick skillet, melt butter; sauté garlic and peppers just until peppers are tender, approximately 4 minutes. Add wine and basil; simmer for 2 minutes.

3. Meanwhile, in small bowl combine stock, milk and flour, stirring until smooth. Add to red pepper mixture and simmer for 4 minutes, or just until sauce slightly thickens, stirring constantly. Add fish pieces and cheese. Simmer for 2 minutes or until fish is just cooked. Pour over pasta, and toss.

 # ANGEL HAIR PASTA WITH MUSHROOMS AND SNAPPER

Serves 4.

TIP

Use any firm white fish or seafood, such as halibut, haddock, scallops or shrimp.

Be certain not to overcook fish or it will be dry. Cook just until it is moist, tender and flaky.

Try oyster mushrooms for a more sophisticated meal.

8 oz	fine strand pasta (angel hair, capellini or spaghettini)	250 g
1 tbsp	margarine or butter	15 mL
1 tsp	crushed garlic	5 mL
8 oz	wild or regular mushrooms, finely sliced	250 g
8 oz	snapper (or any firm fish), cut into 1/2-inch [1-cm] pieces	250 g
2 tbsp	dry white wine	25 mL
8 oz	tomatoes, finely chopped	250 g
1/3 cup	chopped fresh basil (or 1 1/2 tsp [7 mL] dried)	75 mL
3 tbsp	grated Parmesan cheese	45 mL

1. Cook pasta in boiling water according to package instructions or until firm to the bite. Drain and place in serving bowl.

2. In large nonstick skillet, melt margarine; sauté garlic and mushrooms just until cooked. Add snapper and sauté until fish is still slightly underdone, for 3 to 4 minutes. Add wine and cook for 1 minute. Add tomatoes and basil and stir just until combined. Pour over pasta. Sprinkle with cheese, and toss.

PER SERVING

Calories	383
Protein	25 g
Fat, total	7 g
Fat, saturated	2 g
Carbohydrates	55 g
Sodium	180 mg
Cholesterol	27 mg
Fiber	6 g

FETTUCCINE WITH FRESH FISH IN A CREAMY LEEK SAUCE

Serves 4.

TIP

Other firm white fish fillets or seafood, such as Chilean seabass, shrimps, or scallops, can be used.

To wash leeks properly, separate leaves and rinse to remove all trapped dirt.

If leeks are unavailable, substitute another 1 cup (250 mL) of onions (preferrably Vidalia or red onions).

MAKE AHEAD

Prepare sauce a day ahead, without adding dill. Reheat gently, adding more stock if too thick. Then add dill.

PER SERVING

Calories	471
Protein	23 g
Fat, total	10 g
Fat, saturated	2 g
Carbohydrates	70 g
Sodium	263 mg
Cholesterol	21 mg
Fiber	3 g

8 oz	fettuccine	250 g
8 oz	halibut or orange roughy, cut into pieces	250 g
1 tbsp	vegetable oil	15 mL
1 1/2 tsp	crushed garlic	7 mL
1 cup	chopped onions	250 mL
1	medium leek (white part), thinly sliced	1
1 1/2 cups	sliced sweet red peppers	375 mL

Sauce

1 tbsp	margarine or butter	15 mL
2 tbsp	all-purpose flour	25 mL
1 cup	2% milk	250 mL
3/4 cup	fish or chicken stock	175 mL
1/4 cup	dry white wine	50 mL
1/4 cup	chopped fresh dill (or 1 tsp [5 mL] dried)	50 mL
	Pepper	

1. Cook pasta in boiling water according to package instructions or until firm to the bite. Drain and place in serving bowl.

2. Place seafood in simmering water and cook just until opaque, approximately 2 minutes. Drain and add to pasta.

3. In nonstick skillet, heat oil; sauté garlic, onions, leek and sweet peppers until tender, approximately 8 minutes. Add to pasta.

4. Make the sauce: In medium saucepan, melt margarine. Add flour and cook until combined, approximately 1 minute. Slowly add milk, stock and wine. Simmer until thickened, about 5 minutes, stirring constantly. Add dill and pepper. Pour over pasta, and toss.

SPAGHETTINI WITH TOMATOES, BASIL AND FISH

Serves 6.

TIP

For fish fillets, consider orange roughy, haddock or seabass.

MAKE AHEAD

Sauce in Step 3 can be made early in day but substitute 1/3 cup (75 mL) dry white wine for reserved seafood liquid. When cooking seafood, drain wine and cooking liquid.

12 oz	spaghettini	375 g
1/3 cup	dry white wine	75 mL
12 oz	firm white fish fillets, cut into 1-inch (2.5-cm) pieces	375 g
2 tsp	vegetable oil	10 mL
2 tsp	crushed garlic	10 mL
3/4 cup	chopped onions	175 mL
1 3/4 lb	diced tomatoes	875 g
1 tbsp	tomato paste	15 mL
2/3 cup	chopped fresh basil (or 2 tsp [10 mL] dried)	150 mL
1/4 cup	grated Parmesan cheese	50 mL

1. Cook pasta in boiling water according to package instructions or until firm to the bite. Drain and place in serving bowl.

2. Put wine in saucepan; add fish and simmer just until done, approximately 3 minutes. Drain and reserve liquid. Add fish to pasta.

3. In large nonstick saucepan, heat oil; sauté garlic and onions until soft, approximately 3 minutes. Add tomatoes, paste and reserved fish liquid. Simmer on low heat for 15 minutes, until the sauce thickens. Pour over pasta. Sprinkle with basil and cheese, and toss.

PER SERVING

Calories	390
Protein	22 g
Fat, total	7 g
Fat, saturated	2 g
Carbohydrates	58 g
Sodium	185 mg
Cholesterol	22 mg
Fiber	6 g

 # ROTINI WITH FISH, OLIVES AND FETA CHEESE

Serves 6.

TIPS

Try fish fillets such as swordfish, snapper or haddock. Seafood such as shrimp or scallops can also be used.

▼

Goat cheese can substitute for feta cheese.

MAKE AHEAD

Sauce in Step 3 can be made a day ahead. Cover and reheat gently, adding more stock if too thick.

12 oz	rotini	375 g
2 tsp	vegetable oil	10 mL
1 1/2 tsp	crushed garlic	7 mL
1/3 cup	chopped green onions	75 mL
12 oz	halibut or orange roughy, cut into 1-inch (2.5-cm) pieces	375 g
1 tbsp	margarine or butter	15 mL
5 tsp	all-purpose flour	25 mL
1 1/3 cups	seafood or chicken stock	325 mL
2/3 cup	2% milk	150 mL
3 1/2 oz	feta cheese, crumbled	90 g
1/3 cup	sliced black olives	75 mL
1 3/4 tsp	dried oregano	8 mL
	Parsley	

1. Cook pasta in boiling water according to package instructions or until firm to the bite. Drain and place in serving bowl.

2. In large nonstick skillet, heat oil; sauté garlic and onions until soft, approximately 3 minutes. Add fish and sauté until pink, approximately 3 minutes. Add to pasta.

3. In medium nonstick saucepan, melt margarine; add flour and cook for 1 minute. Stir in stock and milk slowly; simmer on medium heat just until thickened, approximately 4 minutes. Add cheese, olives and oregano; cook for 1 minute. Pour over pasta, and toss. Garnish with parsley.

PER SERVING

Calories	407
Protein	21 g
Fat, total	11 g
Fat, saturated	4 g
Carbohydrates	55 g
Sodium	534 mg
Cholesterol	31 mg
Fiber	3 g

CAJUN SPICED FISH WITH ROTINI, ZUCCHINI AND TOMATOES

Serves 6.

TIP

Substitute seafood such as shrimp or scallops for the fish.

Experiment with the seasoning, increasing the intensity if desired.

MAKE AHEAD

Sauce can be made a day ahead and gently reheated. If too thick, add more stock. Fish can be coated with spices and refrigerated until used.

12 oz	rotini	375 g

Spice Mixture

3/4 tsp	cayenne powder	4 mL
1 1/2 tsp	onion powder	7 mL
1 1/4 tsp	garlic powder	6 mL
3/4 tsp	paprika	4 mL
3/4 tsp	dried basil	4 mL
1/2 tsp	dried oregano	2 mL
2 tbsp	unseasoned bread crumbs	25 mL
12 oz	halibut, snapper or Chilean seabass, cut into 1-inch (2.5-cm) strips	375 g
2 tsp	vegetable oil	10 mL
1 1/2 tsp	crushed garlic	7 mL
2/3 cup	chopped onions	150 mL
2/3 cup	chopped zucchini	150 mL
1 1/2 cup	chopped tomatoes	375 mL
1 1/2 tsp	dried basil	7 mL
3/4 tsp	dried oregano	4 mL
5 1/2 tsp	all-purpose flour	27 mL
1 3/4 cups	cold fish stock or chicken stock	425 mL
1/4 cup	chopped green onions	50 mL

PER SERVING

Calories	381
Protein	20 g
Fat, total	5 g
Fat, saturated	0.6 g
Carbohydrates	65 g
Sodium	313 mg
Cholesterol	16 mg
Fiber	3 g

1. Cook pasta in boiling water according to package instructions or until firm to the bite. Drain and place in serving bowl.

2. Prepare the spice mixture: In a small bowl, combine the cayenne, onion powder, garlic powder, paprika, basil, oregano and bread crumbs. Coat fish in mixture.

3. In large nonstick skillet sprayed with vegetable spray, sauté fish just until cooked and browned, approximately 4 minutes. Drain and add to pasta.

4. In same skillet, add oil; sauté garlic, onions and zucchini until tender, approximately 4 minutes. Add tomatoes, basil and oregano. Simmer for 2 minutes.

5. Meanwhile, mix flour and stock together in small bowl. Add to tomato mixture and cook on medium heat until slightly thickened, approximately 5 minutes. Pour over pasta. Sprinkle with onions, and toss.

FETTUCCINE WITH FISH, ASPARAGUS AND CORIANDER

Serves 4 to 5.

TIP

If asparagus is unavailable, substitute chopped broccoli.

▼

Seabass or orange roughy goes well with coriander.

MAKE AHEAD

Prepare sauce early in day but do not add seafood until ready to serve. Reheat gently. Add more stock if sauce thickens, then continue with recipe.

8 oz	fettuccine	250 g
8 oz	asparagus cut into 1-inch (2.5-cm) pieces	250 g
8 oz	any firm white fish, cut into 1-inch (2.5-cm) pieces	250 g
2 tsp	margarine or butter	10 mL
1 1/2 tsp	crushed garlic	7 mL
1 cup	chopped sweet red peppers	250 mL
1/4 cup	chopped onions	50 mL
5 tsp	all-purpose flour	25 mL
2/3 cup	2% milk	150 mL
2/3 cup	seafood or chicken stock	150 mL
1/4 cup	dry white wine	50 mL
1/2 cup	chopped coriander or parsley	125 mL

1. Cook pasta in boiling water according to package instructions or until firm to the bite. Drain and place in serving bowl.

2. Blanch asparagus in boiling water for 3 minutes or until slightly tender. Drain, rinse with cold water, and add to pasta.

3. In small nonstick skillet sprayed with vegetable spray, sauté fish until it flakes, approximately 2 minutes. Add to pasta.

4. In medium nonstick saucepan, melt margarine; sauté garlic, red peppers and onions for 2 minutes. Add flour and cook for 1 minute. Slowly add milk, stock and white wine; simmer on medium heat for 3 minutes or until slightly thickened, stirring constantly. Pour over pasta. Sprinkle with coriander, and toss.

PER SERVING (5)

Calories	315
Protein	18 g
Fat, total	4 g
Fat, saturated	1 g
Carbohydrates	50 g
Sodium	167 mg
Cholesterol	15 mg
Fiber	3 g

Angel Hair Pasta with Fish in a Tomato Pesto Sauce

Serves 6.

TIP

Mild fish such as seabass or orange roughy is ideal.

▼

This pasta dish is best served as an appetizer or side dish.

MAKE AHEAD

Prepare pesto sauce up to 3 days ahead. Prepare sauce early in day and add 1/3 cup (75 mL) dry wine instead of reserved fish liquid. Drain wine from fish after cooking.

10 oz	angel hair pasta (capellini)	300 g
12 oz	firm white fish fillets, cut into chunks	375 g
1/3 cup	dry white wine	75 mL
Sauce		
2 tsp	vegetable oil	10 mL
2 tsp	crushed garlic	10 mL
1 cup	chopped onions	250 mL
1 cup	chopped green peppers	250 mL
8 oz	chopped mushrooms	250 g
3 cups	chopped tomatoes	750 mL
2 tsp	dried oregano	10 mL
1/4 cup	chopped fresh basil (or 2 tsp [10 mL] dried)	50 mL
1 tbsp	tomato paste	15 mL
4 tbsp	prepared pesto sauce, or Basil Pesto Sauce (see page 168)	60 mL
1/4 cup	grated Parmesan cheese	50 mL

1. Cook pasta in boiling water according to package instructions or until firm to the bite. Drain and place in serving bowl.

2. Meanwhile cook fish in wine on medium heat, for approximately 3 minutes. Do not overcook. Drain and save liquid. Add fish to pasta.

3. Make the sauce: In large nonstick saucepan, heat oil; sauté garlic, onions and peppers. Cook until tender, approximately 5 minutes. Add mushrooms, tomatoes, oregano, basil, tomato paste and reserved fish liquid. Simmer on low heat for 15 minutes until thickened. Add pesto sauce and pour over pasta. Add cheese, and toss.

PER SERVING

Calories	398
Protein	23 g
Fat, total	9 g
Fat, saturated	2 g
Carbohydrates	55 g
Sodium	196 mg
Cholesterol	23 mg
Fiber	7 g

SEAFOOD

 SEAFOOD TIPS

1. Store seafood in the coldest part of the refrigerator. Wash, pat dry, then wrap in plastic wrap and keep very cold. Seafood will last up to 3 days like this.

2. Wrap frozen seafood very tightly so no air can penetrate. Avoid seafood with ice crystals or discoloration. These are signs of freezer burn. Seafood such as shrimp, scallops, lobster and squid freeze better and longer than fish, up to 6 months.

3. Defrost seafood in refrigerator on a plate, pouring off excess liquid as necessary, or in microwave following manufacturer's instructions.

4. Sauté seafood in a nonstick skillet, sprayed with nonstick vegetable spray, without any oil or butter. This reduces calories and fat. Sauté just until opaque and just cooked. Do not overcook, or the seafood will be dry. Drain off excess liquid.

5. Firm seafood suits pasta best because it will not flake. Best is shrimp, scallops, squid or lobster.

6. Fish and seafood can replace each other in the following recipes. Be certain not to overcook.

7. Reheat a seafood sauce gently on a low heat to prevent overcooking, or serve at room temperature.

SEAFOOD TOMATO STEW OVER FUSILLI WITH FENNEL

Serves 6.

TIP

Fennel is outstanding in this dish. If it is unavailable, use 1/4 cup (50 mL) licorice liqueur or 1 tbsp (15 mL) fennel seeds. If the licorice taste is not desired, omit fennel and add 1 cup (250 mL) chopped leeks or onions.

Any combination of sea-food can be substituted to make up the total amount. Firm white fish fillets, such as halibut, snapper or haddock, can be substituted for seafood.

MAKE AHEAD

The sauce can be prepared a day ahead and reheated just before seafood is added.

PER SERVING

Calories	469
Protein	32 g
Fat, total	7 g
Fat, saturated	1 g
Carbohydrates	70 g
Sodium	669 mg
Cholesterol	172 mg
Fiber	8 g

1 cup	chopped fennel	250 mL
12 oz	fusilli or rotini	375 g
2 tsp	vegetable oil	10 mL
2 tsp	crushed garlic	10 mL
1 cup	chopped red onions	250 mL
1 cup	chopped sweet green peppers	250 mL
1 cup	sliced mushrooms	250 mL
2	cans (19 oz [540 mL]) crushed tomatoes	2
1/2 cup	fish or chicken stock	125 mL
1/3 cup	sliced black olives	75 mL
1 tbsp	tomato paste	15 mL
2 tsp	dried basil	10 mL
1 tsp	dried oregano	5 mL
1	bay leaf	1
Pinch	cayenne	Pinch
8 oz	fresh mussels or clams	250 g
8 oz	shrimp, peeled and deveined	250 g
8 oz	squid, cleaned and sliced	250 g

1. Cook fennel in boiling water for 8 minutes, or just until barely tender. Drain and set aside.

2. Cook pasta in boiling water according to package instructions or until firm to the bite. Drain and place in serving bowl.

3. In large nonstick saucepan, heat oil; sauté garlic, on-ions, green peppers and fennel for 5 minutes. Add mushrooms and cook for 3 minutes. Add tomatoes, stock, olives, tomato paste, basil, oregano, bay leaf and cayenne. Simmer on medium-low heat for 15 minutes, stirring occasionally.

4. Add seafood. Cover and simmer for 3 minutes, or until mussels are open and seafood just cooked. Pour over pasta.

 LINGUINE WITH SHRIMP
AND MUSSELS IN A CREAMY
VEGETABLE SAUCE

Serves 6.

TIP

Replace shrimp with
12 medium scallops or
8 oz (250 g) of firm white
fish fillets cut into cubes.
Halibut is a good choice.

For a change, try clams
instead of mussels, or use a
combination of both.

If asparagus is unavailable,
substitute 1 1/2 cups
(375 mL) chopped
broccoli.

MAKE AHEAD

The sauce in Steps
5 and 6 can be made
a day ahead and gently
reheated. Add more
stock if too thick.

PER SERVING

Calories	349
Protein	20 g
Fat, total	5 g
Fat, saturated	0.8 g
Carbohydrates	55 g
Sodium	260 mg
Cholesterol	53 mg
Fiber	3 g

12 oz	linguine	375 g
10	medium asparagus, cut into small pieces	10
12	medium shrimp, peeled and deveined	12
1 lb	fresh mussels	500 g
3/4 cup	water or white wine	175 mL
2 tsp	vegetable oil	10 mL
1 1/2 tsp	crushed garlic	7 mL
1/2 cup	diced carrots	125 mL
1/2 cup	diced celery	125 mL
2	medium green onions, chopped	2
1/4 cup	dry white wine	50 mL
3/4 cup	seafood or chicken stock	175 mL
1 cup	2% milk	250 mL
5 tsp	all-purpose flour	25 mL

1. Cook pasta according to package instructions or until firm to the bite. Drain and place in serving bowl.

2. Blanch asparagus in boiling water until barely tender, approximately 2 minutes. Drain and rinse with cold water. Add to pasta.

3. Place shrimp in saucepan and cover with water. Simmer until shrimp turns pink. Drain and add to pasta.

4. Place mussels and water in saucepan. Cover and cook on medium heat until mussels open; discard any that remain closed. Remove mussels from shells and add to pasta.

5. In medium nonstick skillet, heat oil; sauté garlic, carrots and celery just until tender, about 5 minutes. Add green onions and white wine; simmer for 3 minutes.

6. Meanwhile, in small bowl combine stock, milk and flour and stir until smooth. Add to vegetables and simmer for 3 minutes, just until slightly thickened. Remove from heat and purée in food processor. Pour over pasta, and toss.

LINGUINE WITH MUSSELS, SUN-DRIED TOMATOES AND OLIVES

Serves 6.

TIP

Replace mussels with clams or use a combination.

▼

Buy dry sun-dried tomatoes, not ones in oil, to reduce calories and fat.

MAKE AHEAD

Early in the day, prepare entire sauce. Reheat gently, adding some water if sauce appears too thick.

12 oz	linguine	375 g
1/3 cup	sun-dried tomatoes	75 mL
1/4 cup	chopped onions	50 mL
1/4 cup	dry white wine	50 mL
1/4 cup	fish or chicken stock	50 mL
1 lb	mussels	500 g
2 tbsp	olive oil	25 mL
2 tsp	crushed garlic	10 mL
1 1/2 cups	sliced sweet red peppers	375 mL
2 1/2 cups	diced tomatoes	625 mL
1/3 cup	sliced black olives	75 mL
1/2 cup	chopped fresh basil (or 2 tsp [10 mL] dried)	125 mL
	Pepper	

1. Cook pasta in boiling water according to package instructions or until firm to the bite. Drain and place in serving bowl.

2. Pour boiling water over sun-dried tomatoes. Let soak for 15 minutes. Drain and chop.

3. In large saucepan combine onions, wine and stock. Bring to boil. Add mussels. Cover and simmer for approximately 3 minutes, or until mussels open. Discard any that remain closed. Remove mussels from shells and reserve.

4. In medium nonstick skillet, heat oil; sauté garlic, red peppers and tomatoes just until peppers are tender, approximately 4 minutes. Add olives, sun-dried tomatoes and reserved mussels. Pour over pasta. Sprinkle with basil and pepper, and toss.

PER SERVING

Calories	420
Protein	20 g
Fat, total	9 g
Fat, saturated	1 g
Carbohydrates	64 g
Sodium	316 mg
Cholesterol	23 mg
Fiber	6 g

FETTUCCINE WITH MUSSELS, SHRIMP AND PARSLEY

Serves 6.

TIP

Substitute clams for mussels for a variation or use a combination of both.

Shrimp can be replaced with scallops or a firm white fish fillet such as halibut or monkfish.

MAKE AHEAD

The processed sauce in Step 2 can be made up to a day ahead.

12 oz	fettuccine	375 g
2 1/2 slices	stale bread	2 1/2
3 tbsp	red wine vinegar	45 mL
2 tbsp	water	25 mL
2 cups	chopped parsley leaves	500 mL
2 tsp	capers	10 mL
4	anchovy fillets	4
2 tsp	crushed garlic	10 mL
1/4 cup	olive oil	50 mL
1 tbsp	chicken or seafood stock	15 mL
24 (approx.)	mussels	24
1/2 cup	dry white wine	125 mL
1 1/2 tsp	crushed garlic	7 mL
12 oz	shrimp, peeled, deveined, and cut in half	375 g

1. Cook pasta in boiling water according to package instructions or until firm to the bite. Drain and place in serving bowl.

2. In small dish, soak bread in vinegar and water until saturated, approximately 2 minutes. Place bread mixture in food processor. Add parsley, capers, anchovies and garlic. Process until smooth. Add oil and stock and process until smooth. Set aside.

3. In large covered saucepan, steam mussels with wine and garlic just until open, approximately 5 minutes. Discard any that do not open. Remove mussels from shells and save liquid.

4. In large nonstick skillet sprayed with vegetable spray, sauté shrimp just until pink, approximately 3 minutes. Add mussels, reserved liquid and parsley purée. Heat for 1 minute. Toss with pasta.

PER SERVING

Calories	436
Protein	27 g
Fat, total	12 g
Fat, saturated	2 g
Carbohydrates	52 g
Sodium	182 mg
Cholesterol	107 mg
Fiber	2 g

STEAMED MUSSELS WITH CURRIED TOMATOES OVER PENNE

Serves 6.

TIP

Adjust the curry to taste. Clams could substitute for mussels or use a combination.

Use ginger marinated in jars, available in the vegetable section of the grocery store. It keeps for months in the refrigerator.

MAKE AHEAD

Tomato sauce in Step 2 can be made a day ahead and reheated.

12 oz	penne	375 g
1 1/2 tsp	vegetable oil	7 mL
2 tsp	crushed garlic	10 mL
4 cups	crushed tomatoes (canned or fresh)	1 L
2 tsp	curry	10 mL
1 1/2 tsp	minced ginger root	7 mL
1 lb	mussels	500 g
1/4 cup	dry white wine	50 mL
1/3 cup	chopped coriander or parsley	75 mL

1. Cook pasta in boiling water according to package instructions or until firm to the bite. Drain and place in serving bowl.

2. In large nonstick saucepan, heat oil; sauté garlic for 30 seconds. Add tomatoes, curry and ginger. Cover and simmer on low heat for 25 minutes. Set aside.

3. In medium saucepan, combine mussels and wine. Cover and steam just until mussels open, approximately 4 minutes. Discard any mussels that do not open. Drain and reserve mussels.

4. Add tomato sauce to pasta; toss and add mussels. Sprinkle with coriander.

PER SERVING

Calories	368
Protein	20 g
Fat, total	5 g
Fat, saturated	0.7 g
Carbohydrates	60 g
Sodium	437 mg
Cholesterol	23 mg
Fiber	5 g

 # FETTUCCINE WITH CALAMARI, EGGPLANT, FETA CHEESE AND TOMATOES

Serves 6.

12 oz	fettuccine	375 g
1 tbsp	olive oil	15 mL
2 tsp	crushed garlic	10 mL
1/2 cup	diced onions	125 mL
2 cups	diced eggplant	500 mL
1 1/4 cups	diced zucchini	300 mL
2 cups	diced tomatoes	500 mL
1/2 tsp	chili powder	2 mL
2 tsp	dried oregano	10 mL
1 1/4 cups	fish or chicken stock	300 mL
2 tsp	all-purpose flour	10 mL
12 oz	squid, cleaned and sliced	375 g
2 1/2 oz	feta cheese, crumbled	60 g
1/3 cup	chopped parsley	75 mL

1. Cook pasta in boiling water according to package instructions or until firm to the bite. Drain and place in serving bowl.

2. In large nonstick skillet sprayed with vegetable spray, heat oil; sauté garlic, onions, eggplant and zucchini for 5 minutes, or just until eggplant is tender. Add tomatoes, chili powder and oregano. Simmer for 2 minutes.

3. Meanwhile, in small bowl combine stock and flour, stirring until smooth. Add to eggplant mixture, along with squid; simmer for 5 minutes, or just until sauce slightly thickens and squid is just cooked. Add feta cheese. Pour over pasta. Sprinkle with parsley, and toss.

PER SERVING

Calories	390
Protein	21 g
Fat, total	7 g
Fat, saturated	2 g
Carbohydrates	60 g
Sodium	342 mg
Cholesterol	155 mg
Fiber	5 g

PASTA WITH SQUID AND CLAMS IN A SPICY TOMATO SAUCE

Serves 6.

TIP

Replace squid with shrimp, scallops or lobster.

For a spicier version, add 1/4 tsp (1 mL) cayenne pepper.

MAKE AHEAD

Prepare sauce a day ahead up to point where seafood is added. Reheat gently, then continue with recipe.

12 oz	spaghetti	375 g
2 tsp	vegetable oil	10 mL
1 1/2 tsp	crushed garlic	7 mL
1 cup	chopped onions	250 mL
1 cup	chopped sweet green peppers	250 mL
1	can (19 oz [540 mL]) crushed tomatoes	1
2	cans (5 oz [142 mL]) baby clams, liquid reserved from 1 can	2
1 tbsp	tomato paste	15 mL
2 tsp	capers	10 mL
1 1/2 tsp	dried basil	7 mL
3/4 tsp	dried oregano	4 mL
2 tsp	chili powder	10 mL
12 oz	squid, sliced and cleaned	375 g
3 tbsp	grated Parmesan cheese	45 mL
	Parsley	

1. Cook pasta in boiling water according to package instructions or until firm to the bite. Drain and place in serving bowl.

2. In large nonstick saucepan, heat oil; sauté garlic, onions and green peppers until soft, approximately 5 minutes. Add crushed tomatoes, liquid from 1 can of clams, tomato paste, capers, basil, oregano and chili powder. Cover and simmer on low heat until thick, for 15 to 20 minutes, stirring occasionally. Add clams and squid; simmer just until squid is cooked, approximately 3 minutes. Pour over pasta. Sprinkle with cheese, and toss. Garnish with parsley.

PER SERVING

Calories	438
Protein	33 g
Fat, total	6 g
Fat, saturated	1 g
Carbohydrates	62 g
Sodium	335 mg
Cholesterol	180 mg
Fiber	5 g

 LINGUINE WITH BABY CLAMS ✕
AND GOAT CHEESE
IN MARINARA SAUCE

Serves 6.

TIP

For a spicier taste, add 1/4 tsp (1 mL) cayenne pepper.

Try coarsely chopped tomatoes instead of crushed. If using whole canned tomatoes, use juice and break up tomatoes during cooking with back of spoon.

MAKE AHEAD

Prepare sauce up to a day ahead without adding cheese. Reheat gently, add cheese, then continue with recipe.

12 oz	linguine	375 g
2 tsp	vegetable oil	10 mL
2 tsp	crushed garlic	10 mL
1 cup	chopped onions	250 mL
3/4 cup	chopped sweet green peppers	175 mL
2 1/2 cups	crushed tomatoes (canned or fresh)	625 mL
1	can (5 oz [142 mL]) baby clams, drained	1
2 tsp	dried basil	10 mL
2 tsp	dried oregano	10 mL
2 tsp	capers	10 mL
1/4 tsp	chili flakes (or to taste)	1 mL
3 1/2 oz	goat cheese, crumbled	90 g

1. Cook pasta in boiling water according to package instructions or until firm to the bite. Drain and place in serving bowl.

2. In large nonstick skillet, heat oil; sauté garlic and onions until soft. Add sweet peppers and sauté until tender. Add tomatoes, clams, basil, oregano, capers and chili flakes; simmer on low heat for 15 minutes, stirring occasionally. Add cheese and cook for 1 minute. Pour over pasta, and toss.

PER SERVING

Calories	368
Protein	18 g
Fat, total	6 g
Fat, saturated	2 g
Carbohydrates	61 g
Sodium	296 mg
Cholesterol	21 mg
Fiber	4 g

SPAGHETTI WITH CLAMS IN A MUSHROOM SAUCE

Serves 6.

TIP

Try wild mushrooms such as oyster or chanterelle for a sophisticated variation of this recipe.

MAKE AHEAD

Prepare sauce early in day. Before serving, reheat gently, adding more milk if too thick.

12 oz	spaghetti	375 g
1 tbsp	vegetable oil	15 mL
2 tsp	crushed garlic	10 mL
1/2 cup	chopped onions	125 mL
2 1/2 cups	sliced mushrooms	625 mL
2	cans (5 oz [142 mL]) clams, liquid reserved from 1 can	2
1/3 cup	dry white wine	75 mL
1 3/4 cups	2% milk	425 mL
5 1/2 tsp	all-purpose flour	27 mL
1/3 cup	chopped fresh dill (or 2 tsp [10 mL] dried)	75 mL
	Pepper	

1. Cook pasta in boiling water according to package instructions or until firm to the bite. Drain and place in serving bowl.

2. In large nonstick skillet, heat oil; sauté garlic and onions until tender, approximately 4 minutes. Add mushrooms and sauté just until soft, approximately 4 minutes. Add clams, with reserved liquid from 1 can, and wine; simmer for 5 minutes.

3. Meanwhile, in small bowl combine milk and flour until smooth. Add to clam mixture and simmer on medium heat for 4 minutes, or just until sauce begins to thicken, stirring constantly. Pour over pasta. Sprinkle with dill and pepper. Toss.

PER SERVING

Calories	450
Protein	28 g
Fat, total	7 g
Fat, saturated	I g
Carbohydrates	69 g
Sodium	127 mg
Cholesterol	37 mg
Fiber	6 g

CREAMY CLAM SAUCE OVER LINGUINE

Serves 6.

TIP

If you want to lower the fat, omit the margarine or butter. Combine garlic, clam juice, milk and flour in saucepan until smooth. Continue with recipe.

MAKE AHEAD

Prepare sauce early in day. Reheat gently, adding more milk if too thick.

12 oz	linguine	375 g
1 tbsp	margarine or butter	15 mL
2 tsp	crushed garlic	10 mL
5 tsp	all-purpose flour	25 mL
2	cans (5 oz [142 mL]) clams, liquid reserved from 1 can	2
1 1/2 cups	2% milk	375 mL
1/3 cup	chopped fresh dill (or 2 tsp [10 mL] dried)	75 mL
1/3 cup	chopped green onions	75 mL
3 tbsp	grated Parmesan cheese	45 mL

1. Cook pasta in boiling water according to package instructions or until firm to the bite. Drain and place in serving bowl.

2. In medium nonstick saucepan, melt margarine. Add garlic and flour; cook for 1 minute, stirring constantly. Add clam juice from 1 can of clams and milk to saucepan. Simmer on medium heat until slightly thickened, approximately 4 minutes, stirring constantly. Add reserved clams, dill, green onions and cheese. Combine until heated. Pour over pasta, and toss.

PER SERVING

Calories	438
Protein	28 g
Fat, total	8 g
Fat, saturated	2 g
Carbohydrates	62 g
Sodium	246 mg
Cholesterol	42 mg
Fiber	2 g

 # LINGUINE WITH ALMOND ORIENTAL SAUCE AND SHRIMP

12 oz	linguine	375 g
2 cups	sliced sweet red peppers	500 mL
1/4 cup	chopped green onions	50 mL
2 cups	snow peas, cut in half	500 mL
12 oz	shrimp, peeled, deveined, and cut into pieces	375 g

Sauce

1/4 cup	sliced or chopped almonds	50 mL
3 tbsp	soya sauce	45 mL
2 tbsp	sesame oil	25 mL
2 tbsp	honey	25 mL
1/4 cup	chicken stock or water	50 mL
2 tbsp	rice wine vinegar	25 mL
1 1/2 tsp	crushed garlic	7 mL
1 1/2 tsp	minced ginger root	7 mL

1. Cook pasta in boiling water according to package instructions or until firm to the bite. Drain and place in serving bowl along with red peppers and green onions.

2. Blanch snow peas in boiling water for 2 minutes. Drain and rinse with cold water. Add to pasta.

3. Make the sauce: In food processor, combine almonds, soya sauce, oil, honey, stock, vinegar, garlic and ginger. Process until almonds are finely chopped. Set aside.

4. In small nonstick skillet sprayed with vegetable spray, sauté shrimp just until cooked, approximately 3 minutes. Add to pasta along with sauce, and toss.

Serves 6.

TIP

Replace shrimp with other seafood, fish or chicken.

Snow peas can be replaced with chopped broccoli or asparagus.

Red pepper can be replaced with sweet green or yellow pepper.

Try cashews, pecans or macadamias instead of almonds.

MAKE AHEAD

Prepare sauce up to 3 days ahead and refrigerate. Bring to room temperature before using.

PER SERVING

Calories	465
Protein	26 g
Fat, total	11 g
Fat, saturated	1 g
Carbohydrates	66 g
Sodium	529 mg
Cholesterol	95 mg
Fiber	3 g

LINGUINE WITH SHRIMP, RED PEPPERS AND PINE NUTS

Serves 4.

8 oz	linguine	250 g
8 oz	shrimp, shelled, deveined and cut into pieces	250 g
2 tsp	vegetable oil	10 mL
2 tsp	crushed garlic	10 mL
2 cups	chopped sweet red peppers	500 mL
1/3 cup	chopped green onions	75 mL
1/2 cup	chopped fresh basil (or 2 tsp [10 mL] dried)	125 mL
1 1/2 tsp	dried oregano	7 mL
1 1/4 cups	cold fish or chicken stock	300 mL
3 1/2 tsp	all-purpose flour	17 mL
3 1/2 oz	feta cheese, crumbled	90 g
2 tbsp	toasted pine nuts	25 mL

TIP

Shrimp can be replaced with scallops, squid or firm fish fillets such as orange roughy or halibut.

Chicken can be substituted for fish.

▼

Goat cheese can replace feta cheese. Walnuts, pecans or cashews can replace pine nuts.

MAKE AHEAD

Prepare sauce in Steps 3 and 4 early in day. Do not add cheese. Reheat gently. Add cheese and continue with recipe.

PER SERVING

Calories	435
Protein	26 g
Fat, total	12 g
Fat, saturated	4 g
Carbohydrates	56 g
Sodium	599 mg
Cholesterol	116 mg
Fiber	3 g

1. Cook pasta in boiling water according to package instructions or until firm to the bite. Drain and place in serving bowl.

2. In medium nonstick skillet sprayed with nonstick vegetable spray, sauté shrimp just until pink and just cooked, approximately 3 minutes. Drain and add to pasta.

3. In large nonstick skillet, heat oil; sauté garlic and red peppers for 3 minutes. Add onions, basil and oregano; sauté for 3 minutes.

4. Meanwhile, in small bowl, combine stock and flour until smooth. Add to red pepper mixture; simmer, stirring constantly until thickened, approximately 3 minutes. Add cheese and allow to melt. Pour over pasta. Add pine nuts, and toss.

PASTA WITH SALMON IN TERIYAKI SAUCE (PAGE 49) ➤

 # FETTUCCINE WITH SCALLOPS AND SMOKED SALMON

Serves 6.

TIP

For a change, replace scallops with firm fish fillets such as halibut or Chilean seabass.

▼

Remove the small muscle on the side of each scallop; it toughens as it cooks.

MAKE AHEAD

Prepare sauce in Step 3 early in day. Before serving, reheat gently, adding more milk if sauce thickens.

12 oz	fettuccine	375 g
2 tsp	crushed garlic	10 mL
12 oz	scallops, quartered	375 g
1 tbsp	margarine or butter	15 mL
2 tbsp	all-purpose flour	25 mL
1 cup	clam juice or chicken stock	250 mL
1 cup	2% milk	250 mL
2 tbsp	light sour cream	25 mL
1/3 cup	chopped fresh dill (or 2 tsp [10 mL] dried)	75 mL
1/4 cup	grated Parmesan cheese	50 mL
3 oz	smoked salmon, chopped	75 g

1. Cook pasta in boiling water according to package instructions or until firm to the bite. Drain and place in serving bowl.

2. In large nonstick skillet sprayed with vegetable spray, sauté garlic and scallops for 2 minutes, or just until scallops are cooked. Drain and add to pasta.

3. In medium nonstick saucepan, melt margarine. Add flour and cook for 1 minute, stirring constantly. Slowly add clam juice and milk. Simmer on medium heat until slightly thickened, approximately 3 minutes, stirring constantly. Add sour cream, dill and cheese. Mix well and pour over pasta. Add smoked salmon, and toss.

PER SERVING

Calories	432
Protein	29 g
Fat, total	8 g
Fat, saturated	3 g
Carbohydrates	61 g
Sodium	568 mg
Cholesterol	35 mg
Fiber	2 g

◄ SEAFOOD TOMATO STEW OVER FUSILLI WITH FENNEL (PAGE 71)

 # FETTUCCINE WITH SCALLOPS IN TOMATO SAUCE

Serves 6.

TIP

Remove the small muscle on the side of each scallop; it toughens as it cooks.

Firm white fish fillets such as orange roughy or grouper can be substituted for the seafood.

MAKE AHEAD

Tomato sauce can be made a day ahead and gently reheated.

12 oz	fettuccine	375 g
2 tbsp	olive oil	25 mL
1 1/2 tsp	crushed garlic	7 mL
1 cup	thinly sliced red onions	250 mL
3 lb	tomatoes, puréed	1.5 kg
1/2 cup	chopped fresh basil (or 2 tsp [10 mL] dried)	125 mL
	Pepper	
12 oz	medium scallops, halved	375 g
	Basil	

1. Cook pasta in boiling water according to package instructions or until firm to the bite. Drain and place in serving bowl.

2. In large nonstick skillet, heat oil; sauté garlic and onions until tender. Add puréed tomatoes and simmer on medium heat for 15 minutes, stirring occasionally. Add basil and pepper and cook for 2 minutes. Set aside.

3. In small nonstick skillet sprayed with vegetable spray, sauté scallops until seared on both sides and just cooked, approximately 3 minutes. Drain and add to pasta along with sauce. Toss and garnish with basil.

PER SERVING

Calories	398
Protein	21 g
Fat, total	7 g
Fat, saturated	0.9 g
Carbohydrates	65 g
Sodium	127 mg
Cholesterol	21 mg
Fiber	8 g

# FETTUCCINE WITH SCALLOPS, BELL PEPPERS AND BASIL

Serves 6.

TIP

Using a variety of bell peppers gives an attractive sophisticated appearance.

Substitute chopped walnuts or pecans for pine nuts.

MAKE AHEAD

Prepare sauce in Step 4 early in day. Before serving, reheat gently, adding more stock if sauce is too thick.

12 oz	fettuccine	375 g
1 1/2 tsp	crushed garlic	7 mL
1 lb	scallops, sliced in half	500 g
2 tsp	vegetable oil	10 mL
2 cups	diced sweet bell peppers (a combination of green, red, and yellow)	500 mL
2/3 cup	cold fish or chicken stock	150 mL
1/3 cup	dry white wine	75 mL
1 1/3 cups	2% milk	325 mL
2 tbsp	all-purpose flour	25 mL
2 tbsp	toasted pine nuts	25 mL
2/3 cup	chopped coriander, basil or dill	150 mL
	Pepper	

1. Cook pasta in boiling water according to package instructions or until firm to the bite. Drain and place in serving bowl.

2. In large nonstick skillet sprayed with vegetable spray, sauté garlic and scallops just until cooked, 3 minutes, or browned on both sides. Drain and add to pasta.

3. To same skillet, add oil; sauté sweet peppers until tender, approximately 4 minutes. Add to pasta.

4. In medium saucepan, mix fish stock, wine, milk and flour until smooth. Simmer on medium heat until sauce slightly thickens, approximately 3 minutes, stirring constantly. Pour over pasta. Sprinkle with pine nuts, coriander and pepper. Toss.

PER SERVING

Calories	422
Protein	27 g
Fat, total	7 g
Fat, saturated	2 g
Carbohydrates	62 g
Sodium	263 mg
Cholesterol	36 mg
Fiber	5 g

ROTINI WITH SCALLOPS, TOMATOES AND CRABMEAT

Serves 4.

TIP

Penne is a good substitute for rotini.

If fresh garlic is unavailable, use garlic pieces preserved in oil in a jar. The extra oil will not significantly alter the nutritional analysis.

Replace crabmeat with imitation crabmeat, called Surimi, which is less expensive.

MAKE AHEAD

Sauce can be made early in day. Reheat gently so as not to overcook scallops.

PER SERVING

Calories	368
Protein	23 g
Fat, total	5 g
Fat, saturated	0.5 g
Carbohydrates	56 g
Sodium	217 mg
Cholesterol	31 mg
Fiber	5 g

8 oz	rotini	250 g
2 tsp	vegetable oil	10 mL
1 tsp	crushed garlic	5 mL
8 oz	scallops, cut into small pieces	250 g
3 tbsp	dry white wine	45 mL
2 cups	diced tomatoes	500 mL
1/4 cup	chopped green onions	50 mL
1/4 cup	chopped fresh basil (or 1 1/2 tsp [7 mL] dried)	50 mL
1/4 cup	chopped fresh oregano (or 1/2 tsp [2 mL] dried)	50 mL
3 oz	shredded crabmeat	75 g

1. Cook pasta in boiling water according to package instructions or until firm to the bite. Drain and place in serving bowl.

2. In large nonstick skillet, heat oil; sauté garlic and scallops just until barely cooked, approximately 3 minutes. Add wine and simmer for 2 minutes. Add tomatoes, green onions, basil, oregano and crabmeat; simmer for 2 minutes, just until hot. Pour over pasta, and toss.

SEAFOOD PASTA PIZZA WITH DILL AND GOAT CHEESE

Serves 6.

TIP

Small shell pasta or broken spaghetti can be substituted for linguine.

Instead of seafood, any firm white fish fillets can be used, such as orange roughy, swordfish or grouper.

Try 3 tbsp (45 mL) sliced olives for color and texture.

MAKE AHEAD

Crust can be made a day ahead and covered. Filling can be made ahead; add more stock if too thick.

PER SERVING

Calories	286
Protein	22 g
Fat, total	8 g
Fat, saturated	3 g
Carbohydrates	33 g
Sodium	382 mg
Cholesterol	80 mg
Fiber	1 g

Preheat oven to 350°F (180°C)
10- to 11-inch (3L) springform pan sprayed with vegetable spray

6 oz	broken linguine	150 g
1	egg	1
1/3 cup	2% milk	75 mL
3 tbsp	grated Parmesan cheese	45 mL
8 oz	seafood, cut in pieces or left whole (shrimp, scallops, squid)	250 g
1 tsp	vegetable oil	5 mL
1 1/2 tsp	crushed garlic	7 mL
3/4 cup	diced sweet red peppers	175 mL
1/4 cup	chopped green onions	50 mL
1/4 cup	sliced red onions	50 mL
1 cup	cold seafood or chicken stock	250 mL
1 cup	2% milk	250 mL
3 tbsp	all-purpose flour	45 mL
1/3 cup	chopped fresh dill (or 1 tbsp [15 mL] dried)	75 mL
1/2 cup	shredded mozzarella cheese	125 mL
2 oz	goat cheese, crumbled	50 g

1. Cook pasta in boiling water according to package instructions or until firm to the bite. Drain and place in mixing bowl. Add egg, milk and cheese. Mix well. Pour into pan and bake for 20 minutes.

2. In large nonstick skillet sprayed with vegetable spray, sauté seafood just until cooked, approximately 3 minutes. Drain and set seafood aside.

3. In same skillet, heat oil; sauté garlic, red peppers and green and red onions for 4 minutes.

4. Meanwhile, in small bowl combine stock, milk and flour until smooth. Add to skillet and simmer on low heat until thickened, approximately 2 minutes, stirring constantly. Add dill and seafood. Pour into pan. Sprinkle with mozzarella and goat cheese; bake for 10 minutes. Let rest for 10 minutes before serving.

CHICKEN

 CHICKEN TIPS

1. Skinless, boneless chicken breasts are used in all recipes. Pounding is not necessary. Buy chicken breasts with moist skin, tender flesh and a fresh smell.

2. At home, remove the wrapping and wash the chicken with cold water. Wrap chicken loosely in foil and place in the coldest part of the refrigerator for up to 48 hours. If freezing, wrap chicken in a plastic freezer bag and freeze for up to 4 months.

3. Thaw poultry in the refrigerator (5 hours per pound [10 hours per kilogram]), in a bowl of cold water (1 hour per pound [2 hours per kilogram]), or in a microwave. Do not defrost at room temperature; harmful bacteria may develop. Never refreeze raw chicken after thawing. Cooked chicken may be frozen.

   Note: Raw chicken contains bacteria that can cause illness. Thorough cooking destroys bacteria. After working with raw chicken, wash hands, cutting board and utensils with hot water and soap. Never place cooked chicken on a plate where raw chicken has been.

4. Always cook chicken until it is no longer pink and juices run clear. It must never be served rare, since harmful bacteria may remain.

5. For these pasta recipes, sauté chicken in a nonstick skillet sprayed with vegetable spray — oil or butter is not necessary. The liquid from the chicken prevents burning.

6. The chicken can also be grilled, baked, roasted, poached or steamed.

7. Reheat chicken sauces gently to prevent overcooking chicken, which will become dry.

8. Turkey can replace chicken in all recipes.

9. Ground chicken is best replaced with ground veal.

 # ORANGE AND PINEAPPLE CHICKEN STIR-FRY

10 oz	linguine	300 g
10 oz	skinless, boneless chicken breast, thinly sliced	300 g

Sauce

3 tbsp	brown sugar	45 mL
1 cup	chicken stock	250 mL
1/3 cup	orange juice	75 mL
1 1/2 tbsp	cornstarch	20 mL
2 tbsp	soya sauce	25 mL
2 tbsp	sesame oil	25 mL
1 1/2 tsp	crushed garlic	7 mL
1 1/2 tsp	crushed ginger root	7 mL
2 tsp	oil	10 mL
1 1/2 cups	chopped asparagus	375 mL
1 cup	sliced sweet red peppers	250 mL
1 cup	chopped baby corn	250 mL
3/4 cup	sliced water chestnuts	175 mL
1 cup	pineapple pieces	250 mL
3/4 cup	mandarin oranges	175 mL

Serves 6.

TIP

Stir-fry over high heat, stirring constantly.

Broccoli can replace asparagus.

Garnish with chopped cashews and green onions.

When making a stir-fry, have all the ingredients chopped and ready so that you don't overcook.

MAKE AHEAD

Sauce can be prepared up to a day before, but stir before using.

PER SERVING

Calories	427
Protein	22 g
Fat, total	8 g
Fat, saturated	1 g
Carbohydrates	70 g
Sodium	563 mg
Cholesterol	27 mg
Fiber	5 g

1. Cook pasta in boiling water according to package instructions or until firm to the bite. Drain and place in serving bowl.

2. In large nonstick skillet sprayed with vegetable spray, sauté chicken just until it is browned but not cooked through. Remove chicken and set aside.

3. Make the sauce: In small bowl combine sugar, stock, orange juice, cornstarch, soya sauce, sesame oil, garlic and ginger. Mix well. Set aside.

4. In skillet, heat oil; sauté asparagus and red peppers just until barely tender, approximately 2 minutes. Add corn, water chestnuts, pineapple pieces, sauce and chicken. Cook just until chicken is no longer pink and sauce has thickened slightly, approximately 2 minutes, stirring constantly. Add mandarin oranges. Pour over pasta and toss.

PASTA WITH SAUTÉED CHICKEN, SNOW PEAS AND ORIENTAL DRESSING

Serves 6.

TIP

Chicken can be replaced with beef or fish.

▼

Green or yellow sweet peppers can be used.

▼

For extra crunch, add 3/4 cup (175 mL) sliced water chestnuts.

MAKE AHEAD

Prepare sauce up to a day ahead. Stir before using.

12 oz	linguine	375 g
12 oz	skinless, boneless chicken breasts, cut into 1-inch (2.5-cm) cubes	375 g
2 tsp	vegetable oil	10 mL
1 1/2 cups	thinly sliced sweet red peppers	375 mL
1 1/2 cups	snow peas, cut in half	375 mL

Sauce

1 cup	chicken stock	250 mL
3 tbsp	soya sauce	45 mL
3 tbsp	brown sugar	45 mL
1 tbsp	vegetable oil	15 mL
1 tbsp	lemon or lime juice	15 mL
2 tsp	sesame oil	10 mL
1 1/2 tsp	crushed garlic	7 mL
1 1/2 tsp	minced ginger root	7 mL
2 1/2 tsp	cornstarch	12 mL
1/4 cup	chopped green onions	50 mL
1/3 cup	chopped coriander or parsley	75 mL

PER SERVING

Calories	464
Protein	28 g
Fat, total	9 g
Fat, saturated	0.9 g
Carbohydrates	69 g
Sodium	654 mg
Cholesterol	36 mg
Fiber	8 g

1. Make the sauce: In small bowl combine stock, soya sauce, sugar, oil, lemon juice, sesame oil, garlic, ginger and cornstarch. Set aside.

2. Cook pasta in boiling water according to package instructions or until firm to the bite. Drain and place in serving bowl.

3. In large nonstick skillet sprayed with vegetable spray, sauté chicken just until no longer pink, approximately 5 minutes. Remove from pan, and add to pasta. Add oil to skillet; sauté red peppers and snow peas for 3 minutes. Add sauce and cook for 2 minutes, stirring constantly just until slightly thickened. Pour over pasta. Garnish with onions and coriander, and toss.

 # CHICKEN AND TARRAGON PASTA PIZZA

Serves 6.

TIP

Macaroni or small shell pasta can replace fettuccine.

▼

Asparagus is a tasty substitute for the broccoli.

MAKE AHEAD

Crust and filling can be made early in day. Keep separate. Add more stock to filling if it thickens.

Preheat oven to 350°F (180°C)
10-inch (3 L) springform pan sprayed with vegetable spray

6 oz	broken fettuccine	150 g
1	egg	1
1/3 cup	2% milk	75 mL
3 tbsp	grated Parmesan cheese	45 mL
1 cup	chopped broccoli	250 mL
1 1/2 tsp	crushed garlic	7 mL
8 oz	skinless, boneless chicken breasts, cut into 1-inch (2.5-cm) cubes	250 g
2/3 cup	diced sweet green peppers	150 mL
2/3 cup	diced red onions	150 mL
1 cup	cold chicken stock	250 mL
1 cup	2% milk	250 mL
3 tbsp	all-purpose flour	45 mL
1/4 cup	chopped fresh tarragon (or 3 tsp [15 mL] dried)	50 mL
2 1/2 oz	shredded Swiss or mozzarella cheese	60 g

PER SERVING

Calories	304
Protein	24 g
Fat, total	8 g
Fat, saturated	4 g
Carbohydrates	36 g
Sodium	377 mg
Cholesterol	44 mg
Fiber	3 g

1. Cook pasta in boiling water according to package instructions or until firm to the bite. Drain and place in mixing bowl. Add egg, milk and cheese; mix well and pour in pan. Bake for 20 minutes.

2. Blanch broccoli in boiling water just until tender. Drain, rinse with cold water, and set aside.

3. In large nonstick skillet sprayed with vegetable spray, sauté garlic and chicken until chicken is no longer pink, approximately 4 minutes. Set chicken aside.

4. Spray skillet again with vegetable spray; sauté green peppers and onions for 4 minutes. In small bowl, mix stock, milk and flour until smooth. Add to skillet with broccoli, chicken and tarragon. Simmer on low heat until sauce thickens, approximately 4 minutes, stirring constantly. Pour into pan, sprinkle with cheese. Bake for 10 minutes.

BOW-TIE PASTA WITH CHICKEN, OLIVES AND SAUSAGE

Serves 6.

TIP

If a spicy taste is not desired, use sweet sausage and omit red pepper flakes.

Roasted pork or turkey can replace chicken.

MAKE AHEAD

Prepare sauce early in day. Reheat gently, adding more stock if sauce thickens.

12 oz	bow-tie pasta or rotini	375 g
1 tsp	vegetable oil	5 mL
1 tsp	crushed garlic	5 mL
8 oz	spicy sausage, skin removed and chopped	250 g
1/3 cup	sliced black olives	75 mL
1/8 tsp	red pepper flakes	1 mL
2 cups	cold chicken or beef stock	500 mL
2 1/2 tbsp	all-purpose flour	35 mL
1 1/2 cups	thinly sliced roasted or grilled chicken	375 mL
	Parsley	

1. Cook pasta in boiling water according to package instructions or until firm to the bite. Drain and place in serving bowl.

2. In large nonstick skillet, heat oil; sauté garlic and sausage for 5 minutes, or until sausage is no longer pink. Add olives and red pepper flakes.

3. Meanwhile, in a small bowl, combine stock and flour until smooth. Add to sausage mixture and simmer until just slightly thickened, approximately 4 minutes, stirring constantly. Add chicken and cook for 1 minute. Pour over pasta. Sprinkle with parsley, and toss.

PER SERVING

Calories	465
Protein	24 g
Fat, total	16 g
Fat, saturated	5 g
Carbohydrates	54 g
Sodium	689 mg
Cholesterol	54 mg
Fiber	2 g

 PASTA WITH PINEAPPLE, CHICKEN, BELL PEPPERS AND GINGER

Serves 6.

TIP

Pineapple juice from frozen concentrate or the juice from canned pineapple can be used.

Minced ginger can be bought in jars. You'll find it in the vegetable section of the grocery. Store in refrigerator for months.

MAKE AHEAD

Prepare vegetable pineapple sauce early in day. Reheat gently, adding more stock if sauce thickens, being careful not to overcook vegetables.

12 oz	rotini	375 g
12 oz	skinless, boneless chicken breast, cubed	375 g
2 tsp	vegetable oil	10 mL
2 tsp	crushed garlic	10 mL
1 cup	chopped sweet red peppers	250 mL
3/4 cup	chopped sweet green peppers	175 mL
2/3 cup	chopped carrots	150 mL
3/4 cup	pineapple juice	175 mL
1 cup	chicken stock	250 mL
2 tsp	minced ginger root	10 mL
2 3/4 tsp	cornstarch	14 mL
4 tsp	soya sauce	20 mL
1 tbsp	brown sugar	15 mL
1 1/2 cups	pineapple chunks (fresh or canned)	375 mL

1. Cook pasta in boiling water according to package instructions or until firm to the bite. Drain and place in serving bowl.

2. In medium nonstick skillet sprayed with vegetable spray, sauté chicken until no longer pink, approximately 5 minutes. Add to pasta.

3. In large nonstick skillet sprayed with vegetable spray, heat oil; sauté garlic, red and green peppers and carrots until just tender, approximately 8 minutes.

4. Meanwhile, in small bowl combine juice, stock, ginger, cornstarch, soya sauce and brown sugar until smooth. Pour into the skillet and simmer just until thickened, approximately 3 minutes. Add pineapple pieces. Pour over pasta, and toss.

PER SERVING

Calories	427
Protein	24 g
Fat, total	4 g
Fat, saturated	0.5 g
Carbohydrates	74 g
Sodium	384 mg
Cholesterol	40 mg
Fiber	4 g

ROTINI WITH CHICKEN, SWEET PEPPERS AND SUN-DRIED TOMATO SAUCE

Serves 6.

TIP

Parmesan cheese can replace Asiago or Romano.

To reduce fat, use dry sun-dried tomatoes instead of those packed in oil.

Toast pine nuts in a skillet until golden brown, approximately 3 minutes.

MAKE AHEAD

Prepare sauce up to 4 days ahead or freeze up to 4 weeks. If sauce thickens, thin with stock or water.

PER SERVING

Calories	477
Protein	29 g
Fat, total	16 g
Fat, saturated	4 g
Carbohydrates	56 g
Sodium	339 mg
Cholesterol	48 mg
Fiber	5 g

12 oz	rotini	375 g
12 oz	skinless, boneless chicken breasts cut into 1-inch (2.5-cm) strips	375 g
1 1/2 cups	thinly sliced yellow or green sweet peppers	375 mL
1/4 cup	grated Asiago or Romano cheese	50 mL

Sauce

4 oz	sun-dried tomatoes	100 g
2 tsp	crushed garlic	10 mL
1 cup	chicken stock or water	250 mL
1/2 cup	chopped parsley	125 mL
2 tbsp	toasted pine nuts	25 mL
3 tbsp	olive oil	45 mL
3 tbsp	grated Parmesan cheese	45 mL

1. Cover sun-dried tomatoes with boiling water; let soak for 15 minutes. Drain and chop. Set aside.

2. Cook pasta in boiling water according to package instructions or until firm to the bite. Drain and place in serving bowl.

3. In large nonstick skillet sprayed with nonstick vegetable spray, sauté chicken until no longer pink, approximately 5 minutes. Add to pasta.

4. Respray skillet and sauté sweet peppers just until tender, approximately 4 minutes. Add to pasta with Asiago cheese.

5. Make the sauce: In food processor, combine sun-dried tomatoes, garlic, stock, parsley, nuts, oil and cheese. Purée until smooth. Pour over pasta, and toss.

 # PENNE WITH SWEET POTATO, LEEKS AND CHICKEN

Serves 6.

TIP

Instead of chicken, firm fish fillets would be a good substitute, especially seabass or orange roughy.

▼

Apricots can replace dates, or a combination of both.

MAKE AHEAD

Prepare sauce early in day. Add more stock if sauce thickens.

12 oz	penne	375 g
8 oz	skinless, boneless chicken breast cut into 1-inch (2.5-cm) cubes	250 g
2 cups	diced sweet potatoes	500 mL
1	medium leek, thinly sliced	1
2/3 cup	chopped dates	150 mL

Sauce

1 tbsp	margarine or butter	15 mL
1 1/2 tsp	crushed garlic	7 mL
1 tsp	minced ginger root	5 mL
2 tbsp	all-purpose flour	25 mL
1/2 cup	dry white wine	125 mL
2 cups	chicken stock	500 mL
1/2 tsp	cinnamon powder	2 mL
2 tbsp	brown sugar	25 mL

PER SERVING

Calories	418
Protein	19 g
Fat, total	4 g
Fat, saturated	0.7 g
Carbohydrates	74 g
Sodium	307 mg
Cholesterol	24 mg
Fiber	4 g

1. Cook pasta in boiling water according to package instructions or until firm to the bite. Drain and place in serving bowl.

2. In large nonstick skillet sprayed with vegetable spray, sauté chicken until browned on all sides and no longer pink, approximately 5 minutes. Add to pasta.

3. Cook sweet potatoes in boiling water just until tender, approximately 5 to 8 minutes. Drain and set aside. Cook leeks in boiling water until tender, approximately 5 minutes. Drain and add to sweet potatoes. Set aside.

4. Make the sauce: In large nonstick skillet, melt margarine; sauté garlic and ginger for 1 minute. Add flour and cook for 1 minute, stirring constantly. Add wine, stock, cinnamon and sugar. Simmer on medium heat until slightly thickened, approximately 4 minutes. Add sweet potatoes, leek mixture and dates. Cook for 1 minute. Pour over pasta, and toss.

ROTINI WITH CHICKEN, APRICOTS AND DATES IN ORANGE SAUCE

Serves 6.

TIP

An unusual pasta that can use fish or seafood in place of chicken.

MAKE AHEAD

Prepare sauce early in day and reheat gently, adding more stock to thin if necessary. Be careful not to overcook apricots and dates.

| 12 oz | rotini | 375 g |
| 8 oz | skinless, boneless chicken breast cut into 1-inch (2.5-cm) cubes | 250 g |

Sauce

2 tsp	vegetable oil	10 mL
1 1/2 tsp	crushed garlic	7 mL
1 cup	chopped sweet red peppers	250 mL
2 1/4 cups	chicken stock	550 mL
1/4 cup	frozen orange juice concentrate, thawed	50 mL
2 tbsp	all-purpose flour	25 mL
2/3 cup	chopped dried apricots	150 mL
2/3 cup	chopped dried dates	150 mL
2 tbsp	brown sugar	25 mL
1/4 cup	chopped green onions	50 mL

1. Cook pasta in boiling water according to package instructions or until firm to the bite. Drain and place in serving bowl.

2. In large nonstick skillet sprayed with vegetable spray, sauté chicken until browned on both sides, or until no longer pink, approximately 5 minutes. Add to pasta.

3. Make the sauce: In same skillet, heat oil; sauté garlic and red peppers until tender, approximately 4 minutes.

4. Meanwhile in small bowl, combine stock, orange juice concentrate and flour until smooth. Add to the skillet and simmer on medium heat until slightly thickened, approximately 4 minutes, stirring constantly. Add apricots, dates, sugar and green onions and cook for 1 minute. Pour over pasta, and toss.

PER SERVING

Calories	506
Protein	21 g
Fat, total	4 g
Fat, saturated	0.4 g
Carbohydrates	101 g
Sodium	360 mg
Cholesterol	27 mg
Fiber	4 g

PASTA WITH CHICKEN MARSALA SAUCE

Serves 6.

TIP

Use oyster or portobello mushrooms if available. The texture and flavor are exceptional.

▼

Marsala is a sweet distinct wine. If a sweet flavor is not desired, use dry white wine.

MAKE AHEAD

Prepare sauce early in day. Reheat gently, adding more stock if sauce is too thick.

12 oz	fettuccine	375 g
1 1/2 tsp	crushed garlic	7 mL
12 oz	skinless, boneless chicken breasts, cut into 1-inch (2.5-cm) strips	375 g

Sauce

2 tsp	vegetable oil	10 mL
3/4 cup	chopped onions	175 mL
3 1/2 cups	sliced mushrooms (wild or regular)	875 mL
1 1/4 cups	2% milk	300 mL
3/4 cup	chicken stock	175 mL
1/3 cup	Marsala wine	75 mL
2 1/2 tbsp	all-purpose flour	35 mL
	Parsley	

1. Cook pasta in boiling water according to package instructions or until firm to the bite. Drain and place in serving bowl.

2. In large nonstick skillet sprayed with vegetable spray, sauté garlic and chicken until chicken is no longer pink, approximately 8 minutes. Remove chicken and add to pasta.

3. Make the sauce: In same skillet, heat oil; sauté onions until tender, approximately 4 minutes. Add mushrooms and sauté until tender, approximately 5 minutes.

4. Meanwhile, in small bowl combine milk, stock, wine and flour until smooth. Add to mushroom mixture; simmer on medium heat until slightly thickened, approximately 5 minutes, stirring constantly. Pour over pasta. Sprinkle with parsley, and toss.

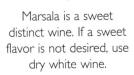

I thought this was good. Dan was unenthusiastic

CAJUN CHICKEN OVER FETTUCCINE

12 oz	fettuccine	375 g
12 oz	skinless, boneless chicken breast cut into 2-inch (5-cm) strips	375 g

Spice Mixture

1 tsp	cayenne	5 mL
1 3/4 tsp	onion powder	8 mL
1 1/4 tsp	garlic powder	6 mL
1 tsp	paprika	5 mL
1 tsp	dried basil	5 mL
3/4 tsp	dried oregano	4 mL
2 1/2 tbsp	unseasoned bread crumbs	35 mL

Sauce

2 tsp	vegetable oil	10 mL
1 tsp	crushed garlic	5 mL
3/4 cup	chopped onions	175 mL
3/4 cup	chopped sweet green peppers	175 mL
4 cups	canned or fresh tomatoes, crushed	1 L
1 1/2 tsp	dried basil	7 mL
1 tsp	dried oregano	5 mL
1/4 tsp	cayenne	1 mL

1. Cook pasta in boiling water according to package instructions or until firm to the bite. Drain and place in serving bowl.

2. Prepare the spices: In small bowl combine cayenne, onion and garlic powders, paprika, basil, oregano and bread crumbs. Coat chicken in mixture.

3. In medium nonstick skillet sprayed with vegetable spray, sauté chicken on medium heat until no longer pink, approximately 4 minutes. Add to pasta.

4. Make the sauce: In same skillet, heat oil; sauté garlic, onions and green peppers for 5 minutes, until tender. Add tomatoes, basil, oregano and cayenne. Simmer for 20 to 25 minutes. Pour over pasta, and toss.

LINGUINE WITH PESTO CHICKEN

Serves 6.

TIP

For a less distinct basil flavor, use half parsley and half basil.

Toast pine nuts on top of stove in skillet until brown, for 2 to 3 minutes.

MAKE AHEAD

Refrigerate sauce for up to 5 days or up to 3 weeks in freezer.

| 12 oz | linguine | 375 g |
| 12 oz | skinless, boneless chicken breasts, thinly sliced | 375 g |

Sauce

2 cups	fresh basil, packed down	500 mL
1/3 cup	chicken stock	75 mL
3 tbsp	olive oil	45 mL
2 tbsp	grated Parmesan cheese	25 mL
2 tbsp	toasted pine nuts or walnuts	25 mL
1 1/2 tsp	crushed garlic	7 mL

1. Cook pasta in boiling water according to package instructions or until firm to the bite. Drain and place in serving bowl.

2. In medium nonstick skillet sprayed with vegetable spray, sauté chicken until no longer pink, approximately 3 minutes. Add to pasta.

3. Make the sauce: In food processor, purée basil, stock, oil, cheese, nuts and garlic until smooth. Pour over pasta, and toss.

PER SERVING

Calories	412
Protein	26 g
Fat, total	13 g
Fat, saturated	2 g
Carbohydrates	48 g
Sodium	154 mg
Cholesterol	40 mg
Fiber	2 g

CHICKEN CACCIATORE OVER PENNE

Serves 6.

TIP

Dark chicken meat can be used but the calories and fat will increase slightly.

MAKE AHEAD

Prepare sauce up to a day ahead. Reheat gently, adding more stock if sauce is too thick.

12 oz	penne	375 g
2 tsp	vegetable oil	10 mL
2 tsp	crushed garlic	10 mL
1 1/3 cups	chopped onions	325 mL
1 1/4 cups	chopped sweet red peppers	300 mL
1 1/2 cups	sliced mushrooms	375 mL
1 lb	skinless, boneless chicken breasts, cubed	500 g
1/2 cup	dry red wine	125 mL
1/3 cup	chicken stock	75 mL
2 3/4 cups	fresh or canned tomatoes, crushed	675 mL
1 tbsp	tomato paste	15 mL
2 tsp	dried basil	10 mL
1 tsp	dried oregano	5 mL
1/4 cup	chopped parsley	50 mL

1. Cook pasta in boiling water according to package instructions or until firm to the bite. Drain and place in serving bowl.

2. In large nonstick skillet, heat oil; sauté garlic, onions and red peppers until soft, approximately 5 minutes. Add mushrooms and sauté until soft, approximately 5 minutes. Add chicken and sauté on medium heat until just no longer pink, approximately 5 minutes.

3. Add wine and stock; simmer for 2 minutes. Add tomatoes, tomato paste, basil and oregano; simmer for 15 minutes, covered, on low heat, stirring occasionally. Pour over pasta. Add parsley, and toss.

PER SERVING

Calories	441
Protein	32 g
Fat, total	5 g
Fat, saturated	0.7 g
Carbohydrates	66 g
Sodium	283 mg
Cholesterol	48 mg
Fiber	6 g

MACARONI WITH CHICKEN
 AND SUN-DRIED TOMATOES

Serves 6.

TIP

Use dry sun-dried tomatoes instead of those in oil.

Smoked chicken or turkey, which you can find in specialty markets, gives this dish an intense flavor.

MAKE AHEAD

Prepare sauce early in day. Reheat gently, adding more stock if sauce thickens. Do not overcook chicken.

1/2 cup	sun-dried tomatoes	125 mL
12 oz	macaroni	375 g

Sauce

2 tsp	margarine or butter	10 mL
1 1/2 tsp	crushed garlic	7 mL
2	large green onions, chopped	2
1 1/2 cups	chicken stock	375 mL
3/4 cup	2% milk	175 mL
2 tbsp	all-purpose flour	25 mL
1 1/2 cups	cooked or smoked chicken, diced	375 mL
1/4 cup	grated Parmesan cheese	50 mL

1. Pour boiling water over sun-dried tomatoes, and let soak for 15 minutes. Drain and chop. Set aside.

2. Cook pasta in boiling water according to package instructions or until firm to the bite. Drain and place in serving bowl.

3. Make the sauce: In large nonstick skillet, heat margarine; sauté garlic, onions and sun-dried tomatoes for 2 minutes. Add stock and simmer for 2 minutes.

4. Meanwhile, combine milk and flour in small bowl; slowly add to stock mixture and cook just until slightly thickened, approximately 3 minutes, stirring constantly. Add chicken and cook for 2 more minutes. Toss with pasta. Sprinkle with cheese.

PER SERVING

Calories	386
Protein	25 g
Fat, total	7 g
Fat, saturated	3 g
Carbohydrates	55 g
Sodium	448 mg
Cholesterol	39 mg
Fiber	3 g

PASTA WITH CHICKEN BOLOGNESE AND ROASTED PEPPERS

Serves 6.

Preheat oven to broil.

2	medium sweet red peppers	2
12 oz	fettuccine	375 g
Sauce		
2 tsp	vegetable oil	10 mL
2 tsp	crushed garlic	10 mL
1 cup	chopped onions	250 mL
12 oz	ground chicken	375 g
1/2 cup	dry white wine	125 mL
2 1/2 cups	fresh or canned tomatoes, crushed	625 mL
1 tbsp	tomato paste	15 mL
2 tsp	dried basil	10 mL
3/4 tsp	dried oregano	4 mL
3 tbsp	grated Parmesan cheese	45 mL

TIP

A quick way to peel peppers after broiling is to put them in a paper or plastic bag to cool for 10 minutes, then peel.

Chicken can be replaced with ground veal.

MAKE AHEAD

Broil peppers early in day. Set aside. Prepare sauce a day ahead and reheat, adding a little water or stock if sauce thickens.

PER SERVING

Calories	413
Protein	28 g
Fat, total	6 g
Fat, saturated	2 g
Carbohydrates	58 g
Sodium	184 mg
Cholesterol	42 mg
Fiber	5 g

1. Broil peppers until charred on all sides, approximately 15 minutes, turning occasionally. Let cool. Peel, and remove top and seeds. Cut into thin strips. Set aside.

2. Cook pasta in boiling water according to package instructions or until firm to the bite. Drain and place in serving bowl.

3. Make the sauce: In large nonstick saucepan, heat oil; sauté garlic and onions until soft, approximately 3 minutes. Add chicken and sauté until no longer pink, approximately 5 minutes. Add wine and cook for 3 minutes. Add tomatoes, paste, basil and oregano. Cover and simmer on low heat for 20 minutes, until sauce thickens, stirring occasionally. Add roasted peppers.

4. Pour sauce over pasta, sprinkle with Parmesan cheese, and toss.

PASTA WITH SPICY TURKEY TOMATO SAUCE

Serves 6.

TIP

As a substitute for the turkey, try using ground veal, beef or chicken.

Rotini can be replaced with any medium-sized pasta.

MAKE AHEAD

Sauce can be prepared up to 2 days before and gently reheated before serving. Do not add coriander or parsley until ready to serve.

12 oz	rotini	375 g
2 tsp	vegetable oil	10 mL
2 tsp	crushed garlic	10 mL
1 cup	diced red onions	250 mL
1 cup	diced red or green peppers	250 mL
12 oz	ground turkey	375 g
3 cups	crushed tomatoes (canned or fresh)	750 mL
1 1/2 tsp	dried basil	7 mL
1 tsp	dried oregano	5 mL
2 tsp	chili powder	10 mL
Pinch	cayenne pepper	Pinch
1/2 cup	coriander leaves or parsley, chopped	125 mL

1. Cook pasta in boiling water according to package instructions or until firm to the bite. Drain and place in serving bowl.

2. In large nonstick saucepan sprayed with vegetable spray, heat oil; sauté garlic, onions and red peppers until soft, approximately 5 minutes. Add turkey and sauté on medium heat until cooked, approximately 5 minutes.

3. Add tomatoes, basil, oregano, chili powder and cayenne. Cover and simmer on low heat for 15 minutes, stirring occasionally. Add coriander. Pour over pasta, and toss.

PER SERVING

Calories	382
Protein	26 g
Fat, total	4 g
Fat, saturated	0.5 g
Carbohydrates	61 g
Sodium	221 mg
Cholesterol	39 mg
Fiber	4 g

 SWEET AND SOUR
ORIENTAL CHICKENBALLS
OVER SPAGHETTI

Serves 6 to 8.

TIP

Replace chicken with beef, veal or pork for a change.

Pineapple juice from frozen concentrate or the juice from canned pineapple can be used.

MAKE AHEAD

Meatballs and sauce can be cooked up to 2 days before. Reheat gently before pouring over pasta.

10 oz	spaghetti	300 g
12 oz	ground chicken	375 g
1 tsp	crushed garlic	5 mL
1 tsp	minced ginger root	5 mL
3 tbsp	finely chopped onions	45 mL
3 tbsp	canned or home-made tomato sauce	45 mL
1	egg	1
3 tbsp	seasoned bread crumbs	45 mL

Sauce

1 cup	ketchup	250 mL
1 1/2 cups	pineapple juice	375 mL
2 tbsp	brown sugar	25 mL
1 cup	thinly sliced carrots	250 mL
1 cup	thinly sliced red peppers	250 mL
1 cup	pineapple chunks	250 mL

1. Cook pasta in boiling water according to package instructions or until firm to the bite. Drain and place in serving bowl.

2. In bowl, mix together chicken, garlic, ginger, onions, tomato sauce, egg and bread crumbs until well combined. Form into small balls of approximately 1 inch (2.5 cm). This will make about 32 balls.

3. Make the sauce: In large nonstick saucepan, combine ketchup, pineapple juice, brown sugar and carrots over medium heat. Add chicken balls. Cover and simmer for 30 to 40 minutes, just until chicken balls are tender.

4. In the last 10 minutes of cooking, add red peppers and pineapple chunks. Pour over pasta, and toss.

PER SERVING (8)

Calories	328
Protein	18 g
Fat, total	2 g
Fat, saturated	0.3 g
Carbohydrates	61 g
Sodium	515 mg
Cholesterol	28 mg
Fiber	5 g

RIGATONI WITH SAUTÉED CHICKEN LIVERS IN BASIL TOMATO SAUCE

Serves 6.

TIP

Large shell pasta can replace rigatoni.

MAKE AHEAD

Prepare entire sauce early in day. Reheat gently, adding a little water or chicken stock if sauce thickens.

12 oz	rigatoni	375 g
1 tbsp	margarine or butter	15 mL
1 1/2 tsp	crushed garlic	7 mL
3/4 cup	diced onions	175 mL
8	medium chicken livers, cubed	8
2 1/2 cups	canned or fresh tomatoes, crushed	625 mL
1/2 cup	chopped fresh basil (or 2 tsp [10 mL] dried)	125 mL
1/4 cup	grated Parmesan cheese	50 mL

1. Cook pasta in boiling water according to package instructions or until firm to the bite. Drain and place in serving bowl.

2. In large nonstick skillet, melt half the margarine; sauté garlic and onions until soft, approximately 5 minutes. Sauté livers in remaining margarine just until no longer pink, approximately 5 minutes. Add tomatoes and basil; simmer on low heat for 10 minutes, stirring occasionally. Pour over pasta. Sprinkle with cheese, and toss.

PER SERVING

Calories	376
Protein	16 g
Fat, total	7 g
Fat, saturated	3 g
Carbohydrates	67 g
Sodium	359 mg
Cholesterol	18 mg
Fiber	4 g

 # GNOCCHI WITH CHICKEN  LIVER AND VEAL SAUCE

Serves 4 to 6.

TIP

Replace gnocchi with small tortellini or ravioli.

Substitute ground chicken or beef for veal.

Replace chicken liver with beef or calves' liver if desired.

MAKE AHEAD

Prepare sauce early in day. Reheat gently, adding more stock if sauce thickens.

PER SERVING (6)

Calories	273
Protein	17 g
Fat, total	14 g
Fat, saturated	3 g
Carbohydrates	17 g
Sodium	287 mg
Cholesterol	194 mg
Fiber	2 g

1 1/2 lb	gnocchi	750 g
2 tsp	vegetable oil	10 mL
2 tsp	crushed garlic	10 mL
1 1/4 cups	chopped onions	300 mL
1/3 cup	finely chopped celery	75 mL
1/3 cup	finely chopped carrots	75 mL
2/3 cup	chopped mushrooms	150 mL
8 oz	ground veal	250 g
4 oz	chicken liver, chopped	125 g
1/3 cup	dry red wine	75 mL
1 cup	cold beef or chicken stock	250 mL
1 tbsp	all-purpose flour	15 mL

1. Cook pasta in boiling water according to package instructions or until firm to the bite. Drain and place in serving bowl.

2. In large nonstick skillet, heat oil; sauté garlic, onions, celery and carrots until tender, approximately 5 minutes. Add mushrooms and sauté for 2 minutes. Add veal and liver. Sauté until no longer pink, approximately 5 minutes. Add wine and cook for 3 minutes, stirring often.

3. Meanwhile, combine stock and flour in small bowl, until dissolved. Add to veal mixture and cook just until sauce thickens, approximately 2 minutes. Pour over pasta.

$\mathcal{M}$EAT

 MEAT TIPS

1. To reduce fat and calories, sauté meat in a nonstick skillet sprayed with vegetable spray, not oil. The liquid released from the meat prevents any sticking, and the meat browns nicely.

2. Marinate lean cuts of meat — preferably for at least 4 hours, or overnight, to become tender.

3. If you don't marinate the meat, you can use cuts such as rib-eye, sirloin, porterhouse or filet. These are the most tender. Remove visible fat before cooking.

4. If sauce is prepared ahead of time, reheat gently before serving so as not to overcook meat.

5. Beef, veal, lamb or pork can be substituted for one another in recipes. Pork should be thoroughly cooked until no longer pink. Do not overcook, or the meat will become dry.

6. Tightly wrapped fresh meat can be kept refrigerated for 2 days in a cold section of the refrigerator. Meat can be frozen for up to 6 months. Do not use meat that has freezer burn or discoloration.

7. Defrost meat in the refrigerator, or wrap in plastic and place in a bowl of cold water to quicken defrosting. An even faster method is to defrost in the microwave. Rotate meat every few minutes to ensure even defrosting.

8. Use meat sauce with larger, heavier pastas, such as rigatoni, large shell pasta or tortellini.

PIZZA PASTA WITH BEEF-TOMATO SAUCE AND CHEESE

Serves 8.

TIP

Any combination of different vegetables can be used as long as you do not exceed 2 1/4 cups (550 mL).

MAKE AHEAD

Prepare pasta crust and sauce early in day. Do not pour sauce over top until ready to bake.

Preheat oven to 350°F (180°C)
10- to 11-inch (25- to 28-cm) pizza or springform baking pan sprayed with vegetable spray

6 oz	macaroni	150 g
1	egg	1
1/3 cup	2% milk	75 mL
3 tbsp	grated Parmesan cheese	45 mL
1 tsp	vegetable oil	5 mL
2 tsp	crushed garlic	10 mL
3/4 cup	finely chopped onions	175 mL
1/2 cup	finely chopped sweet green peppers	125 mL
1/3 cup	finely chopped carrots	75 mL
8 oz	ground beef or chicken	250 g
1	can (19 oz [540 mL]) tomatoes, crushed	1
2 tbsp	tomato paste	25 mL
1 1/2 tsp	dried basil	7 mL
1 tsp	dried oregano	5 mL
1 cup	low-fat mozzarella cheese, shredded	250 mL

PER SERVING

Calories	247
Protein	15 g
Fat, total	9 g
Fat, saturated	4 g
Carbohydrates	23 g
Sodium	264 mg
Cholesterol	29 mg
Fiber	3 g

1. Cook pasta in boiling water according to package instructions or until firm to the bite. Drain and place in serving bowl. Add egg, milk and cheese. Mix well. Place in baking pan as a crust and bake for 20 minutes.

2. Meanwhile, in medium nonstick saucepan sprayed with vegetable spray, heat oil; sauté garlic, onions, green peppers and carrots until tender, approximately 5 minutes. Add beef and sauté until no longer pink, approximately 4 minutes. Add tomatoes, paste, basil and oregano. Cover and simmer on low heat for 15 minutes, stirring occasionally.

3. Pour sauce into pasta crust. Sprinkle with cheese; bake for 10 minutes or until cheese melts.

(handwritten margin notes: 13 1/2 P, 8 v, 12 b, 1/4 M, 5 F, 150 oc, 2 1/2 P, 1/4 v, 1 F, 2 b, 25 c)

BEEF CASSEROLE WITH CREAMY CHEESE PASTA

Serves 8.

TIP

This is an excellent casserole for children and teenagers. Adults love it too!

▼

Substitute ground chicken or veal for beef.

▼

It's great to reheat.

MAKE AHEAD

Prepare up to a day ahead but do not bake until ready to eat.

(handwritten: really yummy, tastes fattening)

PER SERVING

Calories	339
Protein	18 g
Fat, total	15 g
Fat, saturated	6 g
Carbohydrates	34 g
Sodium	513 mg
Cholesterol	38 mg
Fiber	2 g

Preheat oven to 350°F (180°C)
9-inch (2.5 L) baking dish

1 tsp	vegetable oil *(1 f)*	5 mL
2 tsp	crushed garlic	10 mL
1 cup	chopped onions *(2 v)*	250 mL
12 oz	ground beef *(9 p)*	375 g
1/2 cup	beef or chicken stock *(10 oc)*	125 mL
1 2/3 cups	prepared tomato sauce *(6 v)* or Quick Basic Tomato Sauce (for recipe see page 205)	400 mL
8 oz	small shell pasta *(10 1/2 b)*	250 g
1 tbsp	margarine or butter *(4 F)*	15 mL
2 1/2 tbsp	all-purpose flour *(3/4 b)*	35 mL
1 1/4 cups	beef or chicken stock *(25 oc)*	300 mL
1 1/4 cups	2% milk *(1 1/4 M + 35 oc)*	300 mL
1/2 cup	shredded Cheddar cheese *(4 1/2 p)*	125 mL
2 tbsp	grated Parmesan cheese *(8 oc)*	25 mL

(handwritten: 1 (13 3/4) can, 1 (6) oz can)

1. In large nonstick skillet, heat oil; sauté garlic and onions for 4 minutes. Add beef and sauté until no longer pink, approximately 4 minutes. Add stock and tomato sauce; simmer on low heat for 12 minutes or until thickened, stirring occasionally. Set aside.

2. Cook pasta in boiling water according to package instructions or until firm to the bite. Drain and place in baking dish.

3. In medium nonstick saucepan, melt margarine; add flour and cook for 1 minute, stirring constantly. Add stock and milk; simmer on medium heat until slightly thickened, approximately 5 minutes. Add Cheddar cheese and Parmesan cheese.

4. Add tomato sauce mixture to pasta. Mix well. Pour cheese sauce over top. Cover and bake for 15 minutes or until hot. Let rest for 10 minutes before serving.

RIGATONI WITH THICK CREAMY BEEF TOMATO SAUCE

Serves 6 to 8.

TIP

Large shell pasta will also be good.

Processing this sauce makes it more visually appealing to children.

MAKE AHEAD

Refrigerate sauce up to 2 days ahead and reheat gently, adding more milk if too thick.

1 lb	rigatoni	500 g
2 tsp	vegetable oil	10 mL
2 tsp	crushed garlic	10 mL
1 cup	diced onions	250 mL
1/2 cup	finely diced celery	125 mL
1/2 cup	finely diced carrots	125 mL
12 oz	ground beef	375 g
1/2 cup	dry red wine	125 mL
1/2 cup	2% milk	125 mL
1	can (28 oz [796 mL]) tomatoes, crushed	1
1 tbsp	tomato paste	15 mL
1 1/2 tsp	dried basil	7 mL
1 tsp	dried oregano	5 mL
1/3 cup	grated Parmesan cheese	75 mL

1. Cook pasta in boiling water according to package instructions or until firm to the bite. Drain and place in serving bowl.

2. In large nonstick saucepan, heat oil; sauté garlic, onions, celery and carrots until tender, approximately 5 minutes. Add beef and sauté until no longer pink, approximately 4 minutes. Add wine and cook on high for 2 minutes. Add milk and cook for 2 minutes. Add tomatoes, tomato paste, basil and oregano; cover and simmer on low-heat for 20 minutes or until sauce becomes thickened, stirring occasionally.

3. Place in food processor and purée in batches just until still slightly chunky. Pour over pasta; sprinkle with cheese; toss and serve.

PER SERVING (8)

Calories	415
Protein	20 g
Fat, total	11 g
Fat, saturated	4 g
Carbohydrates	56 g
Sodium	232 mg
Cholesterol	31 mg
Fiber	4 g

50-80

EGGPLANT, BEEF AND TOMATO CASSEROLE WITH PASTA SHELLS

Serves 8.

TIP

Leave skin on eggplant for extra fiber.

Replace beef with ground veal or chicken.

For a stronger cheese taste, replace mozzarella with 1/3 cup (75 mL) Swiss cheese or 3 oz (75g) goat cheese.

MAKE AHEAD

Prepare sauce early in day. Reheat gently, adding more tomato sauce if too thick.

Preheat oven to 350°F (180°C)
9 - by 13-inch (3.5 L) baking dish

8 oz	medium shell pasta	250 g
Sauce		
1 tbsp	olive oil	15 mL
2 tsp	crushed garlic	10 mL
3/4 cup	chopped onions	175 mL
2 cups	diced eggplant	500 mL
12 oz	ground beef	375 g
1 3/4 cups	prepared tomato sauce or Quick Basic Tomato Sauce (for recipe see page 205)	425 mL
1 1/2 tsp	dried basil	7 mL
1 tsp	dried oregano	5 mL
2 tsp	chili powder	10 mL
1/4 cup	grated Parmesan cheese	50 mL
3/4 cup	grated mozzarella cheese	175 mL

1. Cook pasta in boiling water according to package instructions or until firm to the bite. Drain and place in baking dish.

2. Make the sauce: In large nonstick skillet sprayed with vegetable spray, heat oil; sauté garlic and onions until soft, approximately 3 minutes. Add eggplant and beef; sauté for 5 minutes or until beef is no longer pink. Add tomato sauce, basil, oregano and chili powder; simmer on low heat for 12 minutes, stirring occasionally. Add Parmesan cheese and mix well. Pour over pasta and toss. Sprinkle with mozzarella cheese. Bake uncovered for 12 to 15 minutes, or until cheese melts.

PER SERVING

Calories	316
Protein	18 g
Fat, total	13 g
Fat, saturated	5 g
Carbohydrates	31 g
Sodium	234 mg
Cholesterol	34 mg
Fiber	3 g

CREAMY SEAFOOD LASAGNA WITH LEEKS AND SWEET BELL PEPPERS (PAGE 194) ➤

OVERLEAF: UPPER LEFT - SPAGHETTI WITH SUN-DRIED TOMATOES AND BROCCOLI (PAGE 137); *LOWER LEFT* - GRILLED BALSAMIC VEGETABLES OVER PENNE (PAGE 150); *RIGHT* - SPINACH CHEESE TORTELLINI IN PURÉED VEGETABLE SAUCE (PAGE 178)

 # ROTINI WITH STIR-FRIED BEEF AND CRISP VEGETABLES

Serves 6.

TIP

Penne can replace rotini.

▼

Ginger is now available minced in jars in the vegetable section of the grocery. It keeps for months in the refrigerator.

MAKE AHEAD

Prepare sauce up to 2 days ahead, stirring before use.

12 oz	rotini (twisted pasta)	375 g
Sauce		
2 tsp	grated ginger root	10 mL
2 tsp	crushed garlic	10 mL
1/4 cup	soya sauce	50 mL
1 cup	cold beef or chicken stock	250 mL
2 1/2 tsp	sesame oil	12 mL
3 tbsp	brown sugar	45 mL
2 1/2 tsp	cornstarch	12 mL
Stir-Fry		
8 oz	lean steak, thinly sliced	250 g
2 tsp	vegetable oil	10 mL
3/4 cup	chopped onions	175 mL
3/4 cup	diced carrots	175 mL
3/4 cup	chopped broccoli	175 mL
3/4 cup	chopped snow peas	175 mL

1. Cook pasta in boiling water according to package instructions or until firm to the bite. Drain and place in serving bowl.

2. Make the sauce: In small bowl, combine ginger, garlic, soya sauce, stock, sesame oil, sugar and cornstarch. Stir until well mixed. Set aside.

3. In large nonstick skillet sprayed with vegetable spray, sauté steak until no longer pink, approximately 2 minutes. Drain and remove steak. Add oil to same skillet; sauté onions and carrots for 5 minutes or until tender. Add broccoli and snow peas and sauté for 2 minutes. Add sauce and simmer, stirring constantly just until slightly thickened, approximately 3 minutes. Add beef and heat thoroughly. Pour over pasta, and toss.

PER SERVING

Calories	419
Protein	22 g
Fat, total	7 g
Fat, saturated	1 g
Carbohydrates	67 g
Sodium	694 mg
Cholesterol	18 mg
Fiber	6 g

 SEAFOOD PASTA PIZZA WITH DILL AND GOAT CHEESE (PAGE 87)

HOISIN BEEF, RED PEPPERS AND SNOW PEAS OVER FETTUCCINE

Serves 6.

TIP

Hoisin sauce can be found in Chinese food section of the grocery store.

▼

Use any lean steak such as rib eye, porterhouse or filet tenderloin.

MAKE AHEAD

Prepare sauce up to a day ahead, stirring before use.

12 oz	fettuccine	375 g
2 tsp	crushed garlic	10 mL
12 oz	sirloin steak cut into 1/2-inch (1-cm) strips	375 g
2 tsp	vegetable oil	10 mL
1 cup	thinly sliced sweet red peppers	250 mL
1 cup	snow peas, cut in half	250 mL
6 oz	sliced mushrooms	150 g
1/3 cup	chopped green onions	75 mL
1/4 cup	sliced water chestnuts	50 mL

Sauce

3/4 cup	cold beef stock	175 mL
1/4 cup	hoisin sauce	50 mL
2 tbsp	soya sauce	25 mL
1 tbsp	rice wine vinegar	15 mL
1 tbsp	cornstarch	15 mL
2 tsp	sesame oil	10 mL
2 tsp	minced ginger root	10 mL

PER SERVING

Calories	409
Protein	25 g
Fat, total	7 g
Fat, saturated	1 g
Carbohydrates	61 g
Sodium	636 mg
Cholesterol	30 mg
Fiber	5 g

1. Cook pasta in boiling water according to package instructions or until firm to the bite. Drain and place in serving bowl.

2. Make the sauce: In small bowl, combine stock, hoisin sauce, soya sauce, rice wine vinegar, cornstarch, oil and ginger. Stir until smooth. Set aside.

3. In large nonstick skillet sprayed with vegetable spray, sauté garlic and steak just until beef is barely cooked, approximately 3 minutes. Drain and set beef aside.

4. In same skillet, heat oil; add red peppers and snow peas; sauté for 2 minutes. Add mushrooms, green onions and water chestnuts; sauté for 3 minutes. Add sauce and beef and simmer on medium heat until sauce thickens slightly, for 3 or 4 minutes, stirring constantly. Pour over pasta, and toss.

FETTUCCINE WITH BEEF TENDERLOIN, GOAT CHEESE AND SUN-DRIED TOMATOES

Serves 6.

TIP

Use any other lean cut of tender steak such as rib eye, porterhouse or sirloin. Remove any visible fat.

Use dry sun-dried tomatoes, not those packed in oil.

MAKE AHEAD

Prepare sauce early in day but do not add beef until ready to serve.

12 oz	fettuccine	375 g
3/4 cup	sun-dried tomatoes	175 mL
2 1/2 tsp	chopped garlic	12 mL
2 tsp	chopped ginger root	10 mL
12 oz	beef tenderloin, sliced	375 g

Sauce

1 1/4 cups	cold beef or chicken stock	300 mL
3/4 cup	2% milk	175 mL
5 tsp	flour	25 mL
2 1/2 oz	goat cheese	60 g
1/2 cup	chopped green onions	125 mL

1. Cook pasta in boiling water according to package instructions or until firm to the bite. Drain and place in serving bowl.

2. Pour boiling water over sun-dried tomatoes. Let soak for 15 minutes. Drain and chop.

3. In large nonstick skillet sprayed with vegetable spray, sauté garlic, ginger and beef just until beef is slightly cooked, approximately 3 minutes. Drain and remove beef. Set aside.

4. Make the sauce: In small bowl, combine beef stock, milk and flour until smooth; add sun-dried tomatoes and place in skillet. Simmer until just thickened, approximately 3 minutes, stirring constantly. Add goat cheese and reserved beef. Pour over pasta. Sprinkle with onions, and toss.

PER SERVING

Calories	400
Protein	25 g
Fat, total	9 g
Fat, saturated	2 g
Carbohydrates	57 g
Sodium	295 mg
Cholesterol	34 mg
Fiber	4 g

VEAL SCALLOPINI WITH SUN-DRIED TOMATO SAUCE OVER FETTUCCINE

Serves 6.

TIP

Skinless, boneless chicken breast can replace veal.

Wild mushrooms such as oyster or shiitake make this dish very sophisticated.

MAKE AHEAD

Prepare sauce early in day and reheat gently, adding more broth if sauce thickens.

12 oz	fettuccine	375 g
1/2 cup	sun-dried tomatoes	125 mL
12 oz	veal scallopini, cut into thin strips	375 g

Sauce

2 tsp	olive oil	10 mL
2 tsp	crushed garlic	10 mL
1 cup	chopped onions	250 mL
8 oz	sliced mushrooms	250 g
2/3 cup	chicken or beef broth	150 mL
2/3 cup	2% milk	150 mL
1/3 cup	dry white wine	75 mL
1 1/4 cups	prepared tomato sauce or Quick Basic Tomato Sauce (for recipe see page 205)	300 mL
1/4 cup	grated Parmesan cheese	50 mL
	Parsley	

PER SERVING

Calories	475
Protein	29 g
Fat, total	9 g
Fat, saturated	3 g
Carbohydrates	66 g
Sodium	475 mg
Cholesterol	57 mg
Fiber	5 g

1. Cook pasta in boiling water according to package instructions or until firm to the bite. Drain and place in serving bowl.

2. Pour boiling water over sun-dried tomatoes. Let soak for 15 minutes. Drain and chop. Set aside.

3. In large nonstick skillet sprayed with vegetable spray, sauté veal until browned, approximately 5 minutes. Add to pasta.

4. Make the sauce: Add oil to same skillet sprayed again with vegetable spray; sauté garlic and onions until soft, approximately 4 minutes. Add mushrooms and sauté approximately 5 minutes. Add broth, milk, wine, tomato sauce and sun-dried tomatoes. Simmer on low heat for 12 minutes, stirring occasionally. Pour over pasta. Sprinkle with cheese and parsley, and toss.

 # FETTUCCINE WITH GOAT CHEESE, TOMATOES AND GROUND VEAL

Serves 4.

TIP

Veal can be replaced with ground chicken, beef or pork.

Feta cheese can replace goat cheese.

MAKE AHEAD

Prepare sauce early in day and reheat gently, adding water or beef stock if sauce thickens.

8 oz	fettuccine	250 g
2 tsp	vegetable oil	10 mL
1 tsp	crushed garlic	5 mL
1/2 cup	diced onions	125 mL
6 oz	ground veal	150 g
1/3 cup	dry white wine	75 mL
1 lb	diced tomatoes (about 2 1/2 cups [625 mL])	500 g
1/3 cup	chopped fresh basil (or 2 tsp [10 mL] dried)	75 mL
2 1/2 oz	crumbled goat cheese	60 g
1/3 cup	sliced black olives	75 mL
	Basil	

1. Cook pasta in boiling water according to package instructions or until firm to the bite. Drain and place in serving bowl.

2. In large nonstick skillet, heat oil; sauté garlic and onions for 4 minutes or until soft. Add veal and sauté until cooked, approximately 5 minutes. Add wine and simmer for 2 minutes. Add tomatoes, basil, cheese and olives; simmer for 5 minutes, stirring occasionally. Pour over pasta, and toss. Sprinkle with basil.

PER SERVING

Calories	412
Protein	19 g
Fat, total	11 g
Fat, saturated	2 g
Carbohydrates	57 g
Sodium	243 mg
Cholesterol	31 mg
Fiber	5 g

 SPAGHETTINI WITH MINCED PORK AND MUSHROOMS IN BLACK BEAN SAUCE

12 oz	spaghettini	375 g
2 tsp	crushed garlic	10 mL
12 oz	ground pork	375 g
2 tsp	vegetable oil	10 mL
2 cups	sliced mushrooms	500 mL
1 cup	chopped sweet red peppers	250 mL
1 tbsp	sesame seeds	15 mL

Sauce

1 1/2 cups	chicken stock	375 mL
1/4 cup	black bean sauce	50 mL
4 tsp	rice wine vinegar	20 mL
4 tsp	soya sauce	20 mL
4 tsp	sesame oil	20 mL
1 tbsp	cornstarch	15 mL
1 tsp	crushed ginger root	5 mL
3 tbsp	brown sugar	45 mL
1/2 cup	chopped green onions	125 mL

1. Cook pasta in boiling water according to package instructions or until firm to the bite. Drain and place in serving bowl.

2. Make the sauce: In small bowl, combine stock, black bean sauce, rice wine vinegar, soya sauce, sesame oil, cornstarch, ginger and sugar; mix well. Set aside.

3. In large nonstick skillet sprayed with vegetable spray, sauté garlic and pork just until cooked, approximately 5 minutes. Add oil and sauté mushrooms, red peppers and sesame seeds until vegetables are tender, approximately 3 minutes.

4. Add sauce to pork mixture and simmer on low heat until slightly thickened, approximately 3 minutes, stirring constantly. Pour over pasta. Sprinkle with green onions, and toss.

PER SERVING

Calories	455
Protein	26 g
Fat, total	10 g
Fat, saturated	2 g
Carbohydrates	68 g
Sodium	468 mg
Cholesterol	31 mg
Fiber	4 g

 ## SPAGHETTINI WITH PORK STIR-FRY IN OYSTER SAUCE

Serves 6 to 8.

TIP

Oyster sauce can be found in the Chinese food section of the grocery store.

Skinless, boneless chicken breasts can replace lean pork.

MAKE AHEAD

Prepare sauce up to a day ahead, stirring just before use.

12 oz	spaghettini	375 g
3/4 cup	thinly sliced carrots	175 mL
12 oz	boneless pork, sliced thinly	375 g
2 tsp	vegetable oil	10 mL
2 cups	chopped snow peas	500 mL
1 1/2 cups	thinly sliced sweet red peppers	375 mL
1 cup	sliced water chestnuts	250 mL
1/4 cup	chopped green onions	50 mL

Sauce

1 1/3 cups	chicken stock	325 mL
1/4 cup	oyster sauce	50 mL
2 tbsp	brown sugar	25 mL
3 tbsp	rice wine vinegar or dry sherry	45 mL
2 tbsp	soya sauce	25 mL
3 1/4 tsp	cornstarch	16 mL
1 tbsp	sesame oil	15 mL
1 1/2 tsp	minced ginger root	7 mL
1 1/2 tsp	crushed garlic	7 mL

PER SERVING (8)

Calories	337
Protein	19 g
Fat, total	5 g
Fat, saturated	0.9 g
Carbohydrates	53 g
Sodium	460 mg
Cholesterol	26 mg
Fiber	4 g

1. Cook pasta in boiling water according to package instructions or until firm to the bite. Drain and place in serving bowl.

2. Make the sauce: In small bowl, combine stock, oyster sauce, sugar, rice wine vinegar, soya sauce, cornstarch, sesame oil, ginger and garlic. Stir until smooth. Set aside.

3. Blanch carrots in boiling water just until barely tender. Drain and rinse with cold water. Set aside.

4. In large nonstick skillet or wok sprayed with vegetable spray, sauté pork for 3 minutes or until browned. Remove pork from pan. Add oil to skillet; sauté carrots, snow peas and red peppers for 4 minutes. Add water chestnuts, oyster sauce mixture and pork; simmer on medium heat just until sauce thickens, approximately 3 minutes, stirring constantly. Pour over pasta. Add green onions, and toss.

ROTINI WITH SAUSAGES AND MUSHROOMS

Serves 6.

TIP

Use either spicy or mild sausages.

For a change, try wild mushrooms, such as oyster.

MAKE AHEAD

Prepare sauce early in day. Reheat gently, adding more milk if too thick.

12 oz	rotini (twisted pasta)	375 g
1 tsp	vegetable oil	5 mL
1 1/2 tsp	crushed garlic	7 mL
1/2 cup	chopped onions	125 mL
8 oz	skinless sausages, chopped	250 g
3/4 cup	chopped mushrooms	175 mL
1/3 cup	dry red or white wine	75 mL
3/4 cup	prepared tomato sauce or Quick Basic Tomato Sauce (for recipe see page 205)	175 mL
2/3 cup	2% milk	150 mL
1 1/2 tsp	dried basil	7 mL
1/4 cup	grated Parmesan cheese	50 mL

1. Cook pasta in boiling water according to package instructions or until firm to the bite. Drain and place in serving bowl.

2. In nonstick skillet sprayed with vegetable spray, heat oil; sauté garlic and onions until tender, approximately 4 minutes. Add sausages; sauté until no longer pink, approximately 4 minutes. Add mushrooms and sauté until soft, approximately 2 minutes. Add wine and simmer for 2 minutes.

3. Add tomato sauce, milk and basil; simmer on low heat for 10 minutes, stirring occasionally. Pour over pasta. Add cheese, and toss.

PER SERVING

Calories	452
Protein	18 g
Fat, total	17 g
Fat, saturated	6 g
Carbohydrates	54 g
Sodium	364 mg
Cholesterol	36 mg
Fiber	3 g

 # LINGUINE WITH SPICY ITALIAN SAUSAGE IN A RED WINE TOMATO SAUCE

Serves 6.

TIP

This dish can be turned into a sweet pasta by replacing spicy sausage with sweet sausage.

White wine can replace red wine.

MAKE AHEAD

Prepare sauce early in day and reheat gently, adding more tomato sauce if it becomes too thick.

12 oz	linguine	375 g

Sauce

2 tsp	vegetable oil	10 mL
1 tsp	crushed garlic	5 mL
1 cup	diced onions	250 mL
8 oz	spicy sausages, skinned and chopped	250 g
1/2 cup	dry red wine	125 mL
2 cups	prepared tomato sauce or Quick Basic Tomato Sauce (for recipe see page 205)	500 mL
3 tbsp	grated Parmesan cheese	45 mL

1. Cook pasta in boiling water according to package instructions or until firm to the bite. Drain and place in serving bowl.

2. Make the sauce: In large nonstick skillet, heat oil; sauté garlic and onions just until soft. Add sausages and sauté until meat loses its pinkness, approximately 5 minutes.

3. Add wine and tomato sauce to sausage mixture; simmer over low heat for 15 minutes, just until sauce thickens, stirring occasionally. Pour over pasta. Sprinkle with cheese, and toss.

PER SERVING

Calories	493
Protein	19 g
Fat, total	19 g
Fat, saturated	6 g
Carbohydrates	58 g
Sodium	578 mg
Cholesterol	35 mg
Fiber	4 g

SHELL PASTA WITH CREAMY ✕ SWEET SAUSAGE

Serves 4.

TIP

For a spicy taste, use spicy sausages.

MAKE AHEAD

Prepare sauce early in day, adding more stock if sauce thickens.

8 oz	small shell pasta	250 g
1 tsp	vegetable oil	5 mL
6 oz	sweet Italian sausages, skinned and chopped	150 g
3/4 cup	beef or chicken stock	175 mL
3/4 cup	2% milk	175 mL
4 tsp	all-purpose flour	20 mL
1/4 cup	grated Parmesan cheese	50 mL
1/4 cup	chopped fresh parsley	50 mL

1. Cook pasta in boiling water according to package instructions or until firm to the bite. Drain and place in serving bowl.

2. In nonstick skillet, heat oil; sauté sausages, breaking with a fork, just until cooked, approximately 5 minutes. Add stock and simmer for 2 minutes.

3. Meanwhile, in small bowl combine milk and flour until smooth; add to sausage mixture and simmer just until slightly thickened, approximately 3 minutes, stirring constantly. Pour over pasta. Sprinkle with cheese and parsley, and toss.

PER SERVING

Calories	431
Protein	18 g
Fat, total	16 g
Fat, saturated	6 g
Carbohydrates	52 g
Sodium	505 mg
Cholesterol	36 mg
Fiber	2 g

ROTINI WITH SAUSAGE IN A CREAMY TOMATO MUSHROOM SAUCE

Serves 6.

TIP

For a milder flavor, try using sweet sausages instead of spicy ones.

Wild mushrooms such as oyster or cremini would complement this dish.

MAKE AHEAD

Prepare sauce early in day, reheating gently and adding more milk if sauce thickens.

12 oz	rotini	375 g
Sauce		
2 tsp	vegetable oil	10 mL
1 tsp	crushed garlic	5 mL
1 cup	chopped onions	250 mL
8 oz	spicy sausages, skinned and chopped	250 g
8 oz	sliced mushrooms	250 g
1/4 cup	dry white wine	50 mL
3/4 cup	prepared tomato sauce or Quick Basic Tomato Sauce (for recipe see page 205)	175 mL
1 1/4 cups	2% milk	300 mL
4 tsp	all-purpose flour	20 mL
1/4 cup	grated Parmesan cheese	50 mL
1/4 cup	chopped parsley	50 mL

1. Cook pasta in boiling water according to package instructions or until firm to the bite. Drain and place in serving bowl.

2. Make the sauce: In large nonstick skillet, heat oil; sauté garlic and onions until soft, about 5 minutes. Add sausages and sauté just until cooked, approximately 5 minutes. Add mushrooms and sauté for 5 minutes. Add wine and tomato sauce and simmer for 3 minutes.

3. Meanwhile, in small bowl combine milk and flour until smooth; add to tomato mixture and simmer until slightly thickened, approximately 3 minutes, stirring constantly. Pour over pasta. Sprinkle with cheese and parsley, and toss.

PER SERVING

Calories	511
Protein	22 g
Fat, total	19 g
Fat, saturated	7 g
Carbohydrates	62 g
Sodium	509 mg
Cholesterol	40 mg
Fiber	5 g

 # RADIATORE WITH SWEET SAUSAGE, ZUCCHINI AND TOMATOES ><

Serves 6 to 8.

TIP

This dish can be made spicier by using spicy sausages and adding 1/4 tsp (1 mL) cayenne pepper.

Beef can be replaced with ground chicken, veal or pork.

MAKE AHEAD

Prepare sauce up to a day ahead, reheating gently before use. Add some water or beef stock if sauce thickens.

12 oz	radiatore or penne	350 g
2 tsp	vegetable oil	10 mL
2 tsp	crushed garlic	10 mL
3/4 cup	chopped onions	175 mL
3/4 cup	chopped sweet green peppers	175 mL
2 cups	chopped zucchini	500 mL
6 oz	sweet sausages, skinned and chopped	150 g
6 oz	ground beef	150 g
2 1/2 cups	canned or fresh tomatoes, crushed	625 mL
1/3 cup	sliced black olives	75 mL
2 tsp	dried basil	10 mL
1 tsp	dried oregano	5 mL

1. Cook pasta in boiling water according to package instructions or until firm to the bite. Drain and place in serving bowl.

2. In large nonstick skillet, heat oil; sauté garlic, onions, green peppers and zucchini until tender, approximately 5 minutes. Add sausage and beef; sauté just until cooked, approximately 10 minutes. Add tomatoes, olives, basil and oregano; simmer for 15 minutes, until sauce thickens, stirring occasionally. Pour over pasta, and toss.

PER SERVING (8)

Calories	335
Protein	14 g
Fat, total	12 g
Fat, saturated	4 g
Carbohydrates	44 g
Sodium	298 mg
Cholesterol	25 mg
Fiber	4 g

WHOLE SWEET BELL PEPPERS ✕ STUFFED WITH SPAGHETTINI, TOMATOES AND PROSCIUTTO

Serves 6.

TIP

A different color combination of sweet peppers makes for a beautiful dinner entrée.

MAKE AHEAD

Broil peppers early in day. Skin can be removed more quickly if, after broiling, peppers are placed in a plastic or paper bag to cool for 10 minutes, then peel. Entire dish can be prepared up to 2 hours early and served at room temperature or reheated gently in microwave.

Preheat oven to broil

6	medium sweet bell peppers (green, red and/or yellow)	6
12 oz	spaghettini	375 g

Sauce

2 tsp	vegetable oil	10 mL
2 tsp	crushed garlic	10 mL
3/4 cup	diced onions	175 mL
1 3/4 cups	diced tomatoes	425 mL
1 1/4 cups	cold chicken or beef stock	300 mL
1 tbsp	all-purpose flour	15 mL
1/4 cup	chopped fresh basil (or 2 tsp [10 mL] dried)	50 mL
1 tbsp	margarine or butter	15 mL
1/2 cup	chopped prosciutto or ham	125 mL
3 tbsp	grated Parmesan cheese	45 mL

PER SERVING

Calories	380
Protein	16 g
Fat, total	10 g
Fat, saturated	3 g
Carbohydrates	57 g
Sodium	631 mg
Cholesterol	18 mg
Fiber	4 g

1. Broil peppers in oven or grill for 15 minutes or until charred, turning often. Let cool for 5 minutes. Remove tops of peppers and save. Peel skin and de-seed, leaving whole pepper intact. This can be done under cool running water.

2. Cook pasta in boiling water according to package instructions or until firm to the bite. Drain and place in large bowl.

3. Make the sauce: In large nonstick skillet, heat oil; sauté garlic and onions until soft, approximately 3 minutes. Add tomatoes and cook for 1 minute.

4. Meanwhile, combine stock and flour in small bowl; add to tomato mixture and simmer just until sauce thickens slightly, approximately 3 minutes, stirring constantly. Pour over pasta; add basil, margarine, prosciutto and cheese. Mix well. Stuff peppers until full, saving remainder as a side dish. Place pepper top over pasta, to act as lid.

ROTINI ALFREDO WITH ASPARAGUS, SWEET RED PEPPER AND PROSCIUTTO

Serves 6.

TIP

For a sharper flavor, try using Romano cheese as a replacement for Parmesan.

Broccoli can replace asparagus.

MAKE AHEAD

Prepare sauce early in day. Reheat gently, adding more stock if sauce thickens.

12 oz	rotini	375 g
2 cups	chopped asparagus	500 mL
1 1/4 cups	thinly sliced sweet red peppers	300 mL
1/3 cup	chopped prosciutto or smoked ham	75 mL

Sauce

1 tbsp	margarine or butter	15 mL
2 tbsp	all-purpose flour	25 mL
1 1/4 cup	2% milk	300 mL
1 cup	chicken or beef stock	250 mL
1/3 cup	grated Parmesan cheese	75 mL
Pinch	nutmeg	Pinch
Pinch	black pepper	Pinch

1. Cook pasta in boiling water according to package instructions or until firm to the bite. Drain and place in serving bowl.

2. Cook asparagus in boiling water just until tender, approximately 3 minutes. Drain and rinse with cold water. Add to pasta. Cook red peppers in boiling water for 1 minute. Drain and rinse with cold water, and add to pasta. Add prosciutto.

3. Make the sauce: In small nonstick skillet, melt margarine; add flour and cook for 1 minute, stirring constantly. Add milk and stock; simmer on medium heat, stirring constantly until slightly thickened, approximately 4 minutes. Add cheese, nutmeg and pepper. Pour over pasta, and toss.

PER SERVING

Calories	338
Protein	15 g
Fat, total	6 g
Fat, saturated	2 g
Carbohydrates	55 g
Sodium	400 mg
Cholesterol	12 mg
Fiber	2 g

 # ROTINI WITH RADICCHIO, HAM, TOMATOES AND CHEESE

Serves 6.

TIP

The radicchio can be increased up to 1 3/4 cups (425 mL) if desired.

▼

For a stronger flavor, use Swiss cheese or 3 oz (75 g) of goat or feta cheese.

MAKE AHEAD

Prepare sauce early in day and reheat gently, adding a little wine if sauce thickens.

| 12 oz | rotini | 375 g |

Sauce

2 tsp	vegetable oil	10 mL
1 tsp	crushed garlic	5 mL
1/2 cup	diced onions	125 mL
1 1/2 cups	coarsely sliced radicchio	375 mL
3/4 cup	dry white wine	175 mL
3 cups	chopped tomatoes	750 mL
2 tbsp	tomato paste	25 mL
4 oz	diced ham	125 g
1/2 cup	shredded mozzarella cheese	125 mL

1. Cook pasta in boiling water according to package instructions or until firm to the bite. Drain and place in serving bowl.

2. Make the sauce: In large nonstick skillet, heat oil; sauté garlic and onions just until tender, approximately 4 minutes. Add radicchio and simmer until wilted, approximately 3 minutes. Add wine and simmer for 3 minutes.

3. Add tomatoes and paste. Simmer over low heat for 10 minutes, stirring occasionally. Add ham. Pour sauce over pasta. Sprinkle with cheese, and toss.

PER SERVING

Calories	333
Protein	14 g
Fat, total	4 g
Fat, saturated	0.7 g
Carbohydrates	56 g
Sodium	317 mg
Cholesterol	10 mg
Fiber	5 g

 # RIGATONI WITH ARTICHOKES, ✕ MUSHROOMS AND HAM

Serves 4 to 6.

TIP

Use smoked or Black Forest ham. For a change, try using prosciutto.

MAKE AHEAD

Prepare sauce early in day, adding more stock if sauce thickens.

12 oz	rigatoni (wide tube pasta)	375 g
1 tsp	vegetable oil	5 mL
1 1/2 tsp	crushed garlic	7 mL
1 cup	diced onions	250 mL
1 cup	sliced mushrooms	250 mL
1/2 cup	sliced sweet red peppers	125 mL
1 1/2	cans (14 oz [390 mL]) artichokes, drained and diced	1 1/2
2/3 cup	frozen green peas	150 mL
2 oz	ham, chopped	50 g

Sauce

1 tbsp	margarine or butter	15 mL
2 tbsp	all-purpose flour	25 mL
1 1/4 cups	chicken or beef stock	300 mL
1/2 cup	dry white wine	125 mL
1/2 cup	2% milk	125 mL
1/4 cup	grated Parmesan cheese	50 mL

1. Cook pasta in boiling water according to package instructions or until firm to the bite. Drain and place in serving bowl.

2. Meanwhile, in large skillet, heat oil; sauté garlic and onions until soft, approximately 4 minutes. Add mushrooms and red peppers and sauté for 2 minutes. Add artichokes and peas and cook just until peas are soft, approximately 2 minutes. Add to pasta along with ham.

3. Make the sauce: In small nonstick saucepan, melt margarine; add flour and cook for 1 minute, stirring constantly. Add stock, wine and milk, and cook on a medium heat, stirring constantly until thickened, approximately 3 minutes. Pour over pasta. Sprinkle with Parmesan cheese, and toss.

PER SERVING (6)

Calories	390
Protein	17 g
Fat, total	6 g
Fat, saturated	2 g
Carbohydrates	66 g
Sodium	639 mg
Cholesterol	8 mg
Fiber	4 g

LEEK AND PROSCIUTTO FETTUCCINE

Serves 6.

TIP

To wash leeks properly, separate leaves and rinse under running water to remove all dirt trapped between leaves.

MAKE AHEAD

Prepare sauce early in day. Reheat gently, adding more stock if sauce thickens.

12 oz	fettuccine	375 g
Sauce		
1 tbsp	margarine or butter	15 mL
2 tsp	crushed garlic	10 mL
2	large leeks, sliced thinly	2
2 tbsp	all-purpose flour	25 mL
1 1/4 cups	beef or chicken stock	300 mL
1 cup	2% milk	250 mL
1 tsp	Dijon mustard	5 mL
1/2 cup	chopped prosciutto or ham	125 mL
1/2 cup	chopped parsley	125 mL
1/4 cup	grated Parmesan cheese	50 mL

1. Cook pasta in boiling water according to package instructions or until firm to the bite. Drain and place in serving bowl.

2. Make the sauce: In large nonstick saucepan sprayed with vegetable spray, melt margarine; sauté garlic and leeks until tender, approximately 5 minutes. Add flour and cook for 1 minute. Slowly add stock, milk and mustard. Simmer on medium heat just until slightly thickened, approximately 5 minutes, stirring constantly. Pour over pasta. Sprinkle with prosciutto, parsley and cheese, and toss.

PER SERVING

Calories	408
Protein	21 g
Fat, total	11 g
Fat, saturated	5 g
Carbohydrates	56 g
Sodium	813 mg
Cholesterol	27 mg
Fiber	3 g

VEGETABLES

 VEGETABLE TIPS

1. Use fresh vegetables that are in season. If out of season vegetables are needed, use frozen, never canned. Canned vegetables have a high salt content and lack good color and texture. Keep vegetables in refrigerator in designated section.

2. If vegetables are to be cooked in advance for a pasta dish, they can be steamed, microwaved, blanched or boiled. Stop cooking vegetables when they are tender-crisp and still retain their color. Drain and rinse with cold water to prevent overcooking. Add to pasta. Overcooked vegetables are dull and soft, and most of the nutrients are lost.

3. Leaving the skin on vegetables, if not discolored or bruised, increases the fiber content.

FETTUCCINE WITH SWEET BELL PEPPERS, SUN-DRIED TOMATOES AND BLACK OLIVES

Serves 4.

Preheat broiler

1	medium sweet red bell pepper	1
15	sun-dried tomatoes	15
8 oz	fettuccine	250 g
1 tsp	vegetable oil	5 mL
1 1/2 tsp	crushed garlic	7 mL
1/4 cup	chopped green onions	50 mL
1/4 cup	sliced black olives	50 mL
1 1/4 cups	chicken stock	300 mL
3/4 cup	prepared tomato sauce or Quick Basic Tomato Sauce (see page 205 for recipe)	175 mL
3 tbsp	grated Parmesan cheese	45 mL

TIP

The skin of sweet peppers will come off easily if, after broiling, you place the peppers in a plastic or paper bag for 10 minutes, then peel.

MAKE AHEAD

Broil peppers and prepare sauce early in day. Reheat sauce gently, adding more stock if sauce thickens.

1. Broil pepper until charred on all sides, for 12 to 15 minutes. Let cool for 5 minutes. Remove top, skin and seeds and slice into thin strips. Set aside.

2. Pour boiling water over sun-dried tomatoes. Let soak for 15 minutes. Drain, cut in half and set aside.

3. Cook pasta in boiling water according to package instructions or until firm to the bite. Drain and place in serving bowl.

4. In large nonstick saucepan, heat oil; add pepper strips, sun-dried tomatoes, garlic, onions and olives. Simmer for 2 minutes. Add stock and simmer on low heat for 5 minutes. Add tomato sauce and simmer on low heat until thickened, approximately 10 minutes, stirring occasionally. Pour over pasta. Sprinkle with cheese, and toss.

PER SERVING

Calories	359
Protein	15 g
Fat, total	8 g
Fat, saturated	3 g
Carbohydrates	57 g
Sodium	697 mg
Cholesterol	9 mg
Fiber	4 g

PASTA WITH SUN-DRIED TOMATOES AND FRESH TOMATOES

Serves 6.

TIP

Finely chop fresh and sun-dried tomatoes when using fine pasta. Use wider pasta if tomatoes are coarsely chopped.

For a different texture, try plum tomatoes instead of field tomatoes.

MAKE AHEAD

Prepare sauce early in day. Before serving, reheat gently, adding more stock if sauce thickens.

2/3 cup	sun-dried tomatoes	150 mL
12 oz	thin pasta (spaghettini)	375 g
1 tbsp	olive oil	15 mL
2 tsp	crushed garlic	10 mL
3 cups	fresh chopped tomatoes	750 mL
1/3 cup	sliced black olives	75 mL
1 cup	cold chicken stock	250 mL
3 tsp	all-purpose flour	15 mL
1/2 cup	chopped fresh basil (or 2 tsp [10 mL] dried)	125 mL
2 tbsp	toasted pine nuts	25 mL

1. Pour boiling water over sun-dried tomatoes. Let soak for 15 minutes. Drain and chop. Set aside.

2. Cook pasta in boiling water according to package instructions or until firm to the bite. Drain and place in serving bowl. Set aside.

3. In large nonstick skillet, heat oil; sauté garlic, sun-dried tomatoes, fresh tomatoes and olives for 3 minutes, stirring constantly.

4. Meanwhile, in small bowl, combine stock and flour until well mixed. Add to tomato mixture and cook for 2 minutes, stirring constantly, until slightly thickened. Add basil and pine nuts. Pour over pasta, and toss.

PER SERVING

Calories	344
Protein	11 g
Fat, total	8 g
Fat, saturated	1 g
Carbohydrates	60 g
Sodium	280 mg
Cholesterol	0 mg
Fiber	6 g

SPAGHETTI WITH SUN-DRIED TOMATOES AND BROCCOLI

Serves 4.

TIP

Buy dry sun-dried tomatoes, not those marinated in oil.

Instead of dried chilies, use 1/8 tsp (1 mL) of cayenne pepper.

MAKE AHEAD

Prepare pasta up to 2 hours earlier, leaving at room temperature. Toss before serving.

8 oz	spaghetti	250 g
1/2 cup	sun-dried tomatoes	125 mL
2 cups	chopped broccoli	500 mL
2 1/2 cups	chopped tomatoes	625 mL
2 tbsp	olive oil	25 mL
1 1/2 tsp	crushed garlic	7 mL
Dash	crushed dried chilies	Dash
1/2 cup	chopped fresh basil (or 2 tsp [10 mL] dried)	125 mL
3 tbsp	grated Parmesan cheese	45 mL

1. Cook pasta in boiling water according to package instructions or until firm to the bite. Drain and place in serving bowl.

2. Pour boiling water over sun-dried tomatoes. Let soak for 15 minutes. Drain, then chop. Add to pasta.

3. Blanch broccoli in boiling water just until barely tender. Rinse with cold water, drain and add to pasta. Add tomatoes, oil, garlic, chilies, basil and cheese. Toss.

PER SERVING

Calories	366
Protein	14 g
Fat, total	9 g
Fat, saturated	2 g
Carbohydrates	60 g
Sodium	125 mg
Cholesterol	4 mg
Fiber	7 g

 # FETTUCCINE WITH CREAMY ✕ WILD MUSHROOM SAUCE

Serves 4 to 6.

TIP

If a sweet sauce is not desired, use dry white or red wine.

MAKE AHEAD

Prepare sauce early in day. Reheat gently, adding more milk if sauce thickens.

12 oz	fettuccine	375 g
2 tsp	oil	10 mL
1 1/2 tsp	crushed garlic	7 mL
2/3 cup	diced onions	150 mL
3 1/2 cups	sliced wild or regular mushrooms (oyster, portobello or shiitake)	875 mL
6 tbsp	sweet wine (port or Madeira)	90 mL
6 tbsp	chicken stock	90 mL
1 1/2 cups	2% milk	375 mL
5 tsp	all-purpose flour	25 mL
1/3 cup	finely chopped chives or green onions	75 mL

1. Cook pasta in boiling water according to package instructions or until firm to the bite. Drain and place in serving bowl.

2. In large nonstick skillet, heat oil; sauté garlic and onions until soft, approximately 3 minutes. Add mushrooms and sauté until soft, approximately 5 minutes. Add wine and cook for 3 minutes.

3. Meanwhile, in small bowl, combine stock, milk and flour until dissolved. Add to mushroom mixture and simmer on medium heat for 5 minutes, stirring often. (Sauce may curdle initially; continue simmering.) Pour over pasta. Sprinkle with chives, and toss.

PER SERVING (6)

Calories	364
Protein	14 g
Fat, total	5 g
Fat, saturated	1 g
Carbohydrates	64 g
Sodium	95 mg
Cholesterol	5 mg
Fiber	6 g

 # PENNE WITH WILD MUSHROOMS

Serves 6.

TIP

The texture and flavor of wild mushrooms warrants the expense. If they are unavailable, use regular mushrooms.

Try plum tomatoes instead of field tomatoes.

MAKE AHEAD

Prepare sauce early in day, leaving at room temperature. Reheat gently, adding more milk if too thick.

12 oz	penne	375 g
1 tsp	margarine or butter	5 mL
3 cups	sliced wild mushrooms (oyster, cremini, portobello)	750 mL
2 tsp	olive oil	10 mL
2 tsp	crushed garlic	10 mL
1 cup	diced onions	250 mL
1 lb	chopped tomatoes (about 3 cups [750 mL])	500 g
2 cups	2% milk	500 mL
4 tsp	all-purpose flour	20 mL
1/2 cup	fresh chopped basil (or 2 tsp [10 mL] dried)	125 mL
	Pepper	

1. Cook pasta in boiling water according to package instructions or until firm to the bite. Drain and place in serving bowl.

2. In large nonstick skillet, melt margarine; sauté mushrooms for 5 minutes. Drain off excess liquid. Add oil; sauté garlic and onions just until tender, approximately 3 minutes. Add tomatoes; simmer on low heat for 10 minutes just until tomatoes become very soft.

3. Meanwhile, in small bowl, mix milk and flour until smooth; add to tomato mixture and simmer on medium heat for 3 minutes or until sauce thickens slightly. Pour over pasta. Sprinkle with basil and pepper, and toss.

PER SERVING

Calories	356
Protein	14 g
Fat, total	5 g
Fat, saturated	1 g
Carbohydrates	66 g
Sodium	49 mg
Cholesterol	3 mg
Fiber	7 g

PASTA WITH CRISP VEGETABLES IN A CREAMY SAUCE

Serves 4 to 6.

TIP

Use green (spinach) linguine for a change.

▼

This is a pasta primavera that works well with any combination of fresh vegetables.

▼

Try asparagus, green peppers or zucchini.

MAKE AHEAD

Make sauce early in day. Reheat gently, adding more stock if too thick.

12 oz	linguine	375 g
1 1/2 cups	chopped broccoli	375 mL
1 1/2 cups	chopped snow peas	375 mL
1 cup	thinly sliced yellow or red peppers	250 mL
1 cup	frozen green peas	250 mL
1 2/3 cups	chopped tomatoes	400 mL
1/2 cup	chopped fresh basil (or 2 tsp [10 mL] dried)	125 mL
1/4 cup	chopped parsley	50 mL
1/3 cup	grated Parmesan cheese	75 mL

Sauce

1 tbsp	margarine or butter	15 mL
2 tbsp	all-purpose flour	25 mL
1 cup	2% milk	250 mL
1 1/4 cups	chicken or vegetable stock	300 mL
1 1/2 tsp	crushed garlic	7 mL
	Salt and pepper	

1. Cook pasta in boiling water according to package instructions or until firm to the bite. Just before the pasta is cooked, add the broccoli, snow peas, yellow peppers and green peas to the boiling water, and cook for 2 minutes. Drain and place in serving bowl. Add tomatoes, basil, parsley and cheese.

2. Meanwhile, make the sauce: In nonstick saucepan, melt margarine; add flour and cook for 1 minute, stirring constantly. Slowly add milk, stock, garlic and salt and pepper; stir constantly until sauce slightly thickens, approximately 4 minutes. Remove from heat. Add to pasta and toss well.

PER SERVING (6)

Calories	367
Protein	16 g
Fat, total	6 g
Fat, saturated	2 g
Carbohydrates	63 g
Sodium	368 mg
Cholesterol	7 mg
Fiber	6 g

 # PASTA WITH FRESH SPRING ⋊ VEGETABLES AND MINT

Serves 6.

TIP

Finely diced vegetables are best suited to the angel hair pasta. If vegetables are chopped in larger pieces, use linguine or fettuccine.

MAKE AHEAD

Sauté vegetables early in day until barely tender, approximately 4 minutes. Add frozen peas, but do not cook. Continue with recipe just before serving.

12 oz	angel hair pasta (fine strand)	375 g
1 tbsp	olive oil	15 mL
2 tsp	crushed garlic	10 mL
4 oz	chopped snow peas	125 g
1 cup	diced zucchini	250 mL
1	small carrot, finely diced	1
1 cup	finely diced sweet red peppers	250 mL
1 cup	frozen green peas	250 mL
2 1/2 cups	cold chicken or vegetable stock	625 mL
2 tbsp and 2 tsp	all-purpose flour	35 mL
1/2 cup	chopped fresh mint (or 1 1/2 tsp [7 mL] dried)	125 mL

1. Cook pasta in boiling water according to package instructions or until firm to the bite. Drain and place in serving bowl.

2. In large nonstick skillet, heat oil; sauté garlic, snow peas, zucchini, carrot and red peppers until just tender, for 5 to 8 minutes. Add peas and sauté for 2 minutes.

3. Meanwhile, in small bowl, combine stock with flour until smooth. Add to vegetables and simmer just until slightly thickened, approximately 4 minutes, stirring constantly. Add mint and pour over pasta. Toss.

PER SERVING

Calories	319
Protein	11 g
Fat, total	4 g
Fat, saturated	0.5 g
Carbohydrates	60 g
Sodium	416 mg
Cholesterol	0 mg
Fiber	4 g

SOBA NOODLES WITH  PEANUT BUTTER DRESSING

Serves 4 to 5.

TIP

Soba noodles are firmer and chewier than fettuccine. The texture goes well with a nutty dressing.

Try almond or cashew butter for a more sophisticated meal.

MAKE AHEAD

Prepare dressing up to 3 days ahead and keep refrigerated. Before continuing with recipe, bring sauce to room temperature.

10 oz	soba noodles or fettuccine	300 g
1 1/2 cups	snow peas, cut in half	375 mL
1 1/2 cups	thinly sliced sweet red peppers	375 mL
1/2 cup	thinly sliced carrots	125 mL
1/3 cup	chopped green onions	75 mL
3/4 cup	sliced water chestnuts	175 mL

Dressing

1/4 cup	peanut butter	50 mL
1/3 cup	chicken stock	75 mL
2 tbsp	rice wine vinegar	25 mL
1 tbsp	lemon juice	15 mL
1 tbsp	soya sauce	15 mL
2 tsp	sesame oil	10 mL
2 tsp	minced ginger root	10 mL
1 1/2 tsp	crushed garlic	7 mL
1 1/2 tsp	brown sugar	7 mL

1. Cook pasta in boiling water according to package instructions or until firm to the bite. Drain and place in serving bowl.

2. Blanch snow peas, red peppers and carrots in boiling water until barely tender, approximately 3 minutes. Drain and refresh with cold water; add to pasta along with green onions and water chestnuts.

3. Make the dressing: In food processor, purée peanut butter, stock, rice wine vinegar, lemon juice, soya sauce, sesame oil, ginger, garlic and brown sugar until smooth. Pour over pasta, and toss.

PER SERVING (5)

Calories	364
Protein	15 g
Fat, total	8 g
Fat, saturated	1 g
Carbohydrates	65 g
Sodium	569 mg
Cholesterol	0 mg
Fiber	4 g

THAI LINGUINE WITH HOISIN ✕ SAUCE AND CRISP VEGETABLES

Serves 5.

TIP

The vegetables should be medium diced for linguine.

Other vegetables you can try are asparagus or green or yellow sweet peppers.

MAKE AHEAD

Salad can be prepared and tossed early in day. Toss again before serving.

PER SERVING

Calories	384
Protein	14 g
Fat, total	7 g
Fat, saturated	1 g
Carbohydrates	68 g
Sodium	472 mg
Cholesterol	0 mg
Fiber	3 g

12 oz	linguine	375 g
1 cup	diced sweet red peppers	250 mL
1 cup	sliced snow peas	250 mL
1 cup	chopped broccoli	250 mL
1/2 cup	chopped coriander or parsley	125 mL
1/4 cup	chopped green onions	50 mL
Sauce		
1/4 cup	rice wine vinegar	50 mL
1/4 cup	hoisin sauce	50 mL
2 tbsp	sesame oil	25 mL
2 tbsp	soya sauce	25 mL
2 tbsp	water	25 mL
1 1/2 tsp	grated ginger root	7 mL
1 1/2 tsp	crushed garlic	7 mL

1. Cook pasta in boiling water according to package instructions or until firm to the bite. Drain and place in serving bowl. Add red peppers.

2. Blanch snow peas for 2 minutes. Repeat with broccoli for 3 minutes. Drain and rinse both vegetables with cold water and add to pasta. Add coriander and green onions.

3. Make the sauce: In small bowl, combine rice wine vinegar, hoisin sauce, oil, soya sauce, water, ginger and garlic until mixed. Pour over pasta, and toss.

 PASTA SALAD WITH ROASTED PEPPERS AND ONIONS

Serves 6.

TIP

A combination of colors of sweet peppers gives this dish a beautiful appearance.

▼

Sweet Vidalia onions in season are excellent in this salad.

▼

The skin of sweet peppers will come off easily if, after broiling, you place the peppers in a plastic or paper bag for 10 minutes, then peel.

MAKE AHEAD

Prepare peppers and sauce early in day and reheat gently. Do not overcook the tomatoes. Serve over hot pasta.

PER SERVING

Calories	354
Protein	12 g
Fat, total	6 g
Fat, saturated	2 g
Carbohydrates	65 g
Sodium	27 mg
Cholesterol	10 mg
Fiber	7 g

Preheat broiler

3	medium red, green and/or yellow sweet bell peppers	3
12 oz	small shell pasta	375 g

Sauce

1 tbsp	olive oil	15 mL
2 tsp	crushed garlic	10 mL
2 1/2 cups	diced onions	625 mL
3 cups	diced tomatoes	750 mL
1 tbsp	paprika	15 mL
3/4 cup	light sour cream	175 mL
	Parsley	

1. Roast peppers, turning occasionally just until blackened, approximately 15 minutes. Let rest for 10 minutes. Rinse under cold water. Peel, and remove top and core and seeds. Slice thinly and reserve.

2. Meanwhile, cook pasta in boiling water according to package instructions or until firm to the bite. Drain and place in serving bowl.

3. Make the sauce: In large nonstick skillet, heat oil; sauté garlic and onions just until soft, approximately 5 minutes. Add tomatoes, paprika and reserved sweet peppers; simmer for 3 minutes. Add sour cream, mix well and pour over pasta. Toss and serve, garnished with parsley.

ROTINI WITH THREE-ONION AND GARLIC SAUCE

Serves 6.

TIP

Instead of white onions, use sweet Vidalia when in season.

MAKE AHEAD

Sauté onions early in day and set aside. Prepare sauce early in day. While cooking pasta, reheat sauce gently, adding more stock if too thick.

12 oz	rotini	375 g
1 tbsp	vegetable oil	15 mL
2 tsp	crushed garlic	10 mL
2 cups	sliced red onions	500 mL
2 cups	sliced white onions	500 mL
1 1/2 cups	chopped green onions	375 mL
1 tbsp	margarine or butter	15 mL
2 tbsp and 1 tsp	all-purpose flour	35 mL
1 cup	chicken or vegetable stock	250 mL
1 cup	2% milk	250 mL
1/4 cup	dry white wine	50 mL
Dash	nutmeg	Dash
1/4 cup	grated Parmesan cheese	50 mL

1. Cook pasta in boiling water according to package instructions or until firm to the bite. Drain and place in serving bowl.

2. In large nonstick skillet sprayed with vegetable spray, heat oil; sauté garlic and red, white and green onions, until tender, approximately 7 minutes. Add to pasta.

3. In medium nonstick saucepan, melt margarine; add flour and cook for 1 minute. Slowly add chicken stock, milk and wine. Stir constantly over medium heat, just until slightly thickened, approximately 4 minutes. Add nutmeg. Pour over pasta. Sprinkle with cheese, and toss.

PER SERVING

Calories	443
Protein	17 g
Fat, total	9 g
Fat, saturated	3 g
Carbohydrates	73 g
Sodium	370 mg
Cholesterol	10 mg
Fiber	6 g

PENNE WITH MUSHROOM AND ONION SAUCE

Serves 6.

TIP

For a different texture, do not purée onions.

Try oyster, portobello or cremini mushrooms.

MAKE AHEAD

Prepare sauce early in day. Reheat gently, adding a little stock if too thick.

12 oz	penne	375 g
1 tbsp	olive oil	15 mL
2 tsp	crushed garlic	10 mL
3 cups	sliced white onions	750 mL
1/2 cup	chicken or vegetable stock	125 mL
1 lb	wild or regular mushrooms, sliced	500 g
1/3 cup	grated Parmesan cheese	75 mL
	Pepper	
	Parsley	

1. Cook pasta in boiling water according to package instructions or until firm to the bite. Drain and place in serving bowl.

2. In large nonstick skillet, heat oil; sauté garlic and onions for 10 to 12 minutes. Purée in food processor with stock. Set aside.

3. In same skillet, sprayed with vegetable spray, sauté mushrooms until tender, approximately 7 minutes. Add onion purée to mushroom mixture; pour over pasta. Sprinkle with cheese and pepper, and toss. Garnish with parsley.

PER SERVING

Calories	352
Protein	14 g
Fat, total	6 g
Fat, saturated	2 g
Carbohydrates	63 g
Sodium	184 mg
Cholesterol	4 mg
Fiber	7 g

BOW-TIE PASTA WITH CHICKEN, OLIVES AND SAUSAGE (PAGE 94) ➤

LINGUINE WITH SWEET PEPPER SAUCE

Serves 4 to 6.

TIP

The skin of sweet peppers will come off easily if, after broiling, you place the peppers in a plastic or paper bag for 10 minutes, then peel.

MAKE AHEAD

Prepare sauce early in day. Reheat gently, adding a little stock if too thick.

12 oz	linguine	375 g
2 tsp	vegetable oil	10 mL
1 1/2 tsp	crushed garlic	7 mL
1/2 cup	chopped onions	125 mL
1	green onion, chopped	1
2	medium sweet yellow or red peppers, sliced	2
1	bay leaf	1
1/2 cup	chicken stock	125 mL
	Salt and pepper	
1 tbsp	margarine or butter	15 mL
	Parsley	

1. Cook pasta in boiling water according to package instructions or until firm to the bite. Drain and place in serving bowl.

2. In large nonstick skillet, heat oil; sauté garlic, onions and green onion until tender, approximately 3 minutes. Add peppers and cook just until tender, approximately 8 minutes. Add bay leaf and stock; simmer for 4 minutes. Add salt and pepper to taste and margarine; remove bay leaf. Purée in food processor. Pour over pasta and garnish with parsley.

PER SERVING (6)

Calories	268
Protein	8 g
Fat, total	3 g
Fat, saturated	0.4 g
Carbohydrates	50 g
Sodium	162 mg
Cholesterol	0 mg
Fiber	2 g

◄ ORANGE AND PINEAPPLE CHICKEN STIR-FRY OVER LINGUINE (PAGE 91)

FETTUCCINE WITH SWEET BELL PEPPERS

Serves 6.

TIP

Different colored peppers give this dish a beautiful appearance.

Try plum tomatoes instead of field tomatoes for a firmer texture.

MAKE AHEAD

Prepare sauce early in day. Reheat gently. Add to hot pasta.

12 oz	fettuccine	375 g
2 tsp	vegetable oil	10 mL
1 1/2 tsp	crushed garlic	7 mL
1 cup	chopped onions	250 mL
4 cups	thinly sliced sweet peppers (combination of green, red and/or yellow)	1 L
2 1/2 cups	chopped tomatoes	625 mL
1/2 cup	chicken or vegetable stock	125 mL
1/3 cup	grated Parmesan cheese	75 mL
	Parsley	

1. Cook pasta in boiling water according to package instructions or until firm to the bite. Drain and place in serving bowl.

2. In large nonstick skillet, heat oil; sauté garlic and onions until softened. Add sweet peppers and cook for 5 to 8 minutes on low heat just until tender.

3. Add tomatoes and stock. Simmer on low heat for 15 minutes, stirring occasionally. Pour over pasta. Sprinkle with cheese, and toss. Garnish with parsley.

PER SERVING

Calories	337
Protein	13 g
Fat, total	5 g
Fat, saturated	1 g
Carbohydrates	62 g
Sodium	198 mg
Cholesterol	4 mg
Fiber	6 g

DOUBLE-BEAN CHILI OVER ROTINI

Serves 6.

TIP

Try other beans such as black, Romano or white kidney beans.

Spice up this chili by adding more cayenne.

MAKE AHEAD

Prepare sauce up to a day ahead. Reheat and add more stock if sauce thickens.

12 oz	rotini	375 g
1 tbsp	vegetable oil	15 mL
2 tsp	crushed garlic	10 mL
1 cup	chopped onions	250 mL
1 cup	chopped zucchini	250 mL
1 3/4 cups	vegetable or chicken stock	425 mL
2 1/2 cups	canned tomatoes, crushed	625 mL
2 tbsp	tomato paste	25 mL
1 cup	diced potatoes	250 mL
2/3 cup	canned red kidney beans, drained	150 mL
2/3 cup	canned chick peas, drained	150 mL
1 tbsp	chili powder	15 mL
2 tsp	dried basil	10 mL
1 tsp	dried oregano	5 mL
Pinch	cayenne pepper	Pinch
1/4 cup	grated Parmesan cheese	50 mL

1. Cook pasta in boiling water according to package instructions or until firm to the bite. Drain and place in serving bowl.

2. In large nonstick saucepan, heat oil; sauté garlic, onions and zucchini until soft, approximately 5 minutes. Add stock, tomatoes and paste, potatoes, kidney beans and chick peas, chili powder, basil, oregano and cayenne. Cover and simmer for 40 minutes or until potatoes are tender, stirring occasionally. Pour over pasta. Sprinkle with cheese. Garnish with parsley.

PER SERVING

Calories	394
Protein	15 g
Fat, total	5 g
Fat, saturated	1 g
Carbohydrates	73 g
Sodium	629 mg
Cholesterol	3 mg
Fiber	8 g

GRILLED BALSAMIC VEGETABLES OVER PENNE

Serves 6 to 8.

TIP

Try alternating different vegetables such as eggplant, yellow zucchini or fennel.

If possible use one green, one red and one yellow or orange sweet pepper for brilliant color.

MAKE AHEAD

Grill vegetables early in day. Chop before cooking pasta.

Preheat oven to broil or start barbecue

1	medium red onion, cut in half horizontally	1
1	medium zucchini, cut lengthwise into 4 strips	1
3	medium sweet peppers (green, red and/or yellow)	3
2	medium tomatoes, cut in half horizontally	2
1 lb	penne	500 g

Dressing

3 tbsp	lemon juice	45 mL
3 tbsp	balsamic vinegar	45 mL
1/4 cup	olive oil	50 mL
2 tsp	crushed garlic	10 mL

1. Place all vegetables on grill or barbecue. Grill onion for 25 minutes, turning until charred. Grill zucchini for 15 minutes until charred, turning as necessary. Grill sweet peppers for 15 minutes until charred. Grill tomatoes for 12 to 15 minutes until charred, rotating as necessary. Let vegetables cool for 10 minutes.

2. Remove top, skin and seeds of sweet peppers. Chop all vegetables into medium diced pieces, keeping juices. Set aside.

3. Meanwhile, cook pasta in boiling water according to package instructions or until firm to the bite. Drain and place in serving bowl. Add vegetables.

4. Make the dressing: Combine lemon juice, vinegar, oil and garlic. Pour over pasta, and toss.

PER SERVING (8)

Calories	322
Protein	10 g
Fat, total	7 g
Fat, saturated	1 g
Carbohydrates	55 g
Sodium	9 mg
Cholesterol	0 mg
Fiber	4 g

 # LINGUINE WITH HUMMUS (CHICK PEA SAUCE)

Serves 6.

TIP

If tahini is unavailable, substitute peanut butter.

If sauce appears too thick, add a little more stock.

MAKE AHEAD

Prepare sauce up to a day ahead. Pour over pasta immediately after pasta is cooked.

12 oz	linguine	375 g
1 1/2 cups	canned chick peas, drained	375 mL
2 1/2 tsp	crushed garlic	12 mL
3 tbsp	lemon juice	45 mL
2 tbsp	olive oil	25 mL
1/3 cup	tahini	75 mL
1 cup	chicken stock	250 mL
1 tsp	dried oregano	5 mL
1/2 cup	chopped parsley	125 mL

1. Cook pasta in boiling water according to package instructions or until firm to the bite. Drain and place in serving bowl.

2. In bowl of food processor, purée chick peas, garlic, lemon juice, oil, tahini, stock and oregano until smooth. Pour over pasta. Sprinkle with parsley, and toss.

PER SERVING

Calories	404
Protein	13 g
Fat, total	12 g
Fat, saturated	2 g
Carbohydrates	62 g
Sodium	300 mg
Cholesterol	0 mg
Fiber	5 g

CORIANDER AND PARSLEY PESTO

Serves 6.

TIP

Serve as a side dish or appetizer.

If milder coriander taste is desired, use 1/4 cup (50 mL) coriander and 1 1/4 cup (300 mL) parsley leaves.

Dry leaves well after washing.

Add 8 to 10 oz (250 to 300 g) cooked chicken or fish to pasta.

MAKE AHEAD

Refrigerate up to 3 days before or freeze up to 6 weeks.

PER SERVING

Calories	291
Protein	10 g
Fat, total	7 g
Fat, saturated	1 g
Carbohydrates	48 g
Sodium	112 mg
Cholesterol	1 mg
Fiber	2 g

12 oz	linguine	375 g
1/2 cup	chopped coriander leaves	125 mL
1 cup	chopped flat Italian parsley	250 mL
1/2 cup	chicken stock	125 mL
2 tbsp	olive oil	25 mL
2 tbsp	toasted pine nuts or walnuts	25 mL
2 tbsp	grated Parmesan cheese	25 mL
1 1/2 tsp	crushed garlic	7 mL

1. Cook pasta in boiling water according to package instructions or until firm to the bite. Drain and place in serving bowl.

2. In food processor, purée coriander and parsley leaves, stock, oil, nuts, cheese and garlic until smooth. Pour over pasta.

MOSTLY

CHEESE

 CHEESE TIPS

1. Don't worry about finding low-fat versions of the goat, feta, Cheddar, Swiss, Brie, and Parmesan cheeses used in my recipes. The amount used in each recipe is relatively small — and besides, low-fat or diet cheeses do not have the same flavor intensity.

2. Ricotta cheese is usually sold with 5% or 10% fat. (The following recipes have all been analyzed with 5% fat.) Either is suitable for use with pasta. Softer types of ricotta cheese provide more moisture.

3. Mozzarella is a mild cheese, so taste will not be affected if you replace the regular type with a low-fat version.

4. If cheese sauces are prepared early in day, add some milk if sauce thickens.

 **FOUR-CHEESE MACARONI** ✕

8 oz	macaroni	250 g
1/4 cup	shredded Swiss cheese	50 mL
3 tbsp	shredded Cheddar cheese	45 mL
2 tbsp	grated Parmesan cheese	25 mL
1 1/2 oz	diced mozzarella cheese	40 g

Sauce

1 tbsp	margarine or butter	15 mL
2 tbsp	all-purpose flour	25 mL
1 cup	2% milk	250 mL
1 1/4 cups	chicken stock	300 mL
	Parsley	

Serves 4.

TIP

Any small shell pasta can be used. Tri-color pasta gives lively appeal to this dish.

Select other favorite cheeses to substitute, such as Jarslberg, Romano or Havarti.

MAKE AHEAD

Prepare sauce early in day. Reheat gently, adding more stock if too thick.

1. Cook pasta in boiling water according to package instructions or until firm to the bite. Drain and place in serving bowl. Add Swiss, Cheddar, Parmesan and mozzarella cheeses.

2. Meanwhile, make the sauce: In nonstick saucepan, melt margarine; add flour and cook for 1 minute, stirring constantly. Slowly add milk and chicken stock; stir constantly until sauce thickens, approximately 4 minutes. Pour over pasta and toss well. Garnish with parsley.

PER SERVING

Calories	386
Protein	17 g
Fat, total	11 g
Fat, saturated	5 g
Carbohydrates	54 g
Sodium	487 mg
Cholesterol	24 mg
Fiber	2 g

ROTINI WITH CAULIFLOWER, BROCCOLI AND GOAT CHEESE CREAM SAUCE

Serves 6.

TIP

Substitute feta or Cheddar for goat cheese.

Use more broccoli or cauliflower according to taste, not using more than 4 cups (1L) of vegetables.

MAKE AHEAD

Prepare sauce early in day, just to the point of adding cheese. Add more stock if sauce thickens.

12 oz	rotini	375 g
2 1/2 cups	chopped broccoli	625 mL
1 1/2 cups	chopped cauliflower	375 mL

Sauce

1 tbsp	margarine or butter	15 mL
2 tbsp	all-purpose flour	25 mL
1 1/2 cups	2% milk	375 mL
1 cup	chicken stock	250 mL
4 oz	crumbled goat cheese	125 g
3/4 cup	diced sweet red peppers	175 mL
2 tsp	crushed garlic	10 mL

1. Cook pasta in boiling water according to package instructions or until firm to the bite. Drain and place in serving bowl.

2. Cook broccoli and cauliflower in boiling water just until tender-crisp, approximately 3 minutes; drain and rinse with cold water. Add to pasta.

3. Make the sauce: In small nonstick saucepan, melt margarine; add flour and cook for 1 minute, stirring constantly. Slowly add milk and stock; simmer on medium heat, stirring constantly just until thickened, for 5 to 7 minutes. Add cheese, red peppers and garlic; cook for 1 minute. Pour over pasta, and toss.

PER SERVING

Calories	376
Protein	16 g
Fat, total	8 g
Fat, saturated	3 g
Carbohydrates	61 g
Sodium	306 mg
Cholesterol	12 mg
Fiber	5 g

PASTA WITH FRESH TOMATOES, BASIL AND CHEESE

Serves 6.

TIP

Finely chop tomatoes when using thin pasta. Chop more coarsely if using wider pasta such as fettuccine.

Romano cheese can replace Parmesan.

MAKE AHEAD

Prepare sauce up to a day ahead. Reheat gently, adding a little stock if too dense.

12 oz	thin pasta (capellini or spaghettini)	375 g
1 tbsp	olive oil	15 mL
2 tsp	crushed garlic	10 mL
1 3/4 lb	chopped tomatoes	875 g
1/3 cup	chicken stock	75 mL
1/3 cup	sliced black olives	75 mL
1/2 cup	chopped fresh basil (or 2 tsp [10 mL] dried)	125 mL
1/3 cup	grated Parmesan cheese	75 mL
	Pepper	

1. Cook pasta in boiling water according to package instructions or until firm to the bite. Drain and place in serving bowl.

2. In large nonstick skillet, heat oil; add garlic, tomatoes, stock and black olives; sauté for 2 minutes or just until hot. Pour over pasta. Add basil, cheese and pepper. Toss.

PER SERVING

Calories	318
Protein	12 g
Fat, total	6 g
Fat, saturated	2 g
Carbohydrates	55 g
Sodium	221 mg
Cholesterol	4 mg
Fiber	5 g

 # ROASTED RED PEPPER AND RICOTTA PURÉE OVER ROTINI

Serves 6.

TIP

The skin of sweet peppers will come off easily if, after broiling, you place the peppers in a plastic or paper bag for 10 minutes, then peel.

Yellow or orange sweet peppers could be used.

MAKE AHEAD

Prepare sauce early in day. Pasta must be hot before adding sauce.

Preheat oven to broil

12 oz	rotini	375 g
1	medium sweet red bell pepper	1
1 2/3 cups	ricotta cheese	400 mL
2 tbsp	vegetable oil	25 mL
1/2 cup	chicken stock	125 mL
2 tbsp	grated Parmesan cheese	25 mL
1 1/2 tsp	crushed garlic	7 mL
1/2 cup	chopped basil (or 2 tsp [10 mL] dried)	125 mL
	Parsley	

1. Broil pepper until charred on all sides, approximately 15 minutes. Let cool; remove top, then skin, de-seed, and cut into quarters. Set aside.

2. Cook pasta in boiling water according to package instructions or until firm to the bite. Drain and place in serving bowl.

3. In food processor, purée ricotta cheese, red pepper, oil, stock, Parmesan cheese, garlic and basil until well combined. Pour over pasta. Toss and garnish with parsley.

PER SERVING

Calories	368
Protein	18 g
Fat, total	10 g
Fat, saturated	4 g
Carbohydrates	51 g
Sodium	241 mg
Cholesterol	30 mg
Fiber	2 g

PASTA WITH RIPE TOMATO, BASIL AND RICOTTA CHEESE SAUCE

Serves 6.

TIP

Use juicy ripe tomatoes for extra moisture.

MAKE AHEAD

Combine all ingredients except pasta early in day. Toss just before serving.

12 oz	rotini	375 g
3 cups	chopped ripe tomatoes	750 mL
1/3 cup	green onions	75 mL
2 tbsp	olive oil	25 mL
2/3 cup	chopped fresh basil (or 1 tbsp [15 mL] dried)	150 mL
1 cup	ricotta cheese	250 mL
2 tsp	crushed garlic	10 mL
1/3 cup	sliced black olives	75 mL

1. Cook pasta in boiling water according to package instructions or until firm to the bite. Drain and place in serving bowl.

2. Add tomatoes, onions, oil, basil, ricotta cheese, garlic and olives. Toss.

PER SERVING

Calories	371
Protein	15 g
Fat, total	10 g
Fat, saturated	3 g
Carbohydrates	57 g
Sodium	226 mg
Cholesterol	13 mg
Fiber	5 g

MACARONI WITH ZUCCHINI, TOMATOES AND RICOTTA CHEESE

Serves 4 to 6.

TIP

Use juicy ripe tomatoes for extra moisture.

Leave skin on zucchini for extra fiber.

12 oz	macaroni	375 g
1 tbsp	vegetable oil	15 mL
1 1/2 tsp	crushed garlic	7 mL
1/2 cup	chopped onions	125 mL
1 1/2 cups	diced zucchini	375 mL
1 1/2 cups	diced tomatoes	375 mL
1/2 cup	chopped fresh basil (or 2 tsp [10 mL] dried)	125 mL
1 3/4 cups	ricotta cheese	425 mL
1/2 cup	2% milk	125 mL
3 tbsp	grated Parmesan cheese	45 mL

1. Cook pasta in boiling water according to package instructions or until firm to the bite. Drain and place in serving bowl.

2. In large nonstick skillet, heat oil; sauté garlic, onions and zucchini for 5 minutes. Add tomatoes and basil; simmer for 4 minutes, stirring often. Remove from heat. Add ricotta cheese, milk and Parmesan cheese. Mix well. Pour over pasta, and toss.

PER SERVING (6)

Calories	407
Protein	22 g
Fat, total	10 g
Fat, saturated	5 g
Carbohydrates	58 g
Sodium	251 mg
Cholesterol	30 mg
Fiber	5 g

 # FETTUCCINE WITH RICOTTA ✂ CHEESE AND SWEET PEAS

Serves 4.

TIP

Tarragon gives a sweet flavor to this dish. For a more subtle flavor, use dill or parsley.

MAKE AHEAD

Prepare sauce early in day. While cooking pasta, add a little more milk to sauce if too thick, and immediately pour over pasta.

8 oz	fettuccine	250 g
2 tsp	vegetable oil	10 mL
1 tsp	crushed garlic	5 mL
1 cup	chopped onions	250 mL
1 cup	frozen green peas	250 mL
1 cup	ricotta cheese	250 mL
3/4 cup	2% milk	175 mL
1/3 cup	chopped fresh tarragon or dill (or 2 tsp [10 mL] dried)	75 mL
3 tbsp	grated Parmesan cheese	45 mL
	Salt and pepper	

1. Cook pasta in boiling water according to package instructions or until firm to the bite. Drain and place in serving bowl.

2. Meanwhile, in nonstick skillet, heat oil; sauté garlic and onions until soft, approximately 5 minutes. Add peas and cook for 2 more minutes. Remove from heat. Add ricotta cheese, milk, tarragon, Parmesan cheese and salt and pepper. Pour over pasta and toss well.

PER SERVING

Calories	421
Protein	22 g
Fat, total	9 g
Fat, saturated	4 g
Carbohydrates	63 g
Sodium	237 mg
Cholesterol	27 mg
Fiber	4 g

 LINGUINE WITH TOMATOES
AND THREE CHEESES

Serves 4.

TIP

Feta cheese can replace goat cheese and Romano can replace Asiago or Parmesan.

▼

Sweet red or white onions such as Vidalia can replace green onions.

MAKE AHEAD

Entire pasta can be made up to 3 hours earlier and left at room temperature. Toss before serving.

8 oz	linguine	250 g
1 3/4 cups	diced tomatoes	425 mL
1/2 cup	chopped green onions	125 mL
1/2 cup	crumbled goat cheese	125 mL
1/4 cup	crumbled Asiago or grated Parmesan cheese	50 mL
3/4 cup	shredded low-fat mozzarella cheese	175 mL
1/2 cup	chopped fresh basil (or 1 1/2 tsp [7 mL] dried)	125 mL
	Pepper	

1. Cook pasta in boiling water according to package instructions or until firm to the bite. Drain and place in serving bowl.

2. Add tomatoes, onions, three cheeses, basil and pepper. Mix well, and toss.

PER SERVING

Calories	402
Protein	20 g
Fat, total	11 g
Fat, saturated	6 g
Carbohydrates	55 g
Sodium	319 mg
Cholesterol	28 mg
Fiber	4 g

RIGATONI WITH SAUTÉED EGGPLANT, TOMATOES AND SWISS CHEESE

Serves 6.

12 oz	rigatoni	375 g
1 tbsp	olive oil	15 mL
2 tsp	crushed garlic	10 mL
3/4 cup	chopped onions	175 mL
3 cups	diced eggplant	750 mL
1	can (28 oz [796 mL]) tomatoes, crushed	1
2 tsp	dried basil	10 mL
1 1/2 tsp	dried oregano	7 mL
1/2 cup	shredded Swiss cheese	125 mL

TIP

Mozzarella can replace Swiss cheese for a milder flavor, fewer calories and less fat.

Large shell pasta can replace rigatoni.

Leave skin on eggplant for extra vitamins and fiber.

Whole canned tomatoes with their juice can be used; just break up with back of spoon while cooking.

MAKE AHEAD

Prepare sauce up to a day ahead. Reheat gently, adding a little water if sauce is too thick.

PER SERVING

Calories	360
Protein	14 g
Fat, total	6 g
Fat, saturated	2 g
Carbohydrates	63 g
Sodium	252 mg
Cholesterol	9 mg
Fiber	7 g

1. Cook pasta in boiling water according to package instructions or until firm to the bite. Drain and place in serving bowl.

2. In large nonstick skillet sprayed with vegetable spray, heat oil; sauté garlic and onions until soft, approximately 4 minutes. Add eggplant and sauté just until tender, approximately 8 minutes. Add tomatoes, basil and oregano; simmer on low heat for 20 minutes, stirring occasionally.

3. Pour over pasta. Sprinkle with cheese, and toss.

PENNE WITH ZUCCHINI, EGGPLANT AND TOMATO RATATOUILLE

Serves 6.

TIP

For vegetarian meals, vegetable stock can be substituted for chicken stock.

Leave skin on eggplant and zucchini for extra fiber.

MAKE AHEAD

Prepare sauce early in day. Reheat gently, adding a little stock if sauce is too thick.

12 oz	penne	375 g
1 tbsp	oil	15 mL
2 tsp	crushed garlic	10 mL
1 cup	diced onions	250 mL
1 3/4 cups	diced eggplant	425 mL
1 3/4 cups	diced zucchini	425 mL
1 3/4 cups	diced tomatoes	425 mL
2/3 cup	chicken stock	150 mL
1/2 cup	chopped fresh basil (or 2 tsp [10 mL] dried)	125 mL
1 tsp	dried oregano	5 mL
1/2 cup	shredded Asiago or Parmesan cheese	125 mL

1. Cook pasta in boiling water according to package instructions or until firm to the bite. Drain and place in serving bowl.

2. In large nonstick skillet, heat oil; sauté garlic and onions until soft, approximately 4 minutes. Add eggplant and zucchini and sauté just until tender, for 5 to 8 minutes. Add tomatoes and stock and simmer on low heat for 5 minutes, stirring occasionally. Add basil and oregano; pour over pasta. Sprinkle with cheese, and toss.

PER SERVING

Calories	353
Protein	14 g
Fat, total	6 g
Fat, saturated	2 g
Carbohydrates	61 g
Sodium	268 mg
Cholesterol	7 mg
Fiber	7 g

ROTINI WITH SUN-DRIED TOMATOES, GOAT CHEESE AND OLIVES

Serves 6.

TIP

Try feta cheese instead of goat cheese.

Use dry sun-dried tomatoes, not those marinated in oil.

MAKE AHEAD

Prepare sauce early in day, just to point of adding cheese. Reheat gently before serving, and continue with recipe.

1/2 cup	sun-dried tomatoes	125 mL
12 oz	rotini	375 g
1 tbsp	vegetable oil	15 mL
2 tsp	crushed garlic	10 mL
1 cup	chopped onions	250 mL
1/2 cup	chopped carrots	125 mL
1/2 cup	chopped celery	125 mL
2 1/2 cups	canned or fresh tomatoes, crushed	625 mL
1/4 cup	dry white wine	50 mL
3 oz	crumbled goat cheese	75 g
1/3 cup	sliced black olives	75 mL
	Parsley	

1. Pour boiling water over sun-dried tomatoes. Let soak for 15 minutes. Drain and chop.

2. Cook pasta in boiling water according to package instructions or until firm to the bite. Drain and place in serving bowl.

3. In large nonstick saucepan sprayed with vegetable spray, heat oil; sauté garlic, onions, carrots and celery until tender, approximately 8 minutes. Add tomatoes, sun-dried tomatoes and wine. Simmer on low heat for 15 minutes, stirring occasionally.

4. Add goat cheese and olives. Pour over pasta. Garnish with parsley.

PER SERVING

Calories	349
Protein	12 g
Fat, total	7 g
Fat, saturated	0.5 g
Carbohydrates	60 g
Sodium	307 mg
Cholesterol	7 mg
Fiber	7 g

 ## ASPARAGUS, SUN-DRIED TOMATO AND FETA CHEESE PASTA PIZZA

Serves 8.

TIP

The vegetables can be replaced with broccoli, snow peas and yellow sweet peppers.

▼

Feta cheese can be replaced with goat cheese

MAKE AHEAD

The crust and vegetable sauce can be made early in day, but do not pour sauce over crust until ready to bake and serve. If the sauce thickens too much, add stock to thin slightly.

PER SERVING

Calories	180
Protein	9 g
Fat, total	6 g
Fat, saturated	3 g
Carbohydrates	23 g
Sodium	298 mg
Cholesterol	15 mg
Fiber	2 g

Preheat oven to 350°F (180°C)
10- to 11-inch (3L) springform pan sprayed with vegetable spray

1/2 cup	sun-dried tomatoes	125 mL
6 oz	broken spaghetti	150 g
1	egg	1
3 tbsp	grated Parmesan cheese	45 mL
1/3 cup	2% milk	75 mL
2 tsp	vegetable oil	10 mL
2 tsp	crushed garlic	10 mL
1/3 cup	chopped onions	75 mL
1 cup	chopped asparagus	250 mL
2/3 cup	chopped sweet red peppers	150 mL
1 cup	cold chicken or vegetable stock	250 mL
1 cup	2% milk	250 mL
3 tbsp	all-purpose flour	45 mL
1/2 cup	chopped fresh basil (or 2 tsp [10 mL] dried)	125 mL
1/2 cup	shredded mozzarella cheese	125 mL
2 oz	crumbled feta cheese	50 g

1. Pour boiling water over sun-dried tomatoes. Let soak for 15 minutes. Drain and chop.

2. Cook pasta in boiling water according to package instructions or until firm to the bite. Drain and place in mixing bowl. Add egg, Parmesan cheese and milk. Mix and pour into baking pan. Bake for 20 minutes.

3. In large nonstick skillet sprayed with vegetable spray, heat oil; sauté garlic, onions, asparagus and red peppers for 8 minutes. Add sun-dried tomatoes and cook on medium heat for 2 minutes.

4. Meanwhile, in small bowl, combine stock, milk and flour until smooth. Add to vegetables and simmer on medium heat until slightly thickened, approximately 4 minutes. Add basil; pour into pasta crust. Sprinkle with cheeses and bake for 10 minutes. Let rest for 10 minutes before serving.

LINGUINE WITH AVOCADO PESTO

**Serves 6 to 8
as an appetizer.**

TIP

Even with lemon juice,
the pesto may discolor;
if this happens, skim off
the darkened surface
and discard.

Toast pine nuts in a skillet
on stove top for 2 to 3
minutes until brown.

This is like a guacamole
dressing with much
less fat due to the
basil and parsley.

For a stronger flavor, use
all basil and no parsley.

1 lb	linguine	500 g
1 cup	chopped fresh basil, well packed down	250 mL
1/4 cup	chopped fresh Italian parsley, well packed down	50 mL
2 tsp	crushed garlic	10 mL
1	ripe avocado, peeled and chopped	1
2 tbsp	olive oil	25 mL
1/4 cup	grated Parmesan cheese	50 mL
1 cup	chicken stock or water	250 mL
2 tsp	lemon juice	10 mL
2 tbsp	toasted pine nuts	25 mL

1. Cook pasta in boiling water according to package instructions or until firm to the bite. Drain and place in serving bowl.

2. In food processor, purée basil, parsley, garlic, avocado, oil, 2 tbsp (25 mL) of the Parmesan cheese, stock and lemon juice until smooth. Pour over pasta. Sprinkle with pine nuts and remaining Parmesan cheese. Toss.

PER SERVING (8)

Calories	300
Protein	11 g
Fat, total	7 g
Fat, saturated	2 g
Carbohydrates	48 g
Sodium	198 mg
Cholesterol	4 mg
Fiber	2 g

BASIL PESTO SAUCE OVER PASTA

Serves 6.

TIP

Dry basil well
after washing.

Toast nuts on top of
stove in skillet for
2 to 3 minutes,
until brown.

If the basil flavor is too
strong, use half basil
and half parsley.

Replace pine nuts with
pecans or walnuts.

MAKE AHEAD

Refrigerate up to 5 days
ahead, or freeze
up to 6 weeks.

12 oz	linguine	375 g
1 1/4 cups	chopped fresh basil, well packed down	300 mL
1/3 cup	chicken stock or water	75 mL
2 tbsp	toasted pine nuts	25 mL
2 tbsp	grated Parmesan cheese	25 mL
3 tbsp	olive oil	45 mL
1 tsp	crushed garlic	5 mL

1. Cook pasta in boiling water according to package instructions or until firm to the bite. Drain and place in serving bowl.

2. In food processor, purée basil, stock, pine nuts, cheese, oil and garlic until smooth. Pour over pasta, and toss.

PER SERVING

Calories	321
Protein	10 g
Fat, total	10 g
Fat, saturated	2 g
Carbohydrates	48 g
Sodium	66 mg
Cholesterol	1 mg
Fiber	2 g

PESTO WITH PARSLEY, DILL AND BASIL LEAVES

Serves 6 to 8.

TIP

Dry leaves well after washing.

Toast pine nuts on top of stove in skillet for 2 to 3 minutes, until brown.

For a different taste, try switching the given amounts of parsley, basil or dill.

Any nuts can replace pine nuts. Walnuts and pecans are delicious.

MAKE AHEAD

Refrigerate up to 3 days or freeze up to 6 weeks.

	PER SERVING (8)	
Calories		277
Protein		10 g
Fat, total		9 g
Fat, saturated		2 g
Carbohydrates		41 g
Sodium		70 mg
Cholesterol		2 mg
Fiber		2 g

12 oz	spaghettini	375 g
2/3 cup	Italian parsley leaves, well packed down	150 mL
1 cup	basil leaves, well packed down	250 mL
1/3 cup	fresh dill, well packed down	75 mL
1/4 cup	olive oil	50 mL
1/3 cup	chicken stock	75 mL
3 tbsp	grated Parmesan cheese	45 mL
2 tsp	crushed garlic	10 mL
2 tbsp	toasted pine nuts	25 mL

1. Cook pasta in boiling water according to package instructions or until firm to the bite. Drain and place in serving bowl.

2. In food processor, purée parsley, basil and dill leaves, oil, stock, cheese and garlic until well combined, approximately 30 seconds. Pour over pasta. Sprinkle with pine nuts, and toss.

PASTA WITH SPINACH PESTO

Serves 4 to 6.

TIP

For variety, add to pasta
8 to 12 oz (250 to 375 g)
of cooked meat,
chicken or fish.

Dry spinach well
after washing.

Toast pine nuts on top
of stove in skillet for
2 to 3 minutes,
until brown.

MAKE AHEAD

Refrigerate sauce up to
3 days ahead or freeze for
up to 6 weeks.

12 oz	pasta (any variety)	375 g
1 1/2 cups	fresh spinach, washed and well packed down	375 mL
1/4 cup	water or chicken stock	50 mL
3 tbsp	olive oil	45 mL
2 tbsp	toasted pine nuts	25 mL
3 tbsp	grated Parmesan cheese	45 mL
1 1/2 tsp	crushed garlic	7 mL
	Pepper	

1. Cook pasta in boiling water according to package instructions or firm to the bite. Drain and place in serving bowl.

2. Meanwhile, in food processor, purée spinach, water, oil, nuts, cheese, garlic and pepper until smooth. Pour over pasta.

PER SERVING (6)

Calories	325
Protein	10 g
Fat, total	10 g
Fat, saturated	2 g
Carbohydrates	48 g
Sodium	73 mg
Cholesterol	2 mg
Fiber	2 g

STUFFED PASTA

 STUFFED PASTA TIPS

1. After cooking manicotti or cannelloni pasta shells, drain, rinse with cold water and cover until ready to use. To stuff easily, slice shell to open and lay flat. Place some filling over top shell, close and place seam side down in baking dish. These shells can be refrigerated up to 1 day ahead, then baked.

2. Filling for manicotti and cannelloni can be used in jumbo pasta shells. Less filling is needed. Filling for 12 manicotti is sufficient for about 24 shells.

3. Lasagna sheets can be prepared early in day, rinsed with cold water, and covered. Rinse again with cold water before using if pasta sticks. Lasagna dishes can be prepared up to a day ahead. After baking, let rest for 10 minutes to make the lasagna easier to cut. Reheat lasagnas at 350°F (180°C) just until warm.

# TORTELLINI WITH CREAMY SUN-DRIED TOMATO SAUCE

Serves 4 to 5.

TIP

Use dry sun-dried tomatoes, not those packed in oil.

Spinach tortellini or a combination of spinach and cheese can be used.

MAKE AHEAD

Prepare sauce early in day, adding more stock to thin if it thickens. Pour over hot pasta.

1 lb	cheese tortellini	500 g
1/2 cup	sun-dried tomatoes	125 mL
2 tsp	margarine or butter	10 mL
1 1/2 tsp	crushed garlic	7 mL
4 tsp	all-purpose flour	20 mL
3/4 cup	chicken or vegetable stock	175 mL
1 cup	2% milk	250 mL
1/4 cup	chopped fresh basil (or 1 1/4 tsp [6 mL] dried)	50 mL

1. Cook pasta in boiling water according to package instructions or until firm to the bite. Drain and place in serving bowl.

2. Pour boiling water over sun-dried tomatoes. Let soak for 15 minutes. Drain and dice. Set aside.

3. Meanwhile, in medium nonstick saucepan, melt margarine; sauté garlic for 1 minute. Add flour and cook on medium heat for 1 minute. Slowly add stock and milk; simmer on medium heat until slightly thickened, approximately 4 minutes. Add sun-dried tomatoes. Pour over pasta. Add basil, and toss.

PER SERVING (5)

Calories	337
Protein	14 g
Fat, total	10 g
Fat, saturated	2 g
Carbohydrates	49 g
Sodium	376 mg
Cholesterol	5 mg
Fiber	2 g

 CHEESE TORTELLINI WITH SWEET RED PEPPER CREAM SAUCE

Serves 6.

TIP

Use yellow or orange sweet peppers instead of red.

Try spinach or cheese tortellini for a change.

To remove skin of peppers more easily, place in plastic or paper bag after broiling, and let cool for 10 minutes, then peel.

MAKE AHEAD

Prepare entire sauce up to a day ahead. Reheat gently, adding more milk if sauce thickens. Pour over hot pasta.

PER SERVING

Calories	328
Protein	14 g
Fat, total	12 g
Fat, saturated	3 g
Carbohydrates	42 g
Sodium	284 mg
Cholesterol	10 mg
Fiber	0.9 g

Preheat oven to broil

1 lb	cheese tortellini	500 g
1	large sweet red pepper	1
1/2 cup	chopped fresh basil (or 1 1/2 tsp [7 mL] dried)	125 mL

Sauce

1 tbsp	margarine or butter	15 mL
5 tsp	all-purpose flour	25 mL
2 cups	2% milk	500 mL
2 tbsp	grated Parmesan cheese	25 mL

1. Cook pasta in boiling water according to package instructions or until firm to the bite. Drain and place in serving bowl.

2. Broil red pepper until charred on all sides, approximately 15 minutes, turning occasionally. Let cool, then skin. Remove top and seeds; slice into quarters.

3. Make the sauce: In small nonstick saucepan, melt margarine; add flour and cook on medium heat for 1 minute, stirring constantly. Slowly add milk and simmer on medium heat for approximately 4 minutes, stirring constantly, just until thickened. Add cheese and cook for 1 minute.

4. In food processor, purée red pepper and sauce until blended. Pour over pasta. Sprinkle with basil, and toss.

 # TORTELLINI WITH SWEET RED PEPPER AND SUN-DRIED TOMATO SAUCE

Serves 5 to 6.

TIP

Use spinach or spinach and cheese tortellini for a change.

▼

Sweet yellow or orange bell peppers can be used.

▼

Use dry sun-dried tomatoes instead of those in oil.

MAKE AHEAD

Prepare sauce up to a day ahead. Reheat gently, adding a little chicken stock or water if sauce becomes too dense.

1 lb	cheese tortellini	500 g
1/2 cup	sun-dried tomatoes	125 mL
2 tsp	vegetable oil	10 mL
1 tsp	crushed garlic	5 mL
2/3 cup	chopped onions	150 mL
1	large sweet red pepper, chopped	1
2 cups	chopped ripe tomatoes	500 mL
1/4 cup	chopped parsley	50 mL
2 tbsp	grated Parmesan cheese	25 mL
	Parsley	

1. Cook pasta in boiling water according to package instructions or until firm to the bite. Drain and place in serving bowl.

2. Pour boiling water over sun-dried tomatoes. Let soak for 15 minutes. Drain and chop. Set aside.

3. Meanwhile, in large nonstick skillet sprayed with vegetable spray, heat oil; add garlic, onions and red pepper and cook on medium high for 5 minutes or until tender. Add tomatoes and cook for 5 minutes.

4. Place in food processor and purée. Add sun-dried tomatoes, parsley and cheese; mix until blended. Pour over pasta. Sprinkle with parsley, and toss.

PER SERVING (6)

Calories	305
Protein	13 g
Fat, total	9 g
Fat, saturated	2 g
Carbohydrates	44 g
Sodium	259 mg
Cholesterol	4 mg
Fiber	4 g

TORTELLINI WITH CREAMY BLUE CHEESE DRESSING

Serves 6.

TIP

Adjust amount of blue cheese to taste.

MAKE AHEAD

Prepare sauce early in day, adding more milk if sauce thickens.

1 1/2 lb	cheese tortellini	750 g
1 tbsp	margarine or butter	15 mL
2 tbsp	all-purpose flour	25 mL
2 1/4 cups	2% milk	550 mL
2 oz	crumbled blue cheese	50 g
1/4 cup	chopped parsley	50 mL

1. Cook pasta in boiling water according to package instructions or until firm to the bite. Drain and place in serving bowl.

2. In medium nonstick saucepan, melt margarine; add flour and cook for 1 minute, stirring constantly. Slowly add milk; simmer just until thickened, approximately 4 minutes, stirring often. Add cheese and stir until melted. Pour over pasta. Sprinkle with parsley, and toss.

PER SERVING

Calories	453
Protein	19 g
Fat, total	15 g
Fat, saturated	4 g
Carbohydrates	60 g
Sodium	437 mg
Cholesterol	14 mg
Fiber	1 g

 # CHEESE TORTELLINI WITH PROSCIUTTO AND GREEN PEAS

Serves 4 to 5.

TIP

Any smoked meat or chicken can be used instead of prosciutto.

MAKE AHEAD

Prepare sauce early in day. Reheat gently, adding more stock if sauce thickens.

1 lb	cheese tortellini	500 g
1/3 cup	chopped prosciutto or smoked ham	75 mL
2/3 cup	cooked green peas	150 mL

Sauce

1 tbsp	margarine or butter	15 mL
2 tbsp	all-purpose flour	25 mL
1 cup	2% milk	250 mL
1 1/4 cups	chicken or beef stock	300 mL
Pinch	nutmeg	Pinch
	Pepper	

1. Cook pasta in boiling water according to package instructions or until firm to the bite. Drain and place in serving bowl.

2. Add prosciutto and peas.

3. Make the sauce: In nonstick saucepan, melt margarine; add flour and cook for 1 minute, stirring constantly. Add milk, stock, nutmeg and pepper to taste. Stir until thickened, approximately 4 minutes. Pour over pasta. Toss.

PER SERVING (5)

Calories	395
Protein	17 g
Fat, total	12 g
Fat, saturated	3 g
Carbohydrates	54 g
Sodium	695 mg
Cholesterol	13 mg
Fiber	2 g

 # SPINACH CHEESE TORTELLINI ✕ IN PURÉED VEGETABLE SAUCE

Serves 6.

TIP

Substitute sweet potatoes for carrots.

MAKE AHEAD

Prepare sauce early in day. Reheat gently, adding more stock if sauce becomes too dense.

1 lb	cheese and/or spinach tortellini	500 g

Sauce

1 tbsp	margarine or butter	15 mL
1 tsp	crushed garlic	5 mL
1 cup	finely diced carrots	250 mL
1 cup	finely diced zucchini	250 mL
1 1/2 cups	chicken or vegetable stock	375 mL
1/3 cup	chopped fresh basil (or 1 1/2 tsp [7 mL] dried)	75 mL
2 tbsp	grated Parmesan cheese	25 mL

1. Cook pasta in boiling water according to package instructions or until firm to the bite. Drain and place in serving bowl.

2. Make the sauce: In small nonstick skillet, melt margarine; add garlic, carrots and zucchini. Cook until tender, approximately 8 minutes. Add stock and basil; simmer on medium heat for 5 minutes. Purée in food processor on and off for 30 seconds. Pour over pasta. Add cheese, and toss.

PER SERVING

Calories	296
Protein	12 g
Fat, total	9 g
Fat, saturated	2 g
Carbohydrates	42 g
Sodium	510 mg
Cholesterol	4 mg
Fiber	3 g

RADIATORE WITH SWEET SAUSAGE, ZUCCHINI AND TOMATOES (PAGE 126) ➤

RAVIOLI WITH SPINACH CREAM SAUCE

Serves 4 to 6.

1 1/2 lb	cheese ravioli	750 g
1 tbsp	margarine or butter	15 mL
2 tbsp	all-purpose flour	25 mL
1 cup	2% milk	250 mL
1 1/4 cups	chicken stock	300 mL
1/2	package (10 oz [300g]) frozen chopped spinach, cooked, drained and squeezed dry	1/2
1 tsp	crushed garlic	5 mL
1 1/2 tsp	lemon juice	7 mL
3 tbsp	grated Parmesan cheese	45 mL

TIP

Use half package of fresh spinach if frozen is not available. Rinse spinach and cook with water clinging to leaves, just until wilted. Drain, rinse well, chop and squeeze out excess moisture.

MAKE AHEAD

Prepare sauce early in day, adding more stock if sauce thickens. Pour over hot pasta.

1. Cook pasta in boiling water according to package instructions or until firm to the bite. Drain and place in serving bowl.

2. In medium nonstick skillet, melt margarine; add flour and cook for 1 minute. Slowly add milk and stock; simmer for 4 minutes, stirring constantly, just until thickened. Pour into food processor. Add spinach, garlic and lemon juice. Purée until smooth. Pour over pasta. Sprinkle with cheese, and toss.

PER SERVING (6)

Calories	444
Protein	19 g
Fat, total	14 g
Fat, saturated	4 g
Carbohydrates	60 g
Sodium	635 mg
Cholesterol	10 mg
Fiber	2 g

WHOLE SWEET BELL PEPPERS STUFFED WITH SPAGHETTINI, TOMATOES AND PROSCUITTO (PAGE 127)

 # RAVIOLI WITH MUSHROOM SAUCE

Serves 4 to 6.

TIP

If using wild mushrooms, try oyster, which are less expensive and have great texture.

MAKE AHEAD

Prepare sauce early in day. Add more stock if sauce thickens.

1 lb	cheese ravioli	500 g
2 tsp	margarine or butter	10 mL
1 1/2 tsp	crushed garlic	7 mL
3 cups	sliced wild or regular mushrooms	750 mL
2 tbsp	all-purpose flour	25 mL
1/3 cup	dry white wine	75 mL
3/4 cup	chicken or vegetable stock	175 mL
3/4 cup	2% milk	175 mL
1/3 cup	finely chopped chives or green onions	75 mL
1/4 cup	grated Parmesan cheese	50 mL
	Pepper	

1. Cook pasta in boiling water according to package instructions or until firm to the bite. Drain and place in serving bowl.

2. In medium nonstick saucepan, melt margarine; sauté garlic and mushrooms for 5 minutes, just until mushrooms are cooked. Add flour and cook for 1 minute, stirring constantly. Add wine and cook for 1 minute. Slowly add stock and milk; simmer on medium heat for 5 minutes, or just until sauce slightly thickens, stirring constantly. Pour over pasta. Sprinkle with chives, Parmesan cheese and pepper. Toss.

PER SERVING (6)

Calories	322
Protein	15 g
Fat, total	9 g
Fat, saturated	2 g
Carbohydrates	45 g
Sodium	373 mg
Cholesterol	6 mg
Fiber	4 g

 PASTA SHELLS STUFFED
WITH THREE CHEESES IN A
CREAMY TOMATO SAUCE

Serves 4 to 6.

TIP

Substitute Swiss, Havarti, or mozzarella cheeses for the Cheddar.

▼

Eight ounces (250 g) of jumbo shells should equal about 24 shells.

MAKE AHEAD

Prepare stuffed shells up to a day ahead with sauce poured over. Do not bake until ready to serve.

Preheat oven to 375°F (190°C)
13- by 9-inch (3L) baking dish

8 oz	jumbo shells or 12 manicotti shells	250 g
1 1/4 cups	ricotta cheese	300 mL
1/3 cup	shredded Cheddar cheese	75 mL
3 tbsp	grated Parmesan cheese	45 mL
1/4 cup	finely chopped chives or green onions	50 mL
3 tbsp	2% milk	45 mL
1	egg	1
1 1/2 cups	prepared tomato sauce or Quick Basic Tomato Sauce (see page 205 for recipe)	375 mL
1/2 cup	milk	125 mL
2 tbsp	grated Parmesan cheese	25 mL

1. Cook shells in boiling water according to package instructions or until firm to the bite. Drain, cover and set aside.

2. In medium bowl combine ricotta, Cheddar and Parmesan cheeses. Add chives, milk and egg; mix until well combined. Fill pasta shells.

3. In small bowl combine tomato sauce and milk until smooth. Pour half of tomato mixture in bottom of large baking dish. Place stuffed shells in baking dish. Pour remaining sauce over top of pasta; sprinkle with cheese. Cover and bake for 15 to 20 minutes, or until hot.

PER SERVING (6)

Calories	289
Protein	18 g
Fat, total	10 g
Fat, saturated	6 g
Carbohydrates	32 g
Sodium	442 mg
Cholesterol	32 mg
Fiber	2 g

MANICOTTI SHELLS FILLED WITH CHEESE AND SMOKED SALMON BITS

Serves 4.

TIP

As an alternative to manicotti, use 24 jumbo shells.

Sprinkle 1/4 cup (50 mL) shredded mozzarella cheese over pasta shells just before serving.

MAKE AHEAD

Prepare stuffed pasta shells up to a day ahead with sauce poured over. Bake just before serving.

Preheat oven to 350°F (180°C)
13- by 9-inch (3 L) baking dish

12	manicotti shells	12
1 1/2 cups	ricotta cheese	375 mL
1	egg	1
2 1/2 oz	chopped smoked salmon	60 g
1/4 cup	finely chopped green onions	50 mL
3 tbsp	fresh chopped dill (or 1 tsp [5 mL] dried)	45 mL
2 tbsp	2% milk	25 mL
2 tbsp	grated Parmesan cheese	25 mL
1 1/2 cups	prepared tomato sauce or Quick Basic Tomato Sauce (see page 205 for recipe)	375 mL

1. Cook pasta in boiling water according to package instructions or until firm to the bite. Drain, cover and set aside.

2. In bowl, combine ricotta cheese, egg, salmon, green onions, dill, milk and Parmesan cheese; mix until smooth. Fill pasta shells.

3. Pour half tomato sauce in bottom of large baking dish. Place pasta shells over sauce and pour other half tomato sauce over pasta. Cover and bake for 15 to 20 minutes or until hot.

PER SERVING

Calories	338
Protein	24 g
Fat, total	11 g
Fat, saturated	5 g
Carbohydrates	39 g
Sodium	570 mg
Cholesterol	38 mg
Fiber	3 g

 # PASTA FILLED WITH CHICKEN
 AND RICOTTA CHEESE

Serves 4 to 6.

TIP

If you do not have a food processor, dice the chicken finely.

Use 12 cannelloni shells instead of jumbo shells.

MAKE AHEAD

Prepare stuffed shells early in day with sauce poured over. Do not bake until ready to eat.

Preheat oven to 350°F (180°C)
Large baking dish

24	jumbo pasta shells	24
1 1/2 tsp	crushed garlic	7 mL
6 oz	skinless, boneless chicken breast, diced	150 g
1/3 cup	chopped spinach, cooked, drained and well packed down	75 mL
1 1/2 cups	ricotta cheese	375 mL
2 tbsp	chopped parsley	25 mL
1	egg	1
3 tbsp	2% milk	45 mL
	Salt and pepper	
1 1/2 cups	prepared tomato sauce, or Quick Basic Tomato Sauce (see page 205 for recipe)	375 mL

1. Cook pasta in boiling water according to package instructions or until firm to the bite. Drain, cover and set aside.

2. In nonstick skillet sprayed with vegetable spray, sauté garlic and chicken; cook until no longer pink, approximately 4 minutes. Place in food processor. Add spinach, cheese, parsley, egg, milk, salt and pepper. Process on and off just until finely diced. Do not purée. Stuff shells.

3. Pour half of tomato sauce in baking dish; place shells in baking dish and pour remaining sauce over top. Cover and bake until hot, for 15 to 20 minutes.

PER SERVING (6)

Calories	242
Protein	18 g
Fat, total	6 g
Fat, saturated	3 g
Carbohydrates	30 g
Sodium	238 mg
Cholesterol	35 mg
Fiber	2 g

 # PUMPKIN AND CHEESE ><
CANNELLONI

Serves 6.

TIP

Use honey or maple
syrup instead of sugar
for a different flavor.

MAKE AHEAD

Prepare stuffed pastas
and sauce early in day,
but do not combine.
Add more milk to sauce
if it thickens. Bake just
prior to serving.

Preheat oven to 350°F (180°C)
13- by 9-inch (3 L) baking dish

12	cannelloni or manicotti shells	12
2 tsp	vegetable oil	10 mL
3/4 cup	finely chopped onions	175 mL
8 oz	canned puréed pumpkin	250 g
1/2 cup	ricotta cheese	125 mL
3 tbsp	grated Parmesan cheese	45 mL
2 tbsp	seasoned bread crumbs	25 mL
2 tbsp	brown sugar	25 mL
1/2 tsp	cinnamon powder	2 mL

Sauce

1 tbsp	margarine or butter	15 mL
1 tbsp	all-purpose flour	15 mL
1 1/4 cup	2% milk	300 mL
1/8 tsp	nutmeg	1 mL

1. Cook pasta in boiling water according to package instructions or until firm to the bite. Drain, cover and set aside.

2. In medium nonstick skillet, heat oil; sauté onions until tender, approximately 5 minutes. Remove from heat.

3. Add pumpkin, both cheeses, bread crumbs, sugar and cinnamon to onions, mixing until well blended. Place 1 heaping tablespoon (about 15 mL) into each shell; place in baking dish.

4. Make the sauce: In nonstick skillet, melt margarine; add flour and cook for 1 minute. Add milk and nutmeg; simmer just until slightly thickened, stirring constantly, approximately 3 minutes. Pour over pasta. Cover and bake for 20 minutes or until hot.

PER SERVING

Calories	241
Protein	10 g
Fat, total	7 g
Fat, saturated	3 g
Carbohydrates	35 g
Sodium	197 mg
Cholesterol	13 mg
Fiber	2 g

 # CANNELLONI STUFFED WITH ⋈ ARTICHOKES AND VEAL WITH CREAM SAUCE

Serves 6.

Preheat oven to 350°F (180°C)
13- by 9-inch (3 L) baking dish sprayed with vegetable spray

TIP

Ground beef can
replace veal.

Substitute chicken or beef
stock for white wine.

MAKE AHEAD

Prepare stuffed cannelloni
and sauce up to a day
ahead. Keep separate until
ready to bake, then heat
gently, adding more stock
if sauce thickens.

12	cannelloni shells (or manicotti)	12
2 tsp	vegetable oil	10 mL
1 1/2 tsp	crushed garlic	7 mL
1/2 cup	chopped onions	125 mL
6 oz	ground veal or chicken	150 g
1/4 cup	dry white wine	50 mL
1 cup	canned artichokes, drained and quartered	250 mL

Sauce

1 tbsp	margarine or butter	15 mL
1 tbsp	all-purpose flour	15 mL
1 cup	2% milk	250 mL
1/2 cup	chicken stock	125 mL
3 tbsp	grated Parmesan cheese	45 mL

1. Cook pasta shells in boiling water according to package instructions or until firm to the bite. Drain, cover and set aside.

2. In medium nonstick skillet, heat oil; sauté garlic and onions until soft, approximately 3 minutes. Add veal and sauté until cooked, approximately 4 minutes. Add wine and simmer on low heat for 3 minutes. Add artichokes. Remove from heat.

3. Make the sauce: In small nonstick saucepan melt margarine; add flour and cook for 1 minute, stirring constantly. Add milk, stock and cheese; simmer just until slightly thickened, stirring constantly, approximately 4 minutes. Pour 1/2 cup (125 mL) sauce into food processor along with artichoke mixture and process on and off just until still chunky. Fill pasta shells with artichoke mixture and place in baking dish. Pour over remaining sauce, cover and bake for 15 minutes or until hot.

PER SERVING

Calories	254
Protein	14 g
Fat, total	9 g
Fat, saturated	3 g
Carbohydrates	28 g
Sodium	374 mg
Cholesterol	30 mg
Fiber	2 g

 CHEESE- AND ARTICHOKE- FILLED CANNELLONI WITH TOMATO SAUCE
===

Serves 6.

TIP

If you do not want to use blue cheese, substitute another cheese such as feta or Swiss.

▼

Use 24 jumbo shells instead of cannelloni.

MAKE AHEAD

Prepare stuffed shells early in day with sauce poured over. Do not bake until ready to serve.

Preheat oven to 350°F (180°C)
13- by 9-inch (3 L) baking dish

12	cannelloni or manicotti shells	12
2 tsp	vegetable oil	10 mL
1 tsp	crushed garlic	5 mL
3/4 cup	diced onions	175 mL
3 tbsp	white wine	45 mL
1 cup	canned artichoke hearts, drained and chopped	250 mL
1/2 cup	ricotta cheese	125 mL
2 oz	blue cheese, crumbled	50 g
1	egg yolk	1
1 tbsp	chopped fresh parsley (or 1 tsp [5 mL] dried)	15 mL
1 1/2 cups	prepared tomato sauce, or Quick Basic Tomato Sauce (see page 205 for recipe)	375 mL
1/4 cup	chopped fresh basil (or 1/2 tsp [2 mL] dried)	50 mL

PER SERVING

Calories	230
Protein	10 g
Fat, total	7 g
Fat, saturated	3 g
Carbohydrates	32 g
Sodium	418 mg
Cholesterol	15 mg
Fiber	5 g

1. Cook pasta shells in boiling water according to package instructions or until firm to the bite. Drain, cover and set aside.

2. In medium nonstick skillet, heat oil; sauté garlic and onions until soft, approximately 4 minutes. Add wine and artichokes and simmer for 3 minutes. Place in food processor and chop until chunky, but do not purée. Add ricotta and blue cheeses, yolk and parsley; process on and off just to combine. Fill pasta shells.

3. Combine tomato sauce and basil; pour half into baking dish. Place shells in baking dish and pour remaining sauce over top. Cover and bake for 15 to 20 minutes or until hot.

CANNELLONI STUFFED WITH BROCCOLI AND GOAT CHEESE IN PARMESAN SAUCE

Serves 6.

TIP

For a change, use 24 jumbo pasta shells.

Chopped asparagus can replace broccoli.

MAKE AHEAD

Prepare filling and sauce early in day, but do not combine. Add more milk to sauce if it thickens.

Preheat oven to 350°F (180°C)
13- by 9-inch (3 L) baking dish sprayed with nonstick spray

12	cannelloni shells	12
2 tsp	vegetable oil	10 mL
1 1/2 tsp	crushed garlic	7 mL
1/2 cup	chopped sweet red peppers	125 mL
1/3 cup	chopped onions	75 mL
6 oz	chopped broccoli	150 g
3 oz	goat cheese	75 g
2/3 cup	ricotta cheese	150 mL
3 tbsp	2% milk	45 mL
2 tsp	lemon juice	10 mL
	Pepper	

Sauce

1 tbsp	margarine or butter	15 mL
1 tbsp	all-purpose flour	15 mL
1 1/4 cups	2% milk	300 mL
2 tbsp	grated Parmesan cheese	25 mL
Pinch	nutmeg	Pinch

1. Cook pasta in boiling water according to package instructions or until firm to the bite. Drain, rinse, cover and set aside.

2. In small nonstick skillet, heat oil; sauté garlic, sweet peppers and onions until tender, approximately 3 minutes. Place in food processor.

3. Blanch broccoli in boiling water until quite tender, approximately 8 minutes. Drain and place in food processor. Add goat and ricotta cheeses, milk, lemon juice and pepper. Process on and off just until blended. Do not over-process. Fill pasta shells and place in baking dish.

4. Make the sauce: In small nonstick saucepan, melt margarine; add flour and cook 1 minute. Add milk and simmer, stirring constantly just until thickened, approximately 4 minutes. Add Parmesan cheese and nutmeg. Pour over pasta; cover and bake for 15 to 20 minutes or until hot.

PER SERVING

Calories	223
Protein	12 g
Fat, total	10 g
Fat, saturated	4 g
Carbohydrates	23 g
Sodium	215 mg
Cholesterol	20 mg
Fiber	1 g

 LAMB CANNELLONI WITH
WALNUT PARMESAN SAUCE

Serves 6.

TIP

Any other cut of lamb can be used. Do not use ground lamb.

▼

Pecans can replace walnuts.

MAKE AHEAD

Prepare filled pasta shells up to a day ahead. Do not bake until ready to serve. Prepare sauce early in day, adding more stock if sauce thickens.

PER SERVING

Calories	229
Protein	14 g
Fat, total	7 g
Fat, saturated	2 g
Carbohydrates	26 g
Sodium	370 mg
Cholesterol	33 mg
Fiber	2 g

Preheat oven to 350°F (180°C)
Large baking dish

12	cannelloni shells	12
Filling		
2 tsp	vegetable oil	10 mL
1 1/2 tsp	crushed garlic	7 mL
1 cup	chopped onions	250 mL
1 tsp	dried rosemary	5 mL
8 oz	leg of lamb or beef steak, cut into 1-inch (2.5-cm) cubes	250 g
2 tbsp	chopped fresh parsley (or 1 1/2 tsp [7 mL] dried)	25 mL
1	egg	1
1/4 cup	seasoned bread crumbs	50 mL
Sauce		
2 tsp	margarine or butter	10 mL
2 tsp	all-purpose flour	10 mL
1 cup	beef or chicken stock	250 mL
1 tbsp	dry white wine	15 mL
1 tbsp	grated Parmesan cheese	15 mL
2 tsp	finely chopped walnuts	10 mL

1. Cook pasta in boiling water according to package instructions or until firm to the bite. Drain, cover and set aside.

2. In nonstick skillet, heat oil; add garlic and onions. Cook until soft, approximately 5 minutes. Add rosemary and lamb; continue cooking until lamb is nearly done, approximately 5 to 8 minutes. Pour into food processor with parsley, egg and bread crumbs. Purée until well blended. Fill pasta shells with meat mixture and place in baking dish.

3. Make the sauce: In nonstick saucepan, melt margarine; add flour and cook for 1 minute, stirring constantly. Add stock and cook over low heat until slightly thickened, approximately 3 minutes. Add wine, cheese and nuts; pour over pasta. Cover and bake until hot for 15 to 20 minutes.

CANNELLONI WITH CHEESE AND BEEF FILLING

Serves 5.

TIP

Great pasta dish for children and teenagers.

Cheddar or Swiss cheese can replace mozzarella for a stronger flavor.

MAKE AHEAD

Prepare stuffed pasta up to a day ahead with sauce poured over. Do not bake until ready to serve.

Preheat oven to 350°F (180°C)
13- by 9-inch (3 L) baking dish

12	cannelloni or manicotti shells	12
2 tsp	vegetable oil	10 mL
1 1/2 tsp	crushed garlic	7 mL
6 oz	ground beef	150 g
1/4 cup	diced onions	50 mL
1/4 cup	diced carrots	50 mL
1/4 cup	diced celery	50 mL
1 tbsp	tomato paste	15 mL
1/4 cup	dry red wine	50 mL
1/4 cup	shredded mozzarella cheese	50 mL
3 tbsp	ricotta cheese	45 mL
2 tbsp	grated Parmesan cheese	25 mL
1	egg	1
1 1/2 cups	prepared tomato sauce or Quick Basic Tomato Sauce (see recipe on page 205)	375 mL

PER SERVING

Calories	298
Protein	15 g
Fat, total	12 g
Fat, saturated	4 g
Carbohydrates	31 g
Sodium	316 mg
Cholesterol	27 mg
Fiber	3 g

1. Cook pasta shells in boiling water according to package instructions or until firm to the bite. Drain, cover and set aside.

2. In medium nonstick skillet, heat oil; sauté garlic, beef, onions, carrots and celery, until beef is cooked and vegetables are just tender, approximately 8 minutes. Add tomato paste and wine; cook for 2 minutes. Remove from heat.

3. Add mozzarella, ricotta and Parmesan cheeses and egg. Place mixture in food processor; with on-and-off pulses, chop until still chunky. Do not purée. Place 1 tbsp (15 mL) filling into each shell. Pour half sauce into pan; add pasta shells, and pour remaining sauce over top. Cover and bake for 20 minutes or until hot.

 # SALMON CANNELLONI
WITH GOAT CHEESE
IN A CREAMY SAUCE

Serves 5.

Preheat oven to 350°F (180°C)
13- by 9-inch (3 L) baking dish

10	cannelloni	10
1 tbsp	margarine or butter	15 mL
1 tsp	crushed garlic	5 mL
3 tbsp	chopped green onions	45 mL
1 tbsp	capers	15 mL
8 oz	salmon fillet, cubed	250 g
1 tbsp	brandy	15 mL
1/4 cup	2% milk	50 mL
1/4 cup	fresh chopped dill (or 2 tsp [10 mL] dried)	50 mL
2 1/2 oz	goat cheese	60 g

Sauce

2 tsp	margarine or butter	10 mL
2 1/2 tsp	all-purpose flour	12 mL
1/3 cup	2% milk	75 mL
3/4 cup	fish or chicken stock	175 mL
1 tbsp	grated Parmesan cheese	15 mL
Pinch	nutmeg	Pinch

TIP

Substitute tuna or swordfish for salmon. Be careful not to overcook.

Use dry white wine to replace brandy if desired.

MAKE AHEAD

Prepare stuffed shells and sauce early in day, keeping separate until ready to bake. Add more milk to sauce if it thickens. Bake just before serving.

PER SERVING

Calories	267
Protein	18 g
Fat, total	11 g
Fat, saturated	3 g
Carbohydrates	23 g
Sodium	358 mg
Cholesterol	35 mg
Fiber	0.8 g

1. Cook pasta in boiling water according to package instructions or until firm to the bite. Drain, cover and set aside.

2. In medium nonstick skillet, heat margarine; add garlic, onions and capers; cook for 2 minutes. Add salmon and brandy and cook for 2 minutes. Salmon will still be raw. Place in food processor; add milk, dill and goat cheese and process on and off until still chunky. Fill pasta shells; place in baking dish.

3. Make the sauce: In nonstick saucepan, melt margarine; add flour and cook for 1 minute. Add milk and stock; simmer on medium heat just until thick, stirring constantly for about 3 minutes. Add Parmesan cheese and nutmeg; pour over pasta. Bake, covered, for 15 to 20 minutes or until hot.

 MANICOTTI WITH EGGPLANT ✕ AND FETA CHEESE FILLING

Serves 6.

TIP

Try goat or Swiss cheese instead of feta.

MAKE AHEAD

Prepare stuffed shells up to a day ahead with sauce poured over. Do not bake until ready to serve.

Preheat oven to 350°F (180°C)
13- by 9-inch (3 L) baking dish

12	manicotti shells	12
1 tbsp	vegetable oil	15 mL
2 tsp	crushed garlic	10 mL
2 cups	eggplant, peeled and diced	500 mL
3/4 cup	chopped onions	175 mL
1 1/4 tsp	dried oregano	6 mL
2 1/2 oz	crumbled feta cheese	60 g
3/4 cup	ricotta cheese	175 mL
1 1/2 cups	prepared tomato sauce, or Quick Basic Tomato Sauce (see recipe on page 205)	375 mL

1. Cook pasta in boiling water according to package instructions or until firm to the bite. Drain, rinse, cover and set aside.

2. In medium nonstick skillet sprayed with vegetable spray, heat oil; sauté garlic, eggplant and onions until eggplant is tender, for 5 to 7 minutes. (If eggplant sticks to skillet, add 2 to 3 tbsp [25 to 45 mL] water.) Add oregano and feta and ricotta cheeses. Mix well and remove from heat. Place in food processor and chop on and off just until still chunky. Fill pasta shells.

3. Pour half tomato sauce in bottom of baking dish. Lay manicotti over the sauce, and pour remaining sauce over top. Cover and bake for 15 to 20 minutes or until hot.

PER SERVING

Calories	247
Protein	10 g
Fat, total	8 g
Fat, saturated	3 g
Carbohydrates	33 g
Sodium	289 mg
Cholesterol	19 mg
Fiber	3 g

JUMBO SHELLS WITH SPINACH, SMOKED SALMON AND CHEESE

Serves 6.

TIP

Substitute chopped chives for green onions.

▼

For a milder flavor, use mozzarella instead of Swiss cheese.

MAKE AHEAD

Prepare stuffed shells early in day with sauce poured over. Do not bake until ready to serve.

Preheat oven to 350°F (180°C)
13- by 9-inch (3 L) baking dish

24	jumbo pasta shells	24
1 1/2 cups	ricotta cheese	375 mL
1/4 cup	chopped spinach, cooked, drained and well packed down	50 mL
3 oz	finely chopped smoked salmon	75 g
	Pepper	
1/4 cup	fresh chopped dill (or 1 tsp [5 mL] dried)	50 mL
3 tbsp	2% milk	45 mL
2 tbsp	chopped green onions	25 mL
1 1/2 cups	prepared tomato sauce, or Quick Basic Tomato Sauce (see recipe on page 205)	375 mL
1/3 cup	shredded Swiss cheese	75 mL

1. Cook pasta in boiling water according to package instructions or until firm to the bite. Drain, cover and set aside.

2. In mixing bowl, combine cheese, spinach, salmon, pepper to taste, dill, milk and green onions. Mix well and stuff pasta shells.

3. Pour half sauce into baking dish, place pasta on sauce and pour remaining sauce over top. Sprinkle with cheese. Cover and bake until hot, for 15 to 20 minutes.

PER SERVING

Calories	277
Protein	18 g
Fat, total	8 g
Fat, saturated	4 g
Carbohydrates	36 g
Sodium	402 mg
Cholesterol	27 mg
Fiber	3 g

CREAMY SEAFOOD LASAGNA WITH LEEKS AND SWEET BELL PEPPERS

Serves 8 to 10.

TIP

Try using other vegetables, such as snow peas, zucchini or asparagus.

Basil, parsley or coriander can replace the dill.

MAKE AHEAD

Entire dish can be prepared a day ahead and refrigerated. Bake just before serving.

Preheat oven to 350°F (180°C)
13- by 9-inch (3 L) baking dish

9	lasagna sheets	9
1 tsp	vegetable oil	5 mL
2 tsp	crushed garlic	10 mL
2/3 cup	diced sweet red or green peppers	150 mL
2/3 cup	diced leeks or red onions	150 mL
1 lb	seafood, cut into small pieces (any combination of firm white fish fillets or scallops or shrimp)	500 g

Cream Sauce

1 tbsp	margarine or butter	15 mL
3 tbsp	all-purpose flour	45 mL
1 2/3 cups	seafood or chicken stock	400 mL
1 1/2 cups	2% milk	375 mL
1/4 cup	chopped fresh dill (or 1 tbsp [15 mL] dried)	50 mL

Cheese Sauce

1 1/2 cups	ricotta cheese	375 mL
1 cup	shredded Cheddar cheese	250 mL
1/3 cup	2% milk	75 mL
1/4 cup	grated Parmesan cheese	50 mL

PER SERVING (10)

Calories	355
Protein	27 g
Fat, total	13 g
Fat, saturated	7 g
Carbohydrates	32 g
Sodium	625 mg
Cholesterol	82 mg
Fiber	0.9 g

1. Cook pasta in boiling water according to package instructions or until firm to the bite. Drain, cover and set aside.

2. In medium nonstick skillet, heat oil; sauté garlic, sweet peppers and leeks just until tender, approximately 5 minutes. Add seafood and sauté until fish is opaque, approximately 5 minutes. Pour off excess liquid. Set aside.

3. Make the cream sauce: In nonstick saucepan, melt margarine. Add flour and cook for 1 minute, stirring often. Slowly add stock and milk, and simmer on medium heat until just thickened, approximately 4 minutes, stirring often. Add seafood mixture and dill; remove from heat.

4. Make the cheese sauce: In small bowl, combine ricotta and Cheddar cheeses, milk and Parmesan cheese until mixed.

5. Assembly: Place 3 lasagna sheets in baking dish. Spread one-third cheese mixture over top, then one-third seafood sauce. Place 3 more lasagna sheets over seafood sauce, repeat with one-third cheese and seafood sauce. Repeat with remaining lasagna, cheese and seafood sauce. Cover and bake approximately 30 minutes, or until hot.

 CLAM LASAGNA

Serves 8.

TIP

For a less salty seafood flavor, use chicken stock instead of clam juice.

MAKE AHEAD

Prepare lasagna up to a day ahead. Bake just before serving.

Preheat oven to 350°F (180°C)
13- by 9-inch (3 L) baking pan sprayed with vegetable spray

9	lasagna sheets	9
1	package (10 oz [300 g]) frozen chopped spinach, cooked, drained and squeezed dry	1
2 cups	ricotta cheese	500 mL
1/4 cup	2% milk	50 mL
8 oz	shredded mozzarella cheese	250 g

Sauce

1 tbsp	margarine or butter	15 mL
2 tbsp	all-purpose flour	25 mL
2/3 cup	bottled clam juice or chicken stock	150 mL
2 tsp	crushed garlic	10 mL
1/2 tsp	each of dried basil and oregano	2 mL
2	cans (5.5 oz [155 g]) clams, liquid reserved	2
1/3 cup	chopped fresh parsley (or 1 tbsp [15 mL] dried)	75 mL
2 tbsp	lemon juice	25 mL
1/4 cup	grated Parmesan cheese	50 mL

PER SERVING

Calories	351
Protein	31 g
Fat, total	13 g
Fat, saturated	7 g
Carbohydrates	27 g
Sodium	552 mg
Cholesterol	68 mg
Fiber	2 g

1. Cook pasta in boiling water according to package instructions or until firm to the bite. Drain, cover and set aside.

2. In bowl combine spinach, ricotta cheese, milk and mozzarella cheese. Set aside.

3. Make the sauce: In medium nonstick saucepan, melt margarine; add flour and cook for 1 minute on low heat. Add clam juice and reserved clam liquid; simmer until sauce thickens, approximately 3 minutes,

stirring constantly. Add garlic, basil, oregano, clams, parsley and lemon juice. Set aside.

4. Assembly: Place 3 lasagna sheets in pan. Add half the spinach mixture over top, and then one-third the clam sauce. Repeat layers and top with remaining lasagna sheets, clam sauce and sprinkle with Parmesan cheese. Bake covered for 30 minutes or until hot. Let stand 10 minutes before serving.

PESTO LASAGNA WITH ROASTED SWEET PEPPERS

Serves 8 to 10.

TIP

To remove skin more easily from peppers, place in a plastic or paper bag for 10 minutes after broiling, then peel.

A combination of different colored peppers to total 2 peppers makes an attractive lasagna.

MAKE AHEAD

Prepare entire lasagna up to a day ahead. Bake just before serving.

Preheat oven to broil
13- by 9-inch (3 L) baking dish

9	lasagna sheets	9
2	red, green or yellow sweet peppers	2

Pesto

1 1/2 cups	basil leaves, well packed down	375 mL
1/4 cup	chicken stock or water	50 mL
3 tbsp	olive oil	45 mL
3 tbsp	toasted pine nuts or walnuts	45 mL
2 tbsp	grated Parmesan cheese	25 mL
3 cups	ricotta cheese	750 mL

Sauce

1 1/4 cups	cold chicken stock	300 mL
1 cup	2% milk	250 mL
2 tbsp	all-purpose flour	25 mL
Pinch	nutmeg	Pinch
1 1/2 cups	low-fat mozzarella cheese, shredded	375 mL
2 tbsp	grated Parmesan cheese	25 mL

1. Cook pasta in boiling water according to package instructions or until firm to the bite. Drain, cover and set aside.

2. Broil sweet peppers until charred on all sides, approximately 15 minutes. Let cool. Remove top, skin and seeds; slice into thin strips. Set aside. Preheat oven to 350°F (180°C).

3. Make the pesto: In food processor, mix basil, stock, oil, nuts and Parmesan cheese until blended. Add ricotta cheese and mix well.

4. Make the sauce: In small nonstick skillet, combine stock, milk, flour and nutmeg until smooth. Simmer on medium heat stirring constantly until slightly thickened, approximately 4 minutes. Set aside.

5. Assembly: Place 3 lasagna in baking dish. Place half pesto-ricotta mixture, half sweet peppers, one-third sauce, and half mozzarella cheese over top. Add 3 more lasagna sheets, remaining ricotta mixture, remaining sweet pepper strips, another third sauce and remaining mozzarella. Finish with 3 lasagna sheets, remaining sauce and sprinkle with Parmesan cheese. Cover and bake for 20 to 25 minutes or until hot. Sprinkle with parsley as garnish. Let rest 10 minutes before serving.

LASAGNA WITH ROASTED PEPPERS, EGGPLANT AND ZUCCHINI

Serves 8.

TIP

Green sweet peppers can replace red or yellow.

Try wild mushrooms such as oyster for a more sophisticated lasagna.

MAKE AHEAD

Prepare lasagna up to a day ahead or freeze uncooked up to a week before. Best if cooked right before eating.

Preheat oven to broil
13- by 9-inch (3 L) baking pan

9	lasagna sheets	9
2	medium red and/or yellow sweet peppers	2
1 tbsp	olive oil	15 mL
2 tsp	crushed garlic	10 mL
2 cups	eggplant, peeled and diced	500 mL
2 cups	diced zucchini	500 mL
3/4 cup	diced onions	175 mL
1 1/2 cups	diced mushrooms	375 mL
1 1/2 cups	ricotta cheese	375 mL
1/3 cup	2% milk	75 mL
3 cups	prepared tomato sauce or Quick Basic Tomato Sauce (see page 205 for recipe)	750 mL
8 oz	shredded mozzarella cheese	250 g
1/3 cup	grated Parmesan cheese	75 mL

PER SERVING

Calories	355
Protein	24 g
Fat, total	16 g
Fat, saturated	8 g
Carbohydrates	32 g
Sodium	597 mg
Cholesterol	42 mg
Fiber	5 g

1. Cook pasta according to package instructions or until firm to the bite. Drain, cover and set aside.

2. Broil peppers until charred on all sides, turning occasionally, approximately 15 minutes. Rinse peppers in cool water; remove top, peel and de-seed. Slice into thin strips. Set aside. Preheat oven to 350°F (180°C).

3. In large nonstick skillet sprayed with vegetable spray, heat oil; sauté garlic, eggplant, zucchini, and onions until just tender, approximately 5 minutes. Add mushrooms and cook for 3 more minutes. Add sweet peppers and set aside.

4. In small bowl, combine ricotta cheese and milk until smooth.

5. Assembly: Pour one-third tomato sauce into bottom of pan. Place 3 lasagna sheets over top. Add half the vegetable mixture, half the ricotta mixture, half the mozzarella and half the Parmesan cheese over top. Repeat with one-third sauce, 3 lasagna sheets, remaining vegetable mixture, ricotta mixture and mozzarella cheese. Add remaining lasagna sheets, tomato sauce, and Parmesan cheese. Cover and bake for 20 to 30 minutes or until hot. Let rest for 10 minutes.

MOSTLY 𝒯OMATO SAUCES

 # TIPS FOR TOMATO SAUCES

1. Many recipes call for canned tomatoes. Canned, crushed or puréed tomatoes can be used, or canned whole tomatoes can be bought and puréed, or used whole with their juices. During cooking, the tomatoes can be broken with the back of a wooden spoon.

2. Use a large nonstick saucepan, sprayed with vegetable spray, before sautéeing vegetables.

3. Cook tomato sauces, covered, on low-medium heat, to avoid letting the liquid evaporate. If the sauce appears too thick when reheating, add more stock, water or puréed canned tomatoes.

4. Plum tomatoes are the best tomatoes for making a fresh tomato sauce. They are drier and meatier and make a denser, more flavorful sauce.

 # QUICK BASIC TOMATO SAUCE

Serves 6 to 8.

TIP

Other finely diced vegetables can be added, as well as basil and oregano to taste.

▼

If a thicker sauce is desired, add 2 tbsp (25 mL) tomato paste during the cooking.

MAKE AHEAD

Refrigerate for up to 2 days, or freeze for up to 6 weeks. After defrosting, add 2 tbsp (25 mL) tomato paste to thicken. Heat for 15 minutes.

1 lb	pasta (any variety)	500 g
2 tsp	olive oil	10 mL
2/3 cup	finely chopped onions	150 mL
2 tsp	crushed garlic	10 mL
1	can (28 oz [796 mL]) plum tomatoes, crushed	1
1/4 cup	grated Parmesan cheese (optional)	50 mL

1. In large nonstick saucepan, heat oil; sauté onions and garlic for 3 minutes, stirring often.

2. Add tomatoes and cook on low heat for 15 to 20 minutes, stirring occasionally, or until reduced slightly. Pour over pasta. Add cheese if using, and toss.

PER SERVING (8)

Calories	270
Protein	9 g
Fat, total	2 g
Fat, saturated	0.4 g
Carbohydrates	53 g
Sodium	167 mg
Cholesterol	0 mg
Fiber	3 g

THICK AND RICH TOMATO SAUCE

Serves 6 to 8.

TIP

For a meat sauce, add 8 oz (250 g) ground beef, chicken, veal or pork after vegetables have been cooked. Sauté meat until no longer pink. Drain all fat. Then continue with recipe.

Canned plum tomatoes are a good choice.

MAKE AHEAD

Refrigerate up to a day ahead or freeze for up to 6 weeks. When reheating add 2 tbsp (25 mL) tomato paste to thicken.

1 lb	pasta (any variety)	500 g
1 tbsp	vegetable oil	15 mL
2 tsp	crushed garlic	10 mL
1/2 cup	chopped onions	125 mL
1/2 cup	chopped sweet green peppers	125 mL
1/2 cup	chopped carrots	125 mL
1	can (28 oz [796 mL]) crushed tomatoes	1
1/4 cup	red wine	50 mL
2 tbsp	tomato paste	25 mL
1	bay leaf	1
1 tsp	dried oregano	5 mL
1 tsp	dried basil	5 mL

1. In large nonstick saucepan, heat oil; sauté garlic, onions, green peppers and carrots until softened, approximately 10 minutes.

2. Add tomatoes, wine, tomato paste, bay leaf, oregano and basil; cover and simmer for approximately 20 minutes, stirring occasionally. Discard bay leaf. Purée if desired.

PER SERVING (8)

Calories	303
Protein	10 g
Fat, total	3 g
Fat, saturated	0.4 g
Carbohydrates	58 g
Sodium	176 mg
Cholesterol	0 mg
Fiber	4 g

 # RIGATONI WITH ROASTED ∝ TOMATO SAUCE

Serves 4 to 6.

Preheat oven to broil

12 oz	rigatoni pasta	375 g
8 to 10	small tomatoes (plum or roma)	8 to 10
2 tsp	olive oil	10 mL
2 tsp	crushed garlic	10 mL
3/4 cup	chopped onions	175 mL
1 cup	sliced mushrooms	250 mL
1/2 cup	frozen green peas, thawed	125 mL
1/2 cup	chopped fresh basil (or 2 tsp [10 mL] dried)	125 mL
1/4 cup	grated Parmesan cheese	50 mL
	Pepper	

1. Cook pasta in boiling water according to package instructions or until firm to the bite. Drain and place in serving bowl.

2. Meanwhile, broil or grill tomatoes until black on the outside, approximately 15 minutes, turning once. Do not peel. Place in food processor and purée. Set aside.

3. In large nonstick skillet, heat oil; sauté garlic and onions until tender, approximately 4 minutes. Add mushrooms and sauté for 2 minutes. Add tomato purée, green peas and basil; cook for 3 minutes.

4. Pour over pasta. Sprinkle with cheese and pepper. Toss.

PER SERVING (6)

Calories	318
Protein	12 g
Fat, total	4 g
Fat, saturated	1 g
Carbohydrates	59 g
Sodium	94 mg
Cholesterol	3 mg
Fiber	6 g

 SUN-DRIED TOMATO SAUCE ✕

Serves 6 to 8.

TIP

If sauce is thicker than you like, add a little more stock.

Toast nuts in 400°F (200°C) oven until golden (approximately 10 minutes) or in a skillet on top of the stove for 2 to 3 minutes.

MAKE AHEAD

Refrigerate up to 2 days ahead or freeze for up to 2 weeks. When reheating, add more stock to thin.

4 oz	sun-dried tomatoes	100 g
12 oz	pasta	375 g
2 tsp	crushed garlic	10 mL
1 cup	chicken stock or water	250 mL
1/2 cup	chopped parsley	125 mL
3 tbsp	olive oil	45 mL
3 tbsp	grated Parmesan cheese	45 mL
2 tbsp	toasted pine nuts	25 mL

1. In bowl, pour enough boiling water over tomatoes to cover; let soak for 10 to 15 minutes. Drain and cut into smaller pieces.

2. Cook pasta in boiling water according to package instructions or until firm to the bite. Drain and place in serving bowl.

3. In food processor, process tomatoes, garlic, stock, parsley, oil, cheese and nuts until well blended. Pour over pasta, and toss.

PER SERVING (8)

Calories	315
Protein	11 g
Fat, total	10 g
Fat, saturated	2 g
Carbohydrates	47 g
Sodium	169 mg
Cholesterol	2 mg
Fiber	6 g

FETTUCCINE WITH BLACK OLIVES IN A SPICY TOMATO SAUCE

Serves 6.

TIP

This sauce suits any type of pasta.

MAKE AHEAD

Refrigerate up to 2 days ahead or freeze up to 1 week. When reheating, add more tomato paste if sauce is too thin.

12 oz	fettuccine	375 g
2 tsp	vegetable oil	10 mL
2 tsp	crushed garlic	10 mL
3/4 cup	finely diced onions	175 mL
1/2 cup	finely diced celery	125 mL
1/2 cup	finely diced carrots	125 mL
1/3 cup	sliced black olives	75 mL
4	anchovies, minced	4
2 tsp	capers	10 mL
2 1/2 cups	crushed tomatoes (canned or fresh)	625 mL
1 tbsp	tomato paste	15 mL
2 tsp	dried basil	10 mL
1 tsp	dried oregano	5 mL
1/4 tsp	cayenne pepper	1 mL
3 tbsp	grated Parmesan cheese	45 mL

1. Cook pasta in boiling water according to package instructions or until firm to the bite. Drain and place in serving bowl.

2. In large nonstick skillet, heat oil; sauté garlic, onions, celery and carrots until soft, approximately 5 minutes. Add olives, anchovies, capers, tomatoes, tomato paste, basil, oregano and cayenne. Simmer 20 minutes on low heat, stirring occasionally. Pour over pasta. Sprinkle with cheese and toss.

PER SERVING

Calories	319
Protein	12 g
Fat, total	5 g
Fat, saturated	1 g
Carbohydrates	58 g
Sodium	337 mg
Cholesterol	4 mg
Fiber	5 g

PASTA WITH CREOLE SAUCE, OLIVES AND SWEET PEPPERS

Serves 6.

TIP

Substitute black olives for green if desired.

Increase spiciness by adding more cayenne.

MAKE AHEAD

Prepare up to a day ahead. Reheat gently, adding a little water if sauce thickens.

12 oz	penne	375 g
2 tsp	vegetable oil	10 mL
2 tsp	crushed garlic	10 mL
1 cup	chopped onions	250 mL
3/4 cup	chopped sweet green bell peppers	175 mL
3/4 cup	chopped sweet red bell peppers	175 mL
2 1/2 cups	canned or fresh crushed tomatoes	625 mL
16	large green olives, pitted and sliced	16
1 tbsp	chili powder	15 mL
1/4 tsp	cayenne	1 mL
	Parsley	

1. Cook pasta in boiling water according to package instructions or until firm to the bite. Drain and place in serving bowl.

2. In large nonstick skillet, heat oil; sauté garlic, onions and green and red peppers. Simmer until soft, approximately 5 minutes. Add tomatoes, olives, chili powder and cayenne. Simmer for 15 minutes, stirring occasionally until thickened. Pour over pasta. Sprinkle with parsley, and toss.

PER SERVING

Calories	312
Protein	10 g
Fat, total	4 g
Fat, saturated	0.3 g
Carbohydrates	61 g
Sodium	210 mg
Cholesterol	0 mg
Fiber	6 g

MANICOTTI SHELLS FILLED WITH CHEESE AND SMOKED SALMON BITS (PAGE 182) ➤

PENNE MARINARA

Serves 4.

TIP

Any pasta suits this dish.

MAKE AHEAD

Refrigerate up to 2 days ahead or freeze up to 2 weeks. When reheating, add 1 tbsp (15 mL) of tomato paste if sauce is too watery.

8 oz	penne	250 g
2 tsp	vegetable oil	10 mL
2/3 cup	diced onions	150 mL
2 tsp	crushed garlic	10 mL
2 tsp	chopped capers	10 mL
1/4 cup	chopped fresh basil (or 1 tsp [5 mL] dried)	50 mL
1/2 tsp	dried oregano	2 mL
1	bay leaf	1
1	can (19 oz [540 mL]) crushed tomatoes	1
1/3 cup	pitted black olives, sliced	75 mL
1 tbsp	tomato paste	15 mL
3 tbsp	grated Parmesan cheese	45 mL
	Parsley	

1. Cook pasta in boiling water according to package instructions or until firm to the bite. Drain and place in serving bowl.

2. In nonstick skillet, heat oil; sauté onions and garlic until onions are soft, approximately 3 minutes. Add capers, basil, oregano, bay leaf, tomatoes, olives and tomato paste. Simmer for 15 minutes, stirring occasionally. Pour over pasta. Sprinkle with cheese and toss well. Garnish with parsley.

PER SERVING

Calories	339
Protein	12 g
Fat, total	7 g
Fat, saturated	2 g
Carbohydrates	58 g
Sodium	471 mg
Cholesterol	4 mg
Fiber	5 g

◄ PASTA WITH CRISP VEGETABLES IN A CREAMY SAUCE (PAGE 140)

FETTUCCINE WITH INDIAN TOMATO SAUCE

Serves 6 to 8 as an appetizer.

TIP

Adjust the curry to taste.

Fresh coriander gives this sauce an authentic Indian flavor.

MAKE AHEAD

Refrigerate up to a day ahead. Freeze for up to 2 weeks. Reheat and add a little tomato paste (1 tbsp [15 mL]) if sauce gets watery.

1 lb	fettuccine	500 g
1 tbsp	vegetable oil	15 mL
1 cup	chopped onions	250 mL
1/2 cup	finely chopped carrots	125 mL
2 tsp	crushed garlic	10 mL
2 tsp	minced ginger	10 mL
1	can (28 oz [796 mL]) crushed tomatoes	1
1 tbsp	curry powder	15 mL
1/2 cup	chopped coriander or parsley	125 mL

1. Cook pasta in boiling water according to package instructions or until firm to the bite. Drain and place in serving bowl.

2. In medium nonstick saucepan, heat oil; sauté onions, carrots, garlic and ginger until tender, approximately 5 minutes. Add tomatoes and curry; cover and simmer on low heat for 20 minutes, stirring occasionally. Pour over pasta. Sprinkle with coriander and toss.

PER SERVING (8)

Calories	299
Protein	10 g
Fat, total	4 g
Fat, saturated	0.3 g
Carbohydrates	57 g
Sodium	179 mg
Cholesterol	0 mg
Fiber	5 g

ROTINI WITH

POMODORO SAUCE

Serves 4.

TIP

Use juicy ripe tomatoes for more liquid.

MAKE AHEAD

Prepare early in day. Reheat gently so as not to overcook tomatoes.

8 oz	rotini	250 g
2 oz	diced smoked ham or prosciutto	50 g

Sauce

2 tsp	vegetable oil	10 mL
1 1/2 tsp	crushed garlic	7 mL
3/4 cup	chopped onions	175 mL
3 cups	chopped tomatoes	750 mL
2 tbsp	dry white wine	25 mL
3 tbsp	chicken stock	45 mL
1/4 cup	chopped fresh basil (or 1 tsp [5 mL] dried)	50 mL
3/4 tsp	dried oregano	4 mL
1 tbsp	margarine or butter	15 mL
3 tbsp	grated Parmesan cheese	45 mL
	Parsley	

1. Cook pasta in boiling water according to package instructions or until firm to the bite. Drain and place in serving bowl. Add ham.

2. Make the sauce: In nonstick skillet, heat oil; sauté garlic and onions until tender, approximately 3 minutes. Add tomatoes and simmer for 5 minutes, stirring occasionally.

3. Add wine, stock, basil and oregano. Simmer for 3 minutes, stirring occasionally. Add margarine; pour over pasta. Sprinkle with cheese, and toss. Garnish with parsley.

PER SERVING

Calories	382
Protein	14 g
Fat, total	10 g
Fat, saturated	2 g
Carbohydrates	60 g
Sodium	334 mg
Cholesterol	11 mg
Fiber	6 g

PASTA WITH SPICY MUSHROOM TOMATO SAUCE

Serves 4 to 6.

TIP

Use wild mushrooms such as oyster for a highlighted texture and flavor.

For a spicier flavor, add 1/4 tsp (1 mL) cayenne pepper.

MAKE AHEAD

Prepare sauce early in day. Reheat, adding more milk if sauce thickens.

12 oz	bow-tie pasta or penne	375 g
2 tsp	vegetable oil	10 mL
2 tsp	crushed garlic	10 mL
1 cup	diced onions	250 mL
3 1/2 cups	chopped mushrooms	875 mL
1 cup	prepared tomato sauce or Quick Basic Tomato Sauce (recipe page 205)	250 mL
3/4 cup	2% milk	175 mL
1 1/2 tsp	dried basil	7 mL
1 tsp	dried oregano	5 mL
2 tsp	chili powder	10 mL
1/3 cup	grated Parmesan cheese	75 mL
	Parsley	

1. Cook pasta in boiling water according to package instructions or until firm to the bite. Drain and place in serving bowl.

2. In large nonstick skillet, heat oil; sauté garlic and onions until soft, approximately 5 minutes. Add mushrooms and sauté for another 5 minutes.

3. Add tomato sauce, milk, basil, oregano and chili. Simmer for 5 minutes, just until sauce begins to thicken. Pour over pasta. Sprinkle with cheese and toss. Garnish with parsley.

PER SERVING (6)

Calories	362
Protein	16 g
Fat, total	7 g
Fat, saturated	2 g
Carbohydrates	62 g
Sodium	221 mg
Cholesterol	6 mg
Fiber	7 g

Spaghetti with Sweet Bell Peppers, Eggplant and Tomato Sauce

Serves 6.

TIP

Keep skin on eggplant for extra fiber.

Linguine also suits this sauce.

MAKE AHEAD

Prepare sauce early in day. Reheat, adding a little water or stock if sauce thickens.

12 oz	spaghetti	375 g
1 tbsp	vegetable oil	15 mL
2 tsp	crushed garlic	10 mL
2 cups	eggplant cut into 1-inch (2.5-cm) cubes	500 mL
1 1/2 cups	thinly sliced sweet red or yellow peppers	375 mL
5	anchovy fillets, chopped	5
1/3 cup	sliced black olives	75 mL
2 1/2 cups	crushed tomatoes (canned or fresh)	625 mL
2 tsp	dried basil	10 mL
1/3 cup	grated Parmesan cheese	75 mL

1. Cook pasta in boiling water according to package instructions or until firm to the bite. Drain and place in serving bowl.

2. In large nonstick skillet sprayed with vegetable spray, heat oil; sauté garlic, eggplant and sweet peppers until tender, approximately 8 minutes. Add anchovies, black olives, tomatoes and basil. Cover and simmer on low heat for 10 minutes, stirring occasionally. Pour over pasta. Sprinkle with cheese, and toss.

PER SERVING

Calories	318
Protein	12 g
Fat, total	6 g
Fat, saturated	2 g
Carbohydrates	56 g
Sodium	340 mg
Cholesterol	6 mg
Fiber	4 g

PASTA WITH FENNEL, TOMATO SAUCE AND CHEESE

Serves 6.

12 oz	linguine	375 g
2 cups	chopped fennel	500 mL
2 1/2 cups	prepared tomato sauce or Quick Basic Tomato Sauce (recipe page 205)	625 mL
3/4 cup	cubed mozzarella cheese	175 mL
	Parsley	

1. Cook fennel in boiling water just until barely tender, approximately 8 minutes. Drain and set aside.

2. Cook pasta in boiling water according to package instructions or until firm to the bite. Drain and place in serving bowl.

3. In medium saucepan combine fennel and tomato sauce. Simmer, covered, until fennel is tender, for 15 to 20 minutes. Pour over pasta. Add cheese, and toss. Garnish with parsley.

TIP

Add 2 tsp (10 mL) fennel seed to sauce while cooking for a heightened licorice flavor.

MAKE AHEAD

Prepare sauce early in day. Reheat gently, adding more tomato sauce or water if sauce thickens.

PER SERVING

Calories	403
Protein	22 g
Fat, total	11 g
Fat, saturated	6 g
Carbohydrates	53 g
Sodium	680 mg
Cholesterol	23 mg
Fiber	5 g

PENNE WITH CREAMY SALSA SAUCE

Serves 6.

TIP

According to your preference, buy mild or medium salsa.

MAKE AHEAD

Prepare sauce early in day, reheating gently before use. Add more milk if sauce thickens.

12 oz	penne	375 g
2 tsp	vegetable oil	10 mL
1 1/2 tsp	crushed garlic	7 mL
3/4 cup	chopped onions	175 mL
3/4 cup	prepared tomato salsa	175 mL
1/2 cup	prepared tomato sauce or Quick Basic Tomato Sauce (recipe page 205)	125 mL
1/2 cup	2% milk	125 mL
1/3 cup	sliced green olives	75 mL
1/3 cup	chopped coriander or parsley	75 mL

1. Cook pasta in boiling water according to package instructions or until firm to the bite. Drain and place in serving bowl.

2. In medium nonstick skillet, heat oil; sauté garlic and onions until soft, approximately 4 minutes. Add salsa, tomato sauce, milk and olives. Simmer on medium heat for 3 minutes. Pour over pasta. Sprinkle with coriander, and toss.

PER SERVING

Calories	304
Protein	10 g
Fat, total	5 g
Fat, saturated	0.8 g
Carbohydrates	54 g
Sodium	480 mg
Cholesterol	2 mg
Fiber	5 g

SPAGHETTI SQUASH WITH TOMATO SAUCE, MUSHROOMS AND BLACK OLIVES

Serves 6.

TIP

Squash can also be baked in 350°F (180°C) oven for 40 to 50 minutes, or until tender.

Leave skin on zucchini for extra fiber.

MAKE AHEAD

Prepare sauce early in day. Reheat gently, adding some water if sauce is too thick.

1/2	spaghetti squash, about 1 to 2 lb (500 g to 1 kg)	1/2
12 oz	spaghetti	375 g
2 tsp	vegetable oil	10 mL
2 tsp	crushed garlic	10 mL
1 cup	chopped onions	250 mL
1 cup	chopped zucchini	250 mL
1 cup	chopped sweet green peppers	250 mL
1 cup	sliced mushrooms	250 mL
4 cups	crushed tomatoes (canned or fresh)	1 L
1/3 cup	sliced black olives	75 mL
2 tsp	dried basil	10 mL
1 tsp	dried oregano	5 mL
1/3 cup	grated Parmesan cheese	75 mL

1. Pierce squash in several places. In microwave, cook squash at High for 8 to 10 minutes, or until soft. Cool and slice in half lengthwise. Discard any seeds and, with fork, scrape out spaghetti-like strands and set aside half the squash. (Use other half for another purpose.)

2. Cook pasta in boiling water according to package instructions or until firm to the bite. Drain and place in serving bowl.

3. In large nonstick saucepan, heat oil; sauté garlic, onions, zucchini and green peppers for 5 minutes, or until vegetables are tender. Add mushrooms and sauté for 3 minutes.

4. Add tomatoes, olives, basil and oregano. Cover and simmer on low heat for 15 minutes. Add squash and cook for 2 minutes. Pour over pasta. Sprinkle with cheese, and toss.

PER SERVING

Calories	396
Protein	15 g
Fat, total	6 g
Fat, saturated	2 g
Carbohydrates	73 g
Sodium	463 mg
Cholesterol	4 mg
Fiber	8 g

PASTA GLOSSARY

There are so many varieties of fresh and dry pasta that it is easy to be confused about which type to match with a particular sauce. Some master pasta chefs have strict guidelines, but pasta is flexible (in more ways than one!), so feel free to combine whatever pasta you like with a sauce that suits you.

That being said, thicker or stuffed pastas are generally better with robust sauces, while thin-strand pastas are best with lighter sauces. With special pastas such as bow-ties or wheels, lighter sauces may be preferable since they will not obscure the shapes. Whichever pasta you choose, be sure to get the best quality you can — whether fresh or dry pasta.

Store-bought fresh pasta should be stored in the refrigerator up to the date on package. Homemade pasta should be used immediately or stored in the refrigerator for up to 2 days. Homemade dry pasta can be stored for 7 days in the refrigerator.

Dried pasta can be stored either in its original packaging or in an airtight container for up to 1 year. Here it's worth remembering that a good dry pasta is always better than stale "fresh" pasta.

With these points in mind, here's a list of some of the more common dry pastas. All of them can be found in grocery stores.

Agnolotti   Similar to ravioli, usually semicircular or square in shape. It is filled with various ingredients such as cheese, meat, or vegetables. You can substitute any stuffed pasta, such as ravioli or tortellini.

Angel Hair   See **Capelli d'Angelo.**

Bow-Ties   See **Farfalle.**

Cannelloni   Usually sold fresh as 4- by 5-inch (9- by 12-cm) flat pieces or as a dried pasta in rolled form. They can be filled with meat or cheese fillings and are usually baked in a sauce. They are smaller than manicotti, but can be used interchangeably with them. Use about 1 tbsp (15 mL) of filling in each.

Capelli d'Angelo (Angel Hair)   Very thin strands of pasta, usually sold in coils.

Capellini   Similar to angel hair pasta, but slightly thicker.

Conchiglie (Shells)   Shaped like conch shells, ranging in size from small bite-size pasta to large shells that can be stuffed with meat, cheese, or vegetable fillings.

Farfalle (Bow-Ties)   Shaped like bow-ties — or butterflies, if you like — they come in a variety of sizes. Most often used in the same way as a wide, flat noodle.

Fettuccine (Tagliatelle)   Long, flat pasta , usually about 1/4 inch (0.5 cm) wide.

Fusilli (Spirals, Rotini)   Shaped like twisted spaghetti or corkscrews, about 3 inches (7 cm) in length.

Gnocchi   Dumpling-like in appearance, but nevertheless a type of pasta. Make your own and freeze them, or buy the packaged gnocchi, which are usually excellent. Gnocchi is made from potatoes and flour, and can be served with a variety of sauces.

Lasagna   Sheets of fresh or dried pasta, usually measuring 13 inches (30 cm) long by 3 inches (7 cm) wide; usually cooked, layered with filling and sauce, and baked.

Linguine   A flat, strand-type pasta, like fettuccine, but not as wide.

Macaroni   Available as long, relatively thin tubes, but are most familiar in "elbow" form — that is, as short, crescent-shaped tubes of pasta used for casseroles or soups.

Manicotti   A rolled pasta like cannelloni, but larger; usually filled with a cheese mixture and baked with a sauce. You can buy them in dried form, or buy sheets of lasagna and cut to desired size, usually 5 by 4 inches (12 by 9 cm). Use about 1 tbsp (15 mL) filling for each shell.

Orzo   Sometimes used as a substitute for rice, which it resembles, but is heavier and fuller. Good in soups.

Penne Rigate Quill shaped, tubular pasta, cut diagonally; comes in various sizes, but most often measuring 2 inches (5 cm) in length. Good with heavier meat sauces.

Radiatore An unusually shaped, bite-sized pasta, featuring fins like those of an old-fashioned hot water radiator.

Ravioli Square pasta, 1 to 2 inches (2 to 4 cm) across, filled with a small amount of cheese or meat filling and crimped at the edges. You can prepare your own or buy ready-made frozen. Serve with a sauce.

Rigatoni Large, ridged tubes of pasta, usually about 1 1/2 inches (3 cm) long. Excellent with a chunky sauce.

Shells See **Conchiglie**

Spaghetti Best known of all pastas, often used as a generic term for any strand-type pasta, ranging from thin capellini to thick spaghettoni.

Spaghettini Thinner than spaghetti, but thicker than vermicelli.

Tagliatelle See **Fettuccine**.

Tortellini Similar to ravioli, but with a twisted, irregular shape; usually filled with cheese or meat. You can prepare your own or use ready-made. Fillings for this pasta are interchangable with manicotti, cannelloni, or jumbo pasta shells.

Vermicelli Thinner than spaghettini, but thicker than capellini.

Wheels Circular, bite-sized pasta with various configurations of "hubs" and "spokes." Good in salads and soups.

Ziti A tubular pasta similar to penne.

MAKING YOUR OWN PASTA

As pasta has grown in popularity, many people have started to make their own pasta. It takes time and patience, but for the true pasta gourmet, it is well worth the effort.

BASIC PASTA DOUGH

Makes 3 to 4 servings, approximately 12 oz (375 g)

2	large eggs	2
2 tsp	oil	10 mL
1 1/2 cups	all-purpose flour	375 mL
Pinch	salt	Pinch

1. In a bowl beat eggs and oil. Sift the flour and salt over the eggs. Mix with a fork and form into a ball. If it is too sticky, add some flour until it is easy to handle. If too dry, add some water.

2. Knead for approximately 8 minutes, until smooth. Wrap in a slightly moistened towel and let rest approximately 30 minutes on the counter before rolling and cutting into various pasta shapes.

If using a food processor or electric mixer, add flour and salt to bowl; with motor running, add the eggs and oil. Mix until the dough becomes a ball. If too sticky, add more flour; if too dry, add a few drops of water. Knead for approximately 5 minutes until smooth. Let rest for 30 minutes.

The classic way of making pasta is to sift the flour and salt together, mounding it on a table. Make a well in the center of the mound and break the eggs into it. Add oil. With a fork begin to gather the flour slowly from the sides into the middle until all is incorporated. Follow the same kneading directions as above.

PASTA VARIATIONS

Some flavorful and colorful variations to the pasta can be added quite simply. Just add the following ingredients and continue with the same method of making the basic pasta dough.

TOMATO PASTA

Add 2 tbsp (25 mL) tomato paste to basic pasta dough. Add more flour if too sticky.

GREEN PASTA (PASTA VERDI)

Make basic pasta dough using only one egg. Add 8 oz (250 g) finely chopped, cooked spinach, well drained. If dough is too wet, add extra flour.

HERB PASTA

Chop 2 tbsp (25 mL) of any herb of your choice, and add to basic pasta dough.

WHOLE WHEAT PASTA

Use 1 cup (250 mL) whole wheat flour and 1/4 cup (50 mL) white flour in place of white flour in the basic pasta dough recipe. Note that this produces a heavier pasta. For a lighter version, substitute half whole wheat flour and half white flour.

BLACK PEPPER PASTA

Add 2 tsp (10 mL) freshly ground black pepper to basic recipe.

GARLIC PASTA

Finely chop 5 cloves of garlic and add to basic pasta dough along with 1 tbsp (15 mL) water.

SEMOLINA PASTA

In my opinion, this is the best-tasting of all types of pasta dough. Substitute semolina flour for all-purpose flour in basic pasta dough. You may find the dough very hard to knead, however, and it can tend to clog the holes of electric machines. So use with care.

BLACK PASTA

Use only 1 egg in basic pasta dough. Mix 2 tbsp (25 mL) squid ink with 1/4 cup (50 mL) water. Combine ink mixture with the other ingredients and proceed in the usual manner.

ROLLING THE DOUGH

ROLLING PASTA BY HAND

A long rolling pin and fairly large working space is essential. Work quickly or the pasta will crack and dry.

Roll the dough away from you, stretching it as you roll. After each roll, give the dough a quarter turn to keep the circular shape.

If the dough is sticking to your working surface, dust it with a little flour. Pull and stretch the dough instead of rolling it. To stretch it, place the dough on top of the rolling pin and pull carefully.

Once the dough covers a large area, let it hang over the counter to stretch more. In a few minutes the dough will look smooth and should be very thin, about 1/8 inch (2 mm) thick.

If the dough is to be used for unfilled pasta, spread it on a towel to dry for approximately 30 minutes. Use it immediately for filled pasta such as ravioli or tortellini.

Now the dough is ready to cut into shapes of your choice.

PASTA MACHINES

Two types of wringer-style pasta machines are available. One has a motor and the other is turned by hand.

Using a Manual Pasta Machine

After the dough is rested, divide into 3 or 4 pieces. Keep the pieces not being used wrapped in plastic.

Flatten a piece of dough with your hand just so that it will fit through the pasta machine at the widest setting. Feed the pasta into the machine with one hand while working the machine with the other hand.

After the pasta comes out, fold it over and feed it again into the machine. When the dough begins to get smooth and elastic, start to narrow the roller openings. Continue this process until the dough achieves the desired thickness.

Lay the pieces on a well-floured surface. If the dough is to sit for any length of time, cover it with a towel. Now attach the cutting attachment desired to the pasta machine.

Follow the manufacturer's instructions.

Sprinkle the freshly cut pasta with some flour. Toss in a pile, or gather in strands. Now you can lay the pasta on a drying rack. Alternatively, you can place it in the refrigerator, where it will stay fresh for up to 1 week, or in the freezer for up to 2 months.

ELECTRIC PASTA MACHINES

An electric machine pushes the dough through a die that creates the desired pasta shape. Some of the more elaborate machines will also mix and knead the dough. After a few minutes, it comes out of the other end in various shapes, depending upon the attachment affixed.

The biggest problem with these machines is that the various attachments are easily clogged with flour, and the time cleaning them can be considerable.

FINISHING THE PASTA

FETTUCCINE (TAGLIATELLE) OR ANY FLAT NOODLE

Roll up the dough like a jelly roll and cut in even widths to desired shape, approximately 1/4 inch (0.5 cm) thick. Cook immediately or let dry for a few days before storing.

MANICOTTI, CANNELLONI, LASAGNA

Cut flat sheets of pasta to width and length desired. The most common size for manicotti or cannelloni is 4 by 5 inches (9 by 12 cm).

In boiling water with a little oil added to prevent sticking, cook pasta for about 2 to 3 minutes. Do not place too many pieces in pot, or they may stick together. Drain and rinse with cold water.

The pasta sheets can then be filled with meat, cheese or vegetable stuffing; later, they can be covered and baked with a sauce over top so the pasta does not dry out.

To store the pasta sheets, layer them with plastic or wax paper. Fresh pasta is best cooked immediately, but can be stored in the refrigerator for up to 1 week, or in the freezer for as long as 2 months.

RAVIOLI AND TORTELLINI

Prepare the desired filling and set aside. Roll the pasta dough into strips approximately 12 inches (30 cm) long and 4 inches (9 cm) wide. Keep unused strips covered with a damp towel.

Brush each strip of dough with a little beaten egg. Place a small amount of filling (approximately 1/2 tsp [2 mL]) at intervals of 1 1/2 inches (4 cm) on the pasta.

Lay a second sheet over top and press down firmly. For square shapes, cut between the fillings with a knife, pastry wheel, or special pasta cutter.

For round shapes, cut circles about 1 to 2 inches (2 to 5 cm) in diameter. For tortellini, cut 2-inch (5-cm) circles, and place a small amount of filling in one half of the circle. Fold the pasta and crimp the edges together.

Cataloguing Information

IN THE U.S.

Canadian Cataloguing in Publication Data

Reisman, Rose, 1953–

    Rose Reisman brings home light pasta

Published as a fund raising project of Y-ME
National Breast Cancer Organization

Includes index.

ISBN 1-896503-06-3 (bound) ISBN 1-896503-04-7 (pbk.)

1. Cookery (Pasta). 2. Low-fat diet – Recipes.
3. Nutrition. I. Title.

TX809.M17R35 1995a   641.8'22   C95-931249-8

IN CANADA

Canadian Cataloguing in Publication Data

Reisman, Rose, 1953–

    Rose Reisman brings home light pasta

Published as a fund raising project of the Canadian
Breast Cancer Foundation

Includes index.

ISBN 1-896503-02-0

1. Cookery (Pasta). 2. Low-fat diet – Recipes.
3. Nutrition. I. Title.

TX809.M17R35 1995   641.8'22   C95-931242-0

Index

MAKE A DIFFERENCE!

**Buy a book, wear a Pink Ribbon pin, make a donation...
Here's how you can join Rose Reisman in supporting the
Canadian Breast Cancer Foundation.**

Thank you for buying this book — and for your support of the Canadian Breast Cancer Foundation.

As you may know, the sales of this book are helping us toward our goal of raising awareness and funds for breast cancer research, treatment, and educational programs. Here are some of the other ways that you can help the work of the Foundation:

✔ Purchase Rose Reisman's previous bestselling book, *Rose Reisman Brings Home Light Cooking*;

✔ Buy one of our **Pink Ribbon pins**, and show your personal commitment to finding a cure;

✔ Become a **member** of the Foundation; or

✔ Just make a **donation** of whatever amount you can.

Your help is so important. So please, fill out the form below and mail it back to us at:

Canadian Breast Cancer Foundation • 790 Bay Street, Suite 1000 • Toronto, Ontario M5G 1N8

Or call us at **1-800-387-9816** for more information or to place your order by phone.

Your support will make a difference.

- -

YES, I want to help the Canadian Breast Cancer Foundation. Please send me

_____ copies of *Rose Reisman Brings Home Light Cooking* @ $19.95 $ _____

_____ enameled Pink Ribbon pins @ $5.00 $ _____

Shipping and handling (Please add $4 for each book; $2 for each pin) $ _____

❏ I would like to become a member of the Foundation - $25.00 $ _____
❏ I would like to make a donation in the amount of:
　❏ $25　　❏ $35　　❏ $50　　❏ $100　　❏ Other $_____ $ _____

TOTAL $ _____

Name _____

Address _____

City _____ Province _____ Postal Code _____

Phone No. _____ Res.   _____ Bus.

▼ Payment Method:

❏ Cheque, payable to Canadian Breast Cancer Foundation

❏ Visa _____   ❏ Mastercard _____   Expiry Date _____

Name on card if different from above _____

We regret that tax receipts are not available for memberships, cookbooks or pins. However, we will be pleased to provide tax receipts for donations of $25 or more.

Charitable Registration No. 0973719-11

Y-ME

∎∎∎∎∎∎∎∎∎∎∎∎∎∎∎∎∎∎∎∎∎∎∎∎∎∎∎∎∎∎

If you would like more information about the Y-ME National Breast Cancer Organization, please complete the form below and mail to:

Y-ME National Breast Cancer Organization
212 W. Van Buren St.
Chicago, IL 60607

Name _____

Address _____

_____

Phone (day) _____

Please send information about:

❑ Early detection

❑ Treatment

❑ Y-ME services

❑ Y-ME membership (includes subscription to bimonthly newsletter)

❑ Other _____

∎∎∎∎∎∎∎∎∎∎∎∎∎∎∎∎∎∎∎∎∎∎∎∎∎∎∎∎∎∎